I NEVER LIKED YOU

Also by Chester Brown:
Ed The Happy Clown (1989)
The Playboy (1992)
The Little Man: Short Strips, 1980—1995 (1998)

I NEVER LIKED YOU

A COMIC-STRIP NARRATIVE

CHESTER BROWN

DRAWN AND QUARTERLY PUBLICATIONS
MONTREAL

I Never Liked You was originally serialized in issues 26 through 30 of the comic book series *Yummy Fur.*

Publisher: Chris Oliveros

Second Edition: January 2002
Printed in Canada
ISBN 1-896597-14-9
10 9 8 7 6 5 4 3 2

Drawn & Quarterly
P.O. Box 48056
Montreal, Quebec
Canada H2V 4S8

Free catalogue available upon request.

Website: www.drawnandquarterly.com
E-mail: info@drawnandquarterly.com

As I was finishing this piece
in late 1992 and early 1993,
I was obsessively thinking about
Sook-Yin, so I'm dedicating
this book to her with love.

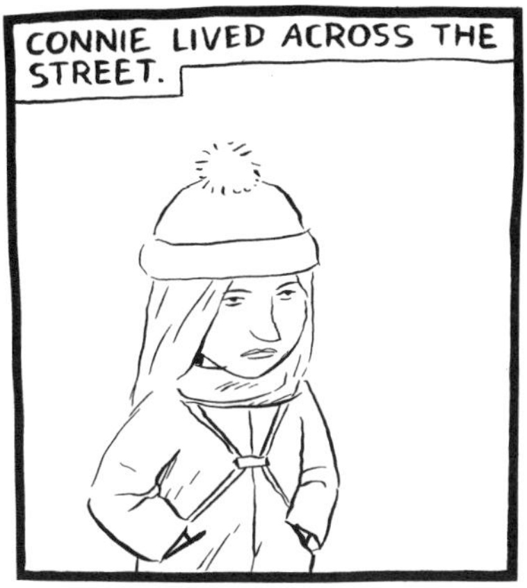
CONNIE LIVED ACROSS THE STREET.

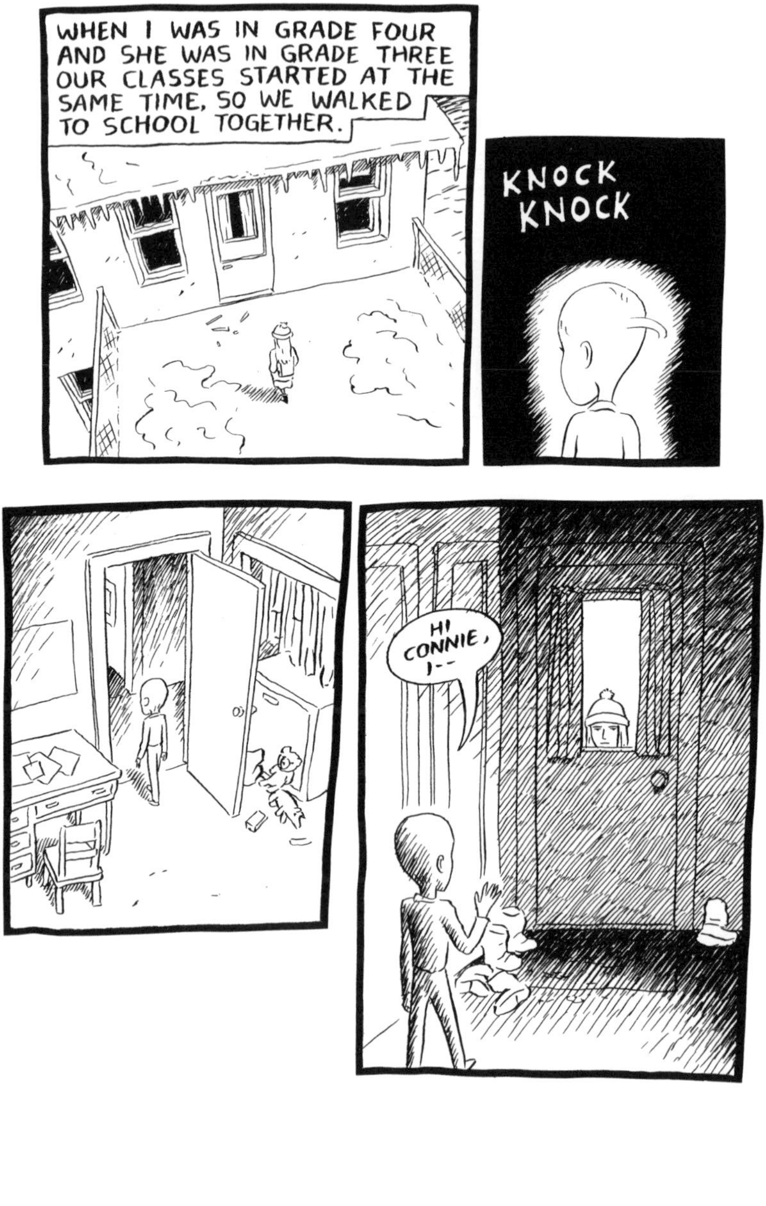
WHEN I WAS IN GRADE FOUR AND SHE WAS IN GRADE THREE OUR CLASSES STARTED AT THE SAME TIME, SO WE WALKED TO SCHOOL TOGETHER.
KNOCK KNOCK
HI CONNIE, I--

--I SHIT IT WAS YOU!
THUMP
THUMP
THUMP
THUMP
DON'T YOU EVER USE THAT WORD AGAIN! DO YOU HEAR ME?!
Y-YES --YES

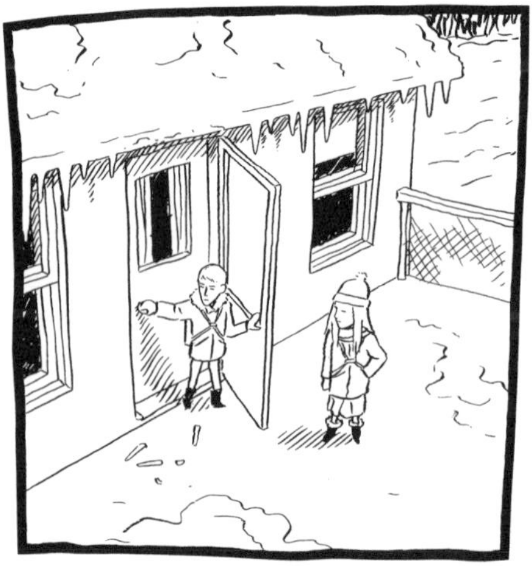

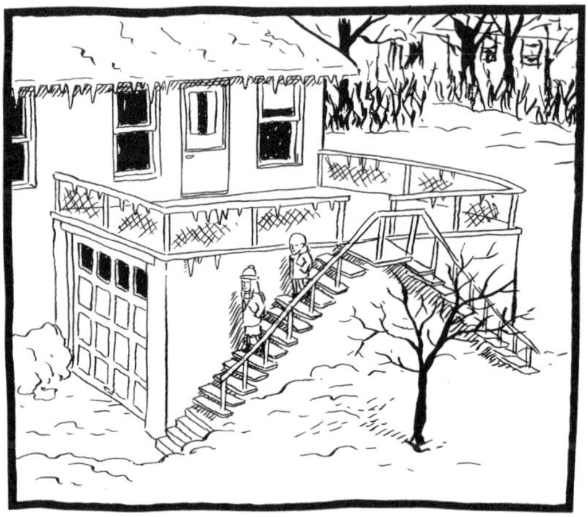

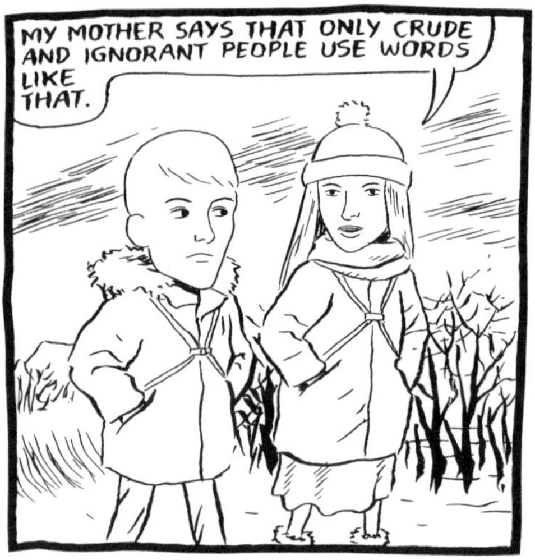
MY MOTHER SAYS THAT ONLY CRUDE AND IGNORANT PEOPLE USE WORDS LIKE THAT.

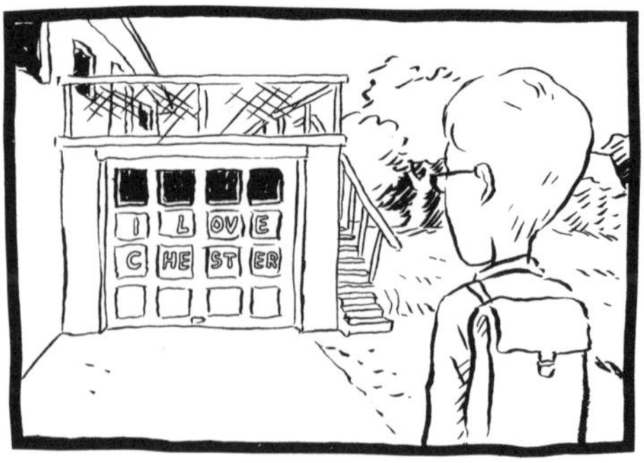
I LOVE
CHESTER

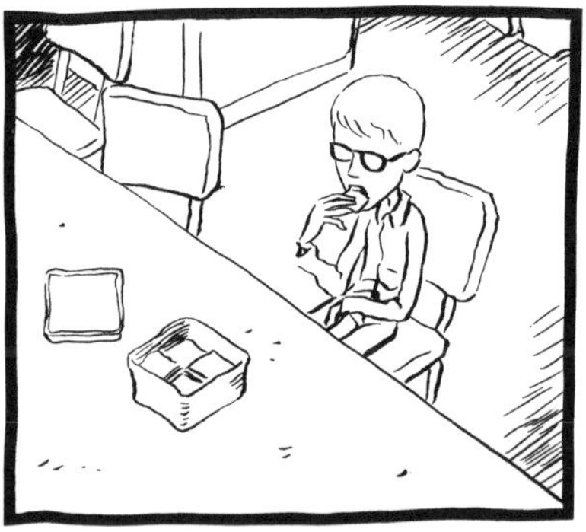

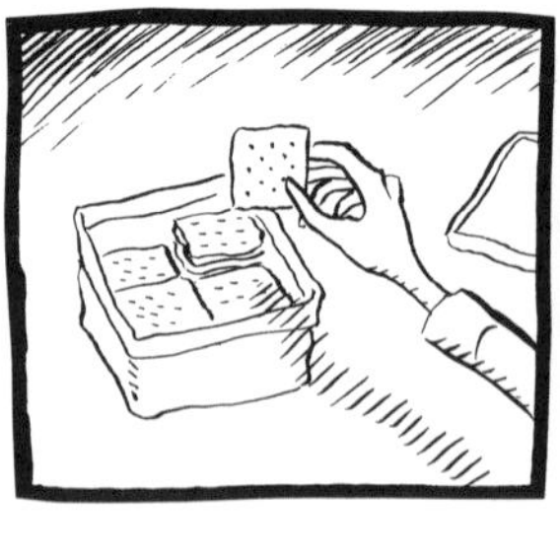

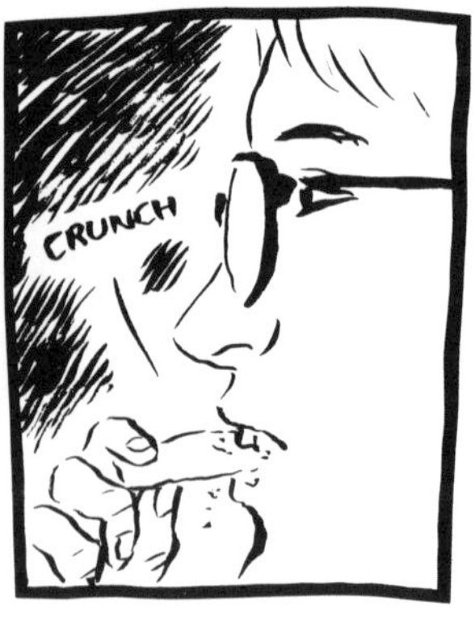
CRUNCH

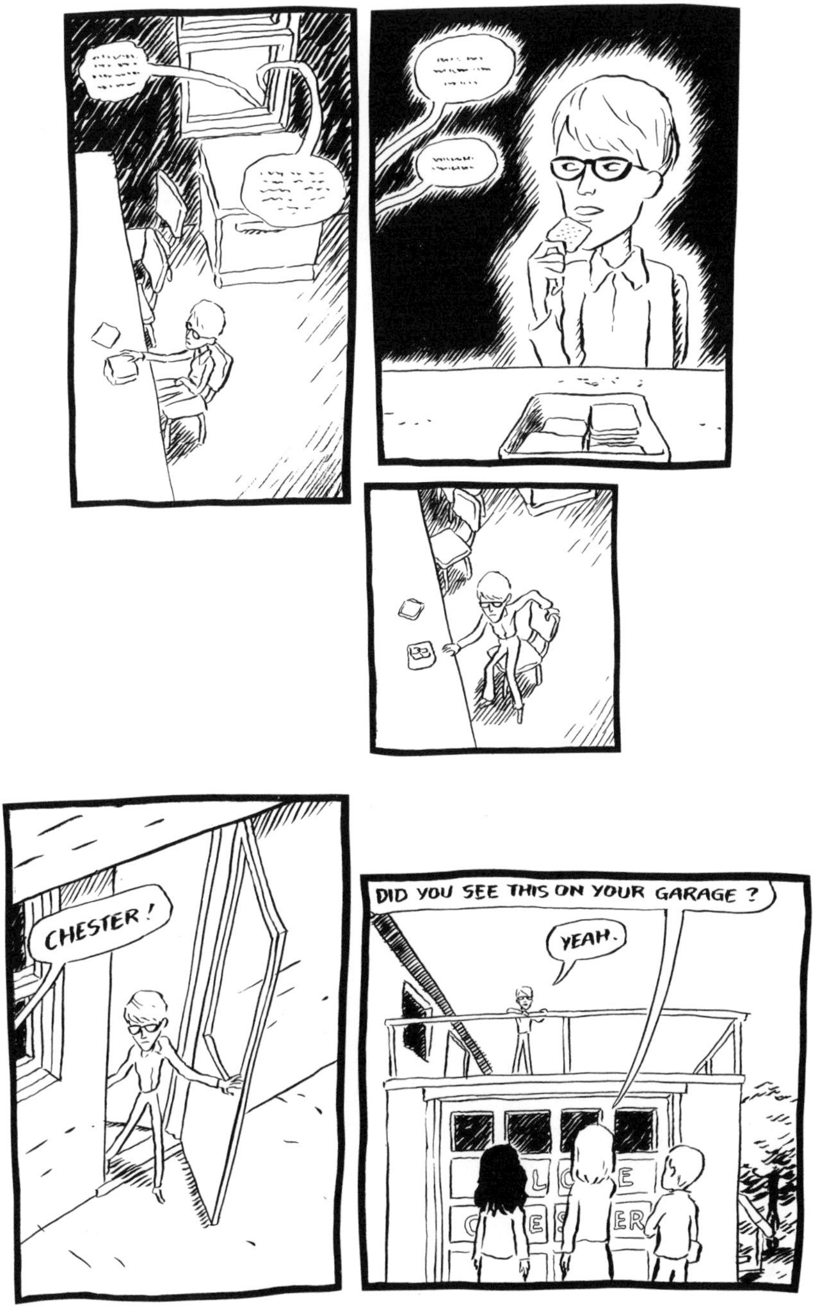
CHESTER!
DID YOU SEE THIS ON YOUR GARAGE?
YEAH.

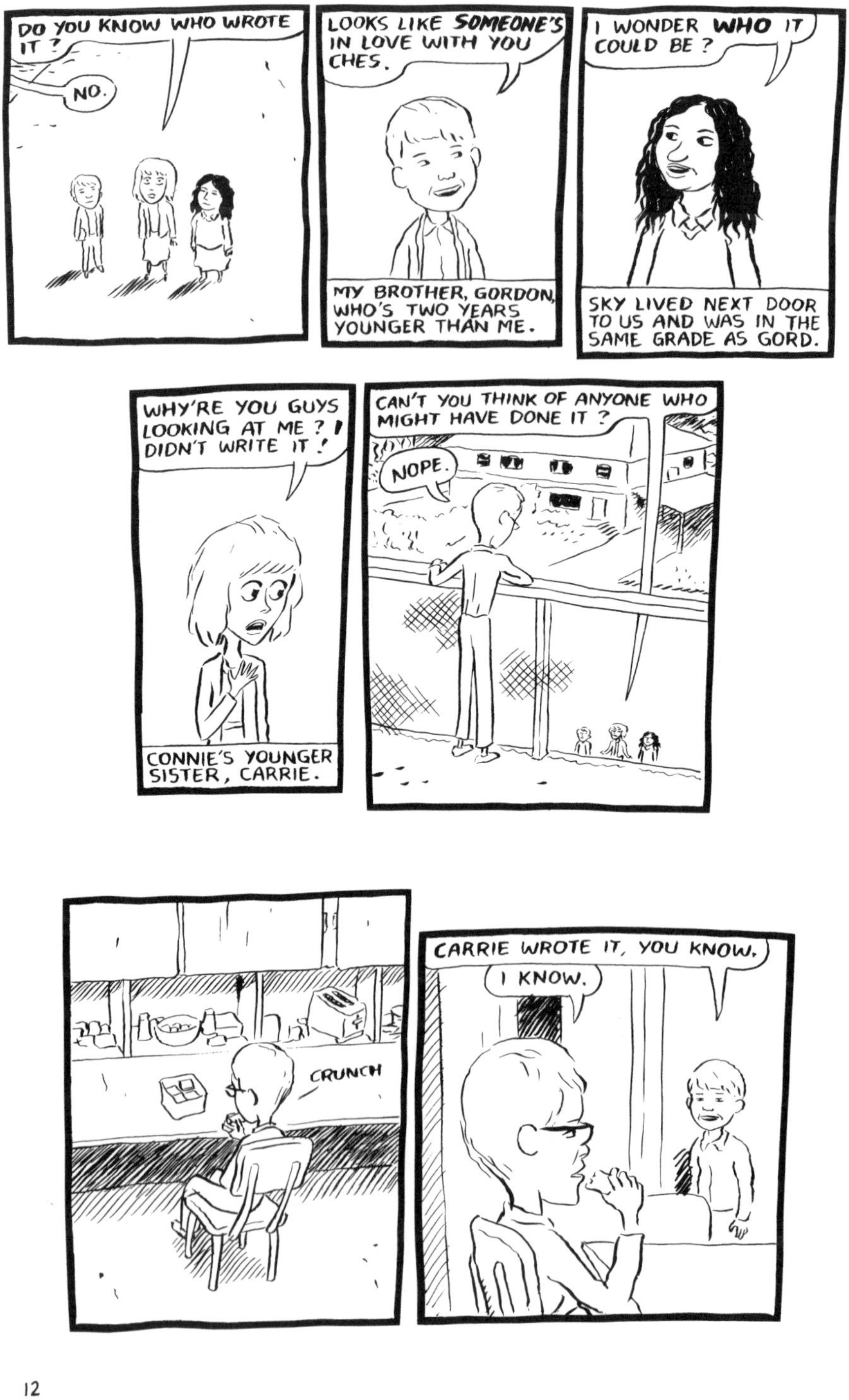
DO YOU KNOW WHO WROTE IT ?
NO.
LOOKS LIKE SOMEONE'S IN LOVE WITH YOU CHES.
MY BROTHER, GORDON, WHO'S TWO YEARS YOUNGER THAN ME.
I WONDER WHO IT COULD BE ?
SKY LIVED NEXT DOOR TO US AND WAS IN THE SAME GRADE AS GORD.
WHY'RE YOU GUYS LOOKING AT ME ? I DIDN'T WRITE IT !
CONNIE'S YOUNGER SISTER, CARRIE.
CAN'T YOU THINK OF ANYONE WHO MIGHT HAVE DONE IT ?
NOPE.
CRUNCH
CARRIE WROTE IT, YOU KNOW.
I KNOW.

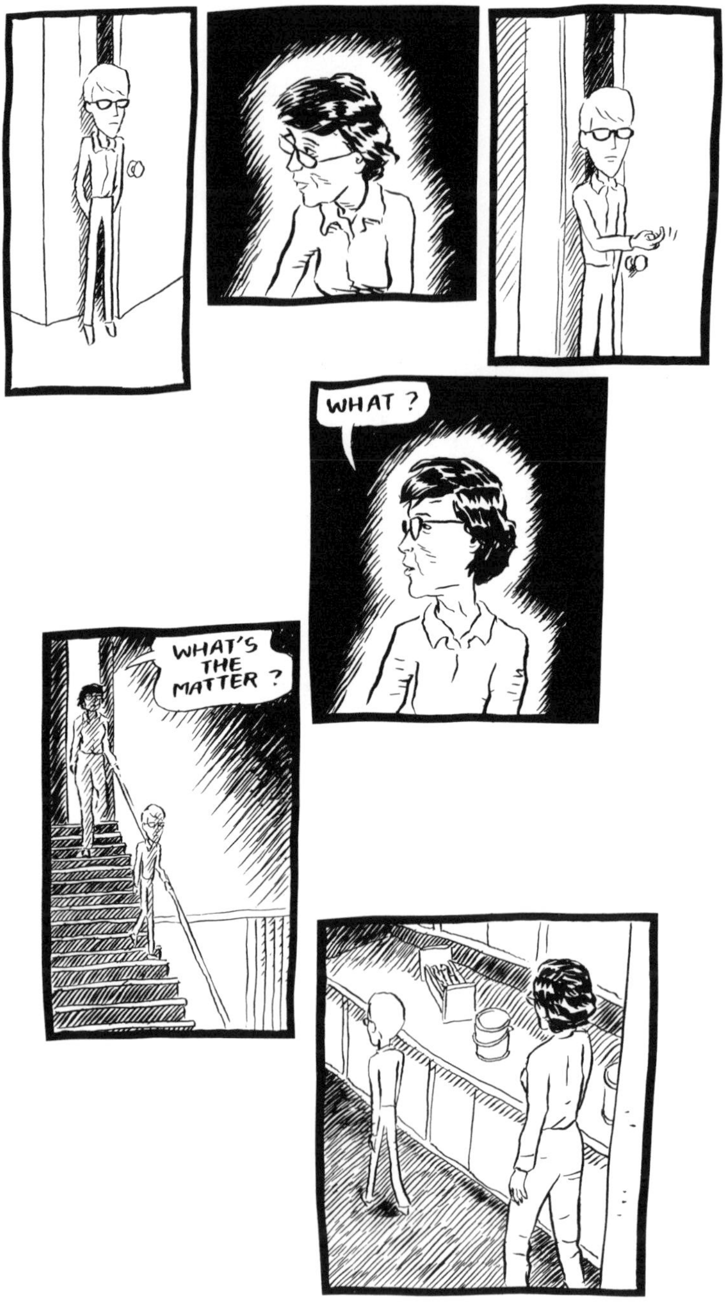
WHAT ?
WHAT'S THE MATTER ?

I WAS JUGGLING.
OH DEAR--
DID YOU THINK I WAS GOING TO BE MAD ? COME HERE.

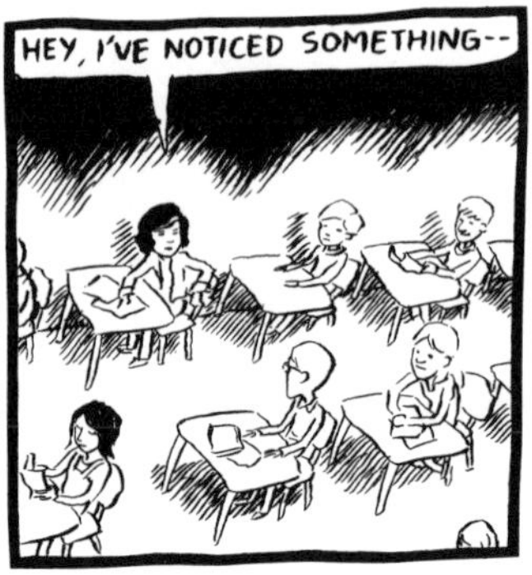
HEY, I'VE NOTICED SOMETHING--

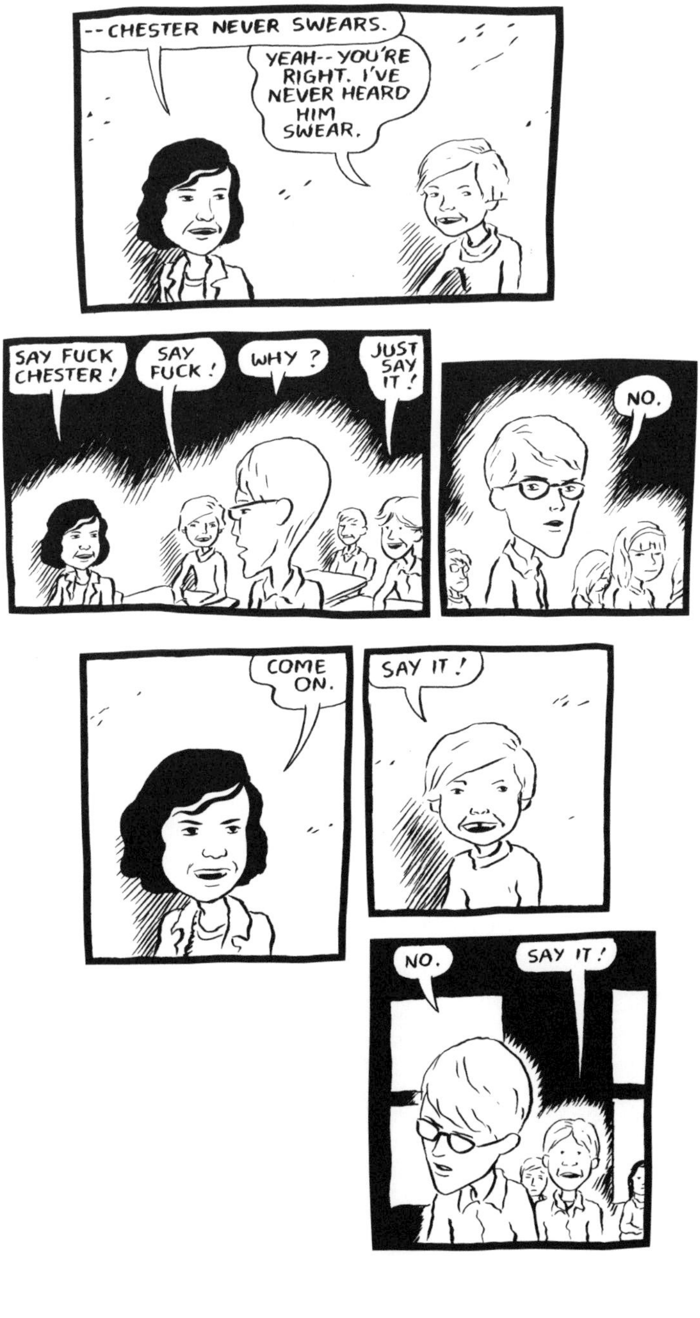
--CHESTER NEVER SWEARS.
YEAH--YOU'RE RIGHT. I'VE NEVER HEARD HIM SWEAR.
SAY FUCK CHESTER!
SAY FUCK!
WHY?
JUST SAY IT!
NO.
COME ON.
SAY IT!
NO.
SAY IT!

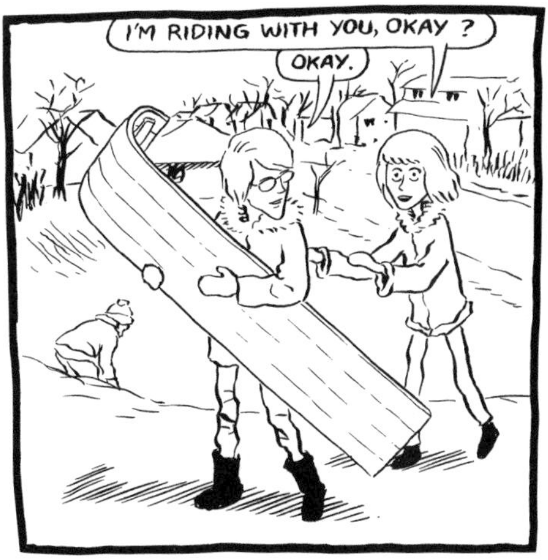
I'M RIDING WITH YOU, OKAY ?
OKAY.

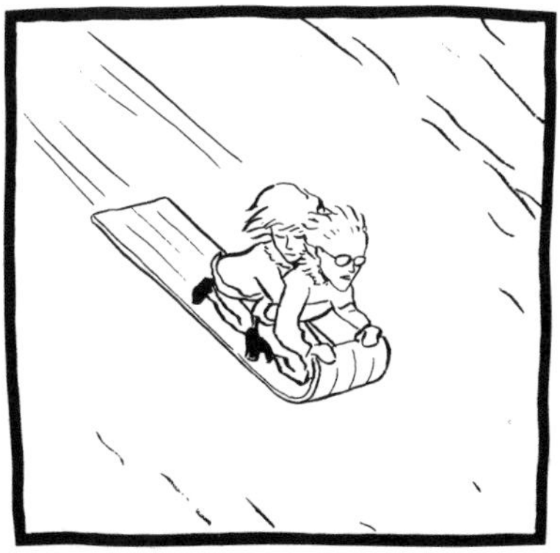

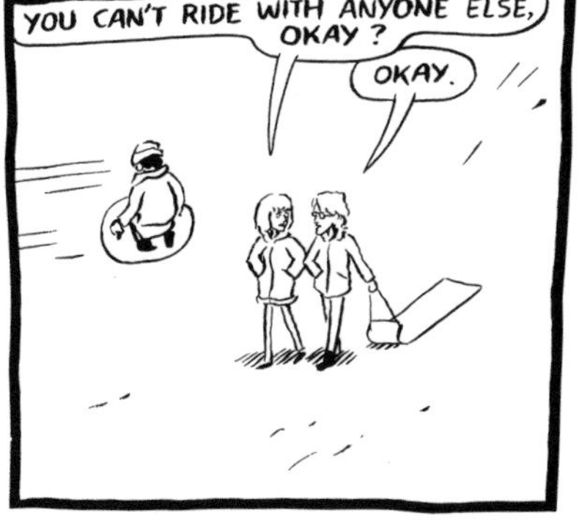
YOU CAN'T RIDE WITH ANYONE ELSE, OKAY ?
OKAY.

CRUNCH

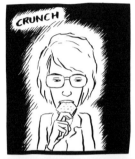

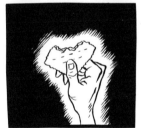

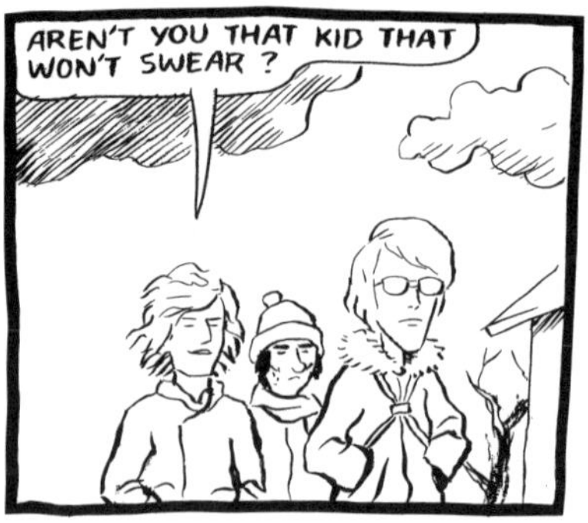
AREN'T YOU THAT KID THAT WON'T SWEAR ?

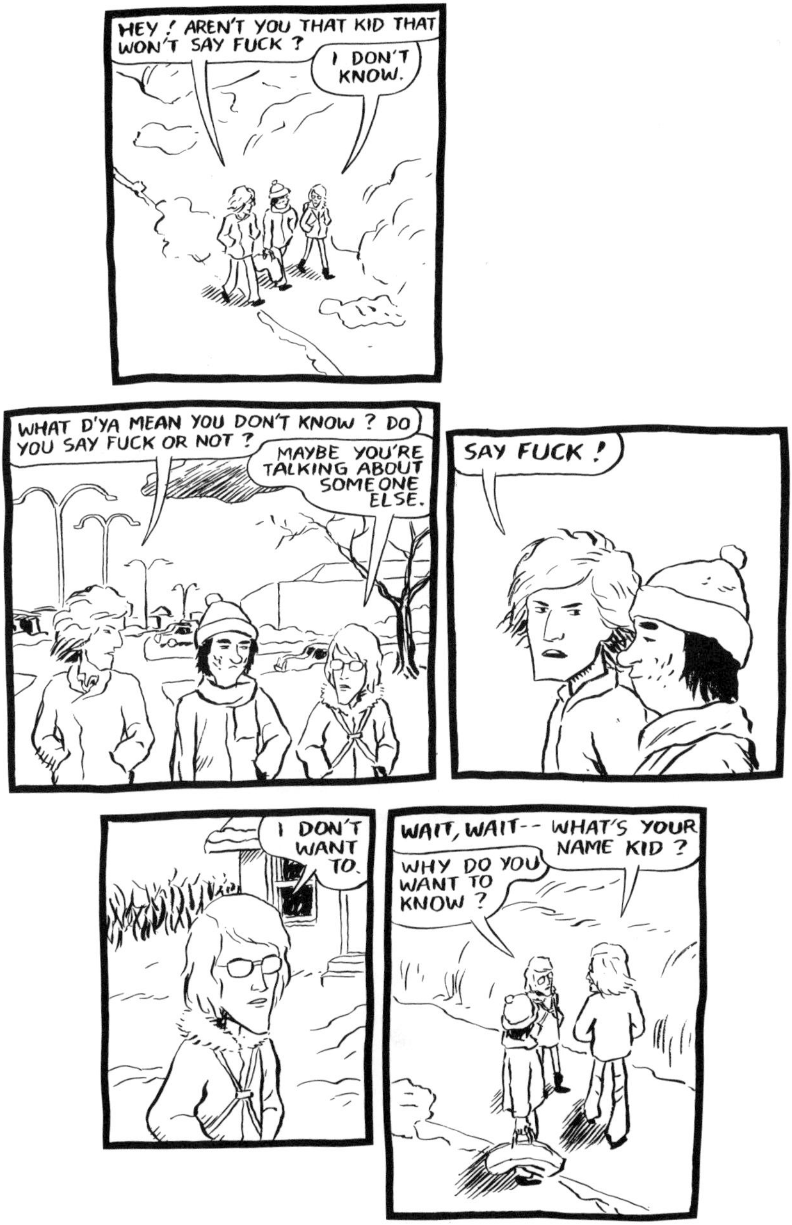
HEY! AREN'T YOU THAT KID THAT WON'T SAY FUCK?
I DON'T KNOW.
WHAT D'YA MEAN YOU DON'T KNOW? DO YOU SAY FUCK OR NOT?
MAYBE YOU'RE TALKING ABOUT SOMEONE ELSE.
SAY FUCK!
I DON'T WANT TO.
WAIT, WAIT-- WHAT'S YOUR NAME KID?
WHY DO YOU WANT TO KNOW?

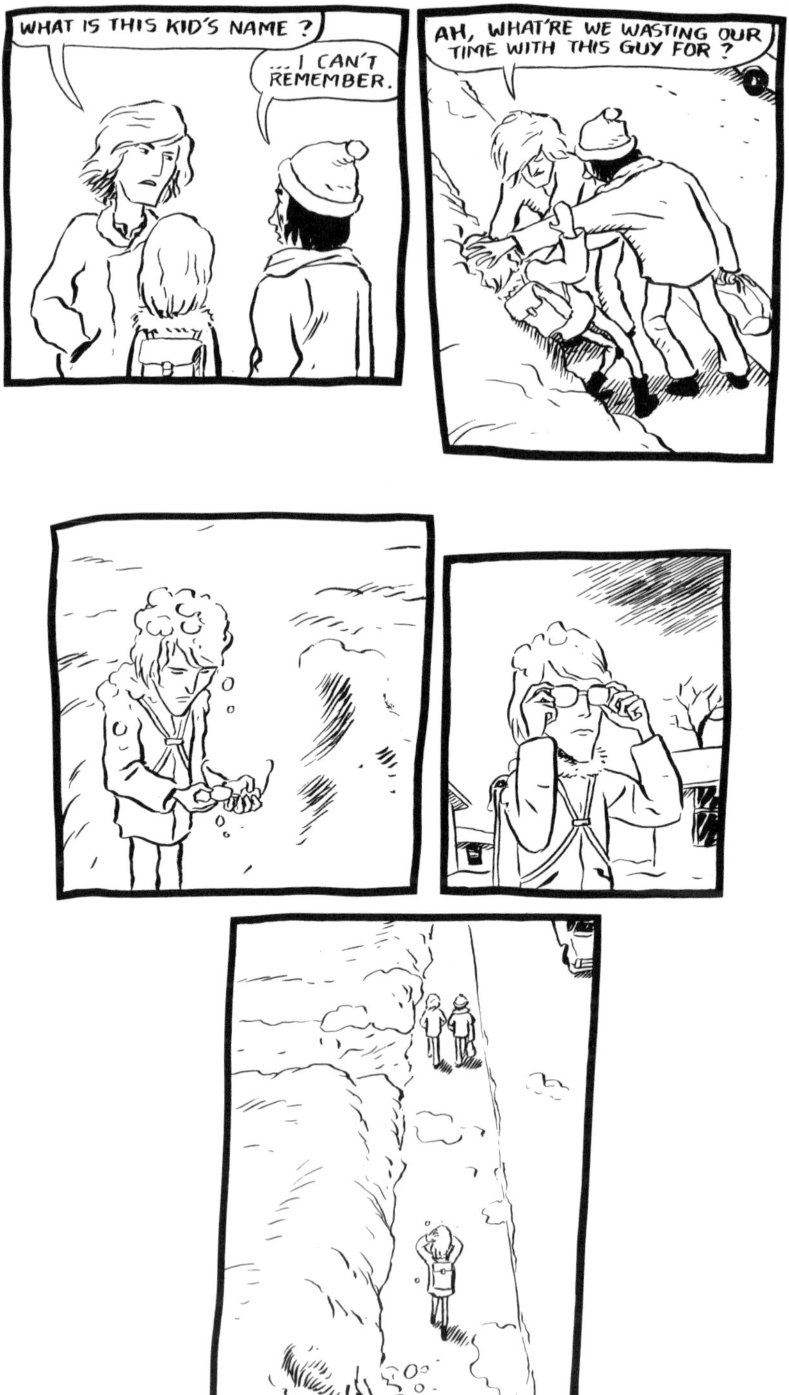
WHAT IS THIS KID'S NAME ?
... I CAN'T REMEMBER.
AH, WHAT'RE WE WASTING OUR TIME WITH THIS GUY FOR ?

BOYS-- I THINK YOU'RE OLD ENOUGH NOW THAT I CAN TALK ABOUT...CERTAIN TOPICS WITH YOU.

YOU KNOW, MOST MEN EXPECT A WOMAN'S BODY TO LOOK A CERTAIN WAY, AND NOT ALL OF THEM DO LOOK THAT WAY.

SO SOMETIMES A WOMAN HAS TO DO SOMETHING THAT WILL CHANGE HER APPEARANCE SO THAT SHE'LL BE ACCEPTED BY THE PEOPLE AROUND HER.

PEOPLE EXPECT A WOMAN'S BREASTS TO BE A CERTAIN SIZE, AND MINE AREN'T THAT SIZE. THEY'RE SMALLER.
SO I WEAR A PADDED BRASSIERE--IT MAKES IT LOOK LIKE MY BREASTS ARE THE SIZE THAT MOST WOMEN'S ARE.

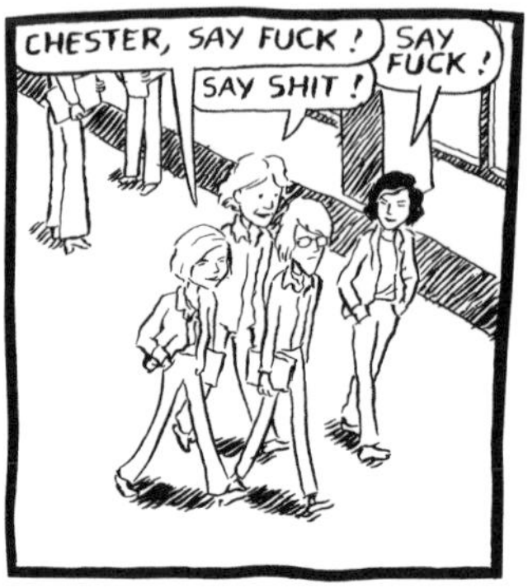
CHESTER, SAY FUCK!
SAY SHIT!
SAY FUCK!

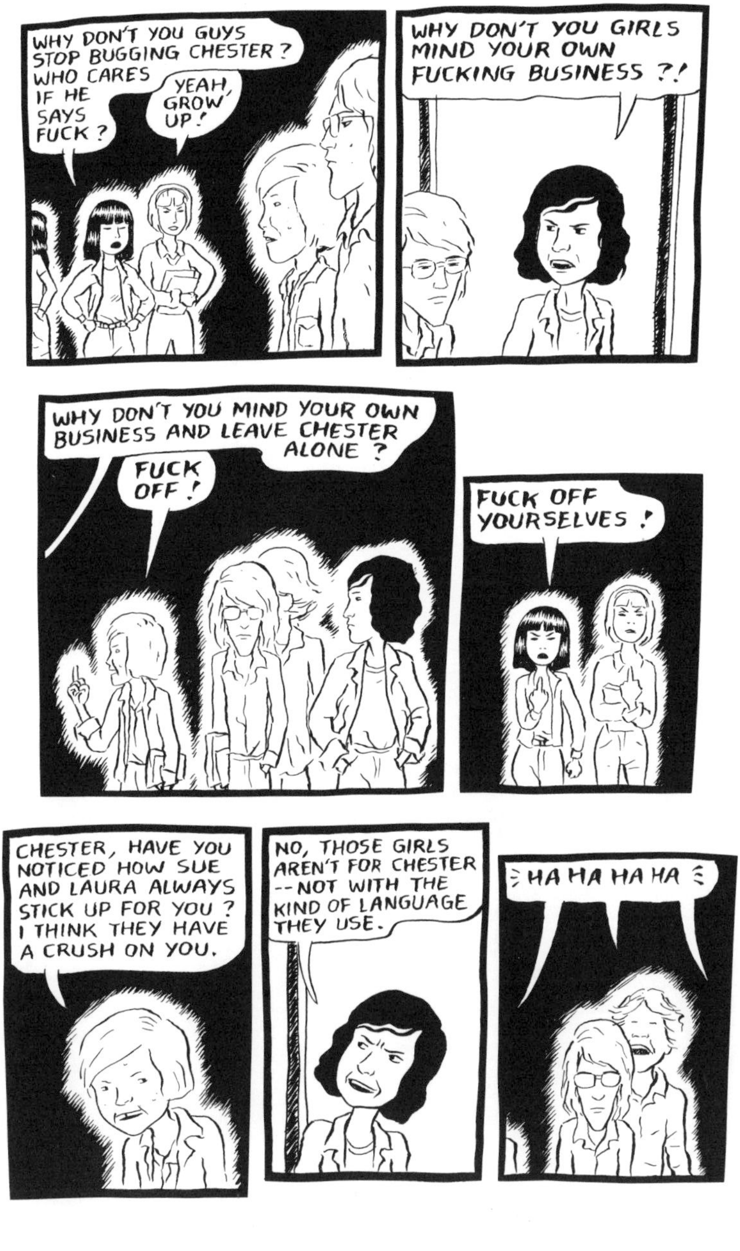
WHY DON'T YOU GUYS STOP BUGGING CHESTER? WHO CARES IF HE SAYS FUCK?
YEAH, GROW UP!
WHY DON'T YOU GIRLS MIND YOUR OWN FUCKING BUSINESS?!
WHY DON'T YOU MIND YOUR OWN BUSINESS AND LEAVE CHESTER ALONE?
FUCK OFF!
FUCK OFF YOURSELVES!
CHESTER, HAVE YOU NOTICED HOW SUE AND LAURA ALWAYS STICK UP FOR YOU? I THINK THEY HAVE A CRUSH ON YOU.
NO, THOSE GIRLS AREN'T FOR CHESTER --NOT WITH THE KIND OF LANGUAGE THEY USE.
HA HA HA HA

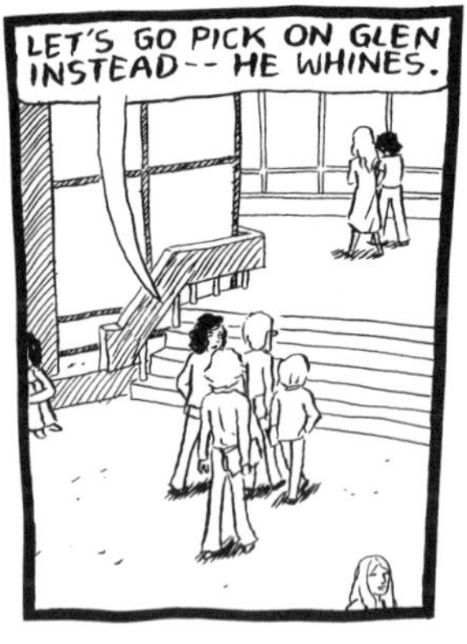
LET'S GO PICK ON GLEN INSTEAD-- HE WHINES.

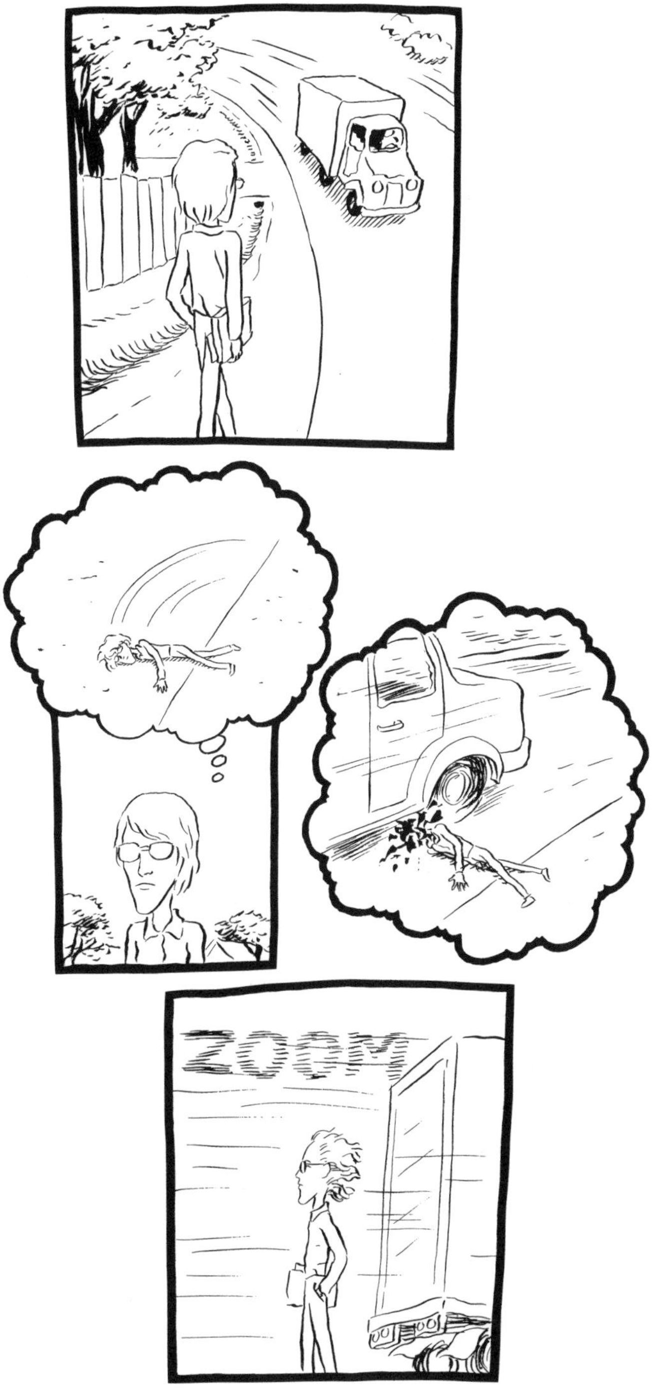
ZOOM

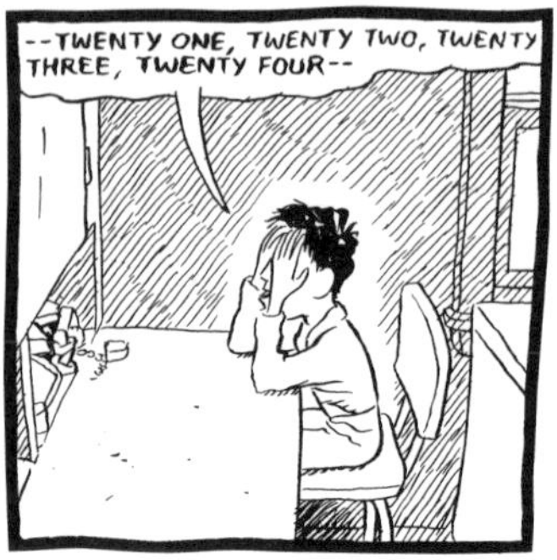
--TWENTY ONE, TWENTY TWO, TWENTY THREE, TWENTY FOUR--

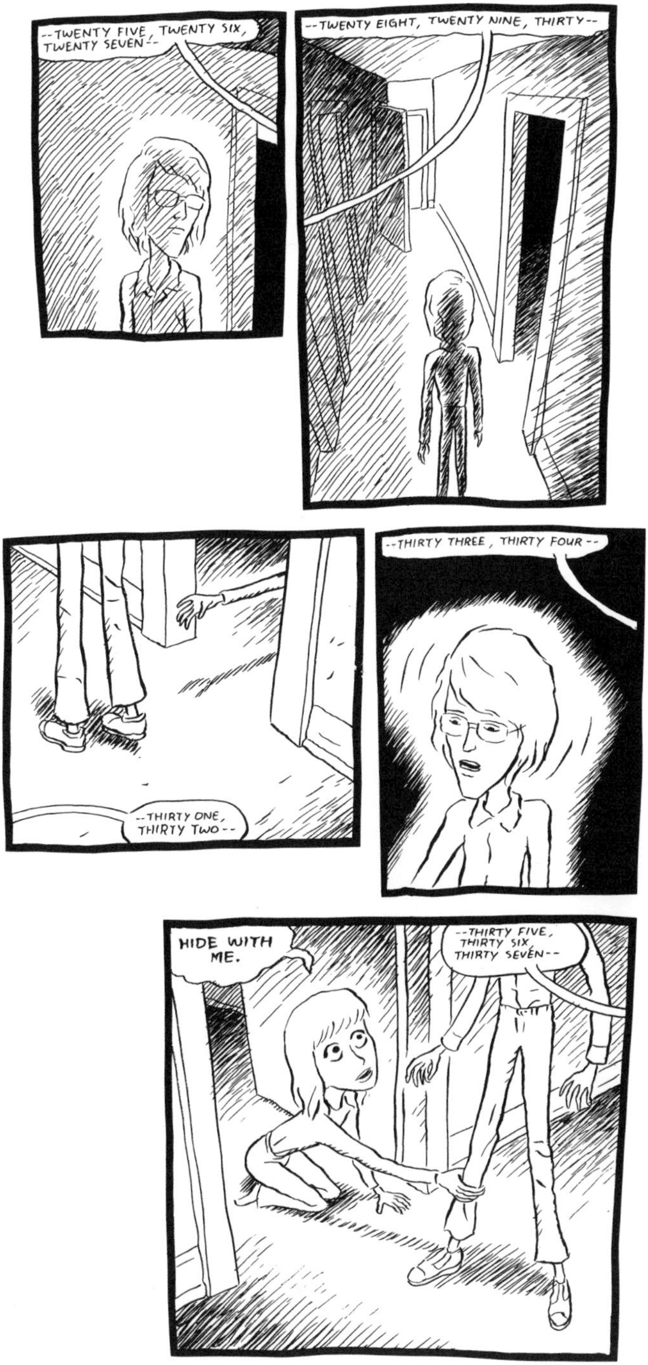
--TWENTY FIVE, TWENTY SIX, TWENTY SEVEN--
--TWENTY EIGHT, TWENTY NINE, THIRTY--
--THIRTY ONE, THIRTY TWO--
--THIRTY THREE, THIRTY FOUR--
HIDE WITH ME.
--THIRTY FIVE, THIRTY SIX, THIRTY SEVEN--

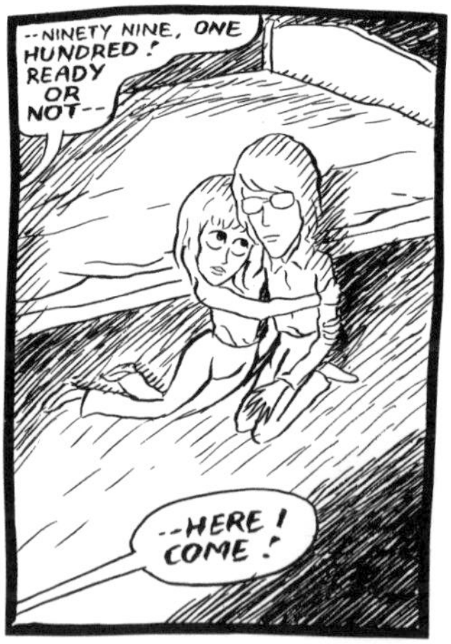
--NINETY NINE, ONE HUNDRED! READY OR NOT--
--HERE! COME!

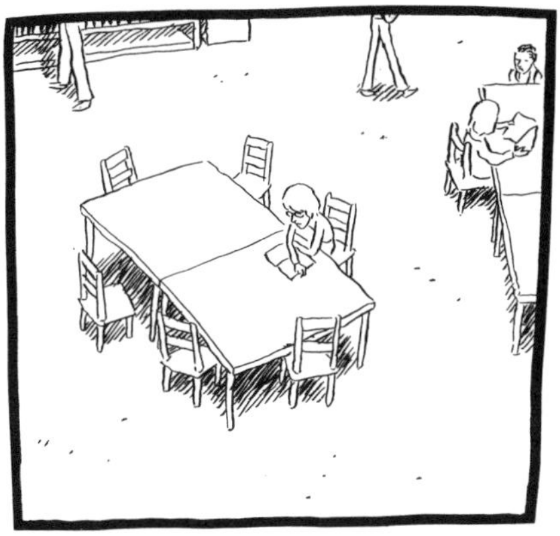

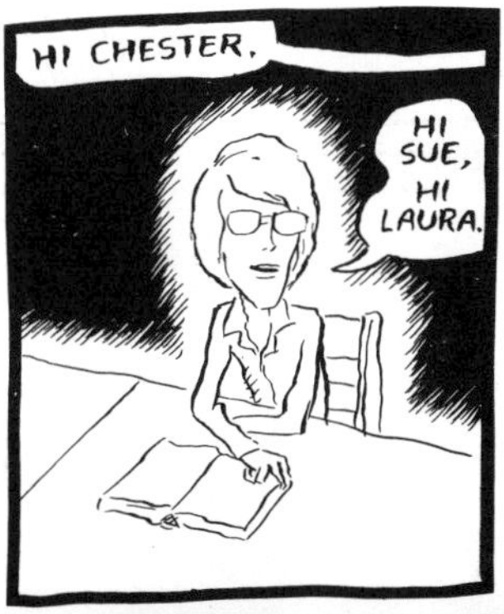
HI CHESTER.
HI SUE, HI LAURA.

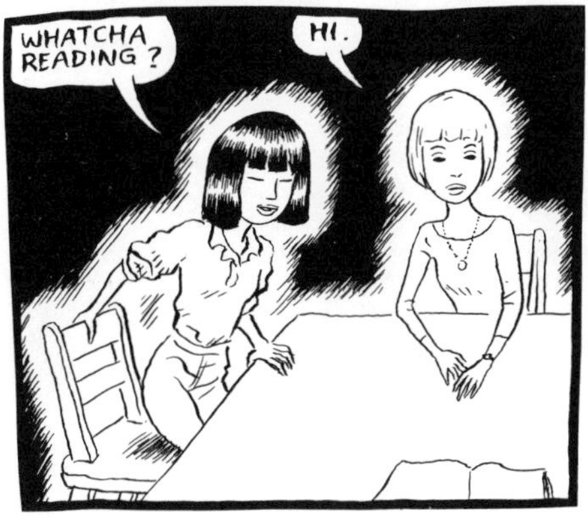
WHATCHA READING?
HI.

OH, IS IT GOOD ?
IT'S OKAY.
WE WANTED TO TALK TO YOU.
YEAH, WE'VE GOT A SECRET TO TELL YOU.
UH-HUNH ?

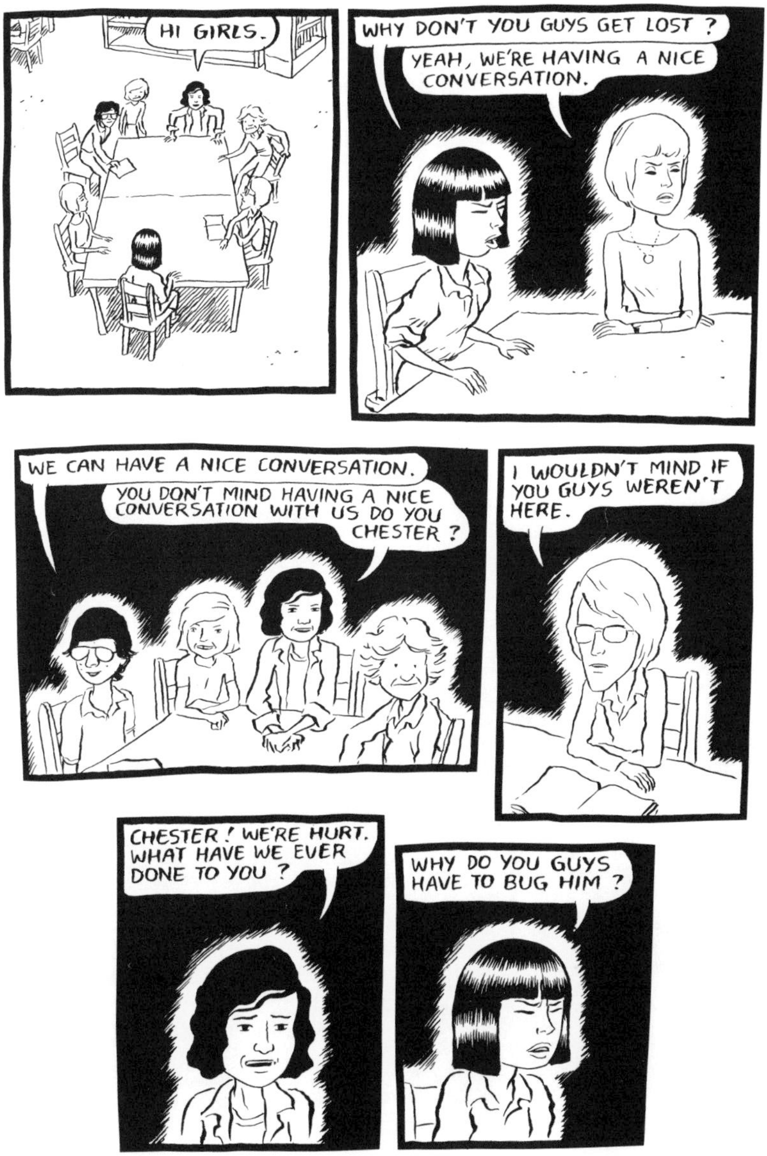
HI GIRLS.
WHY DON'T YOU GUYS GET LOST ?
YEAH, WE'RE HAVING A NICE CONVERSATION.
WE CAN HAVE A NICE CONVERSATION.
YOU DON'T MIND HAVING A NICE CONVERSATION WITH US DO YOU CHESTER ?
I WOULDN'T MIND IF YOU GUYS WEREN'T HERE.
CHESTER ! WE'RE HURT. WHAT HAVE WE EVER DONE TO YOU ?
WHY DO YOU GUYS HAVE TO BUG HIM ?

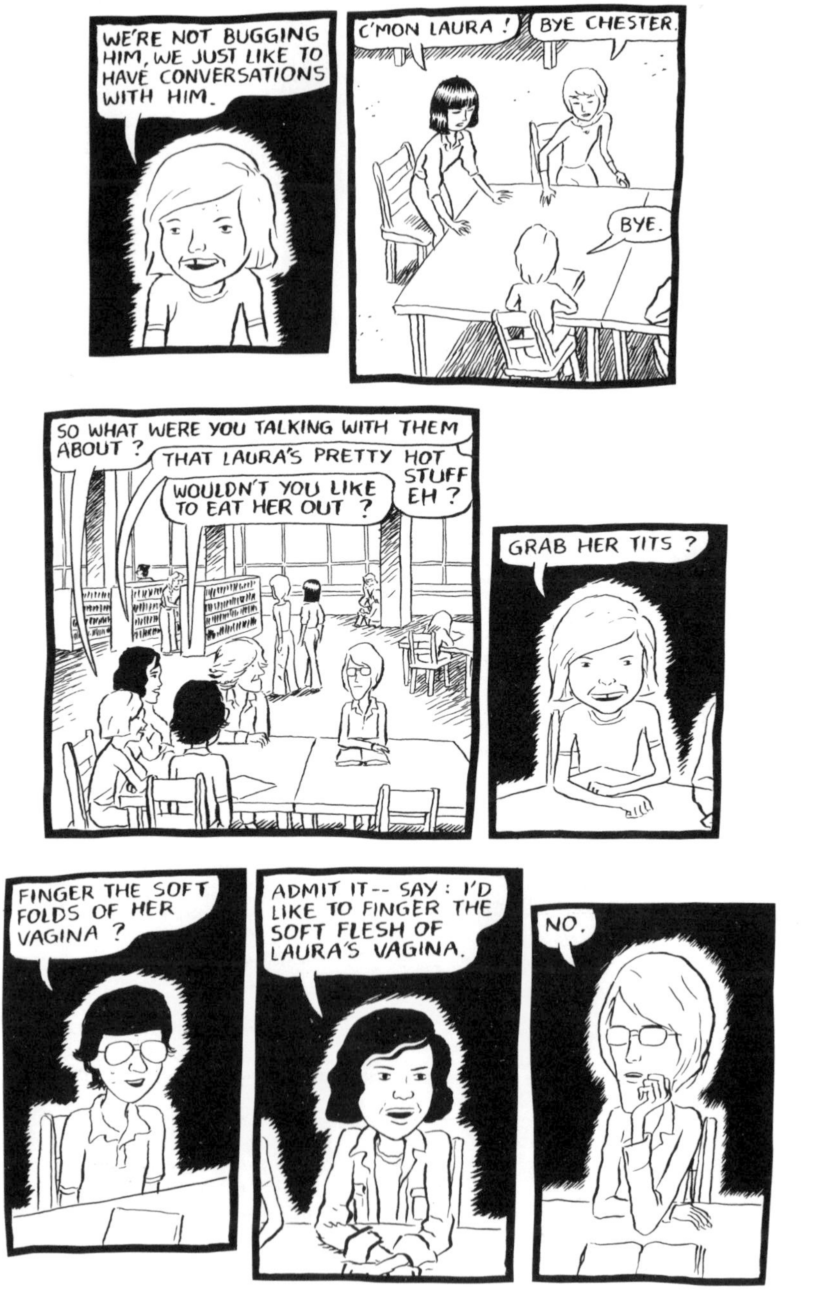
WE'RE NOT BUGGING HIM, WE JUST LIKE TO HAVE CONVERSATIONS WITH HIM.
C'MON LAURA!
BYE CHESTER.
BYE.
SO WHAT WERE YOU TALKING WITH THEM ABOUT?
THAT LAURA'S PRETTY HOT STUFF EH?
WOULDN'T YOU LIKE TO EAT HER OUT?
GRAB HER TITS?
FINGER THE SOFT FOLDS OF HER VAGINA?
ADMIT IT-- SAY: I'D LIKE TO FINGER THE SOFT FLESH OF LAURA'S VAGINA.
NO.

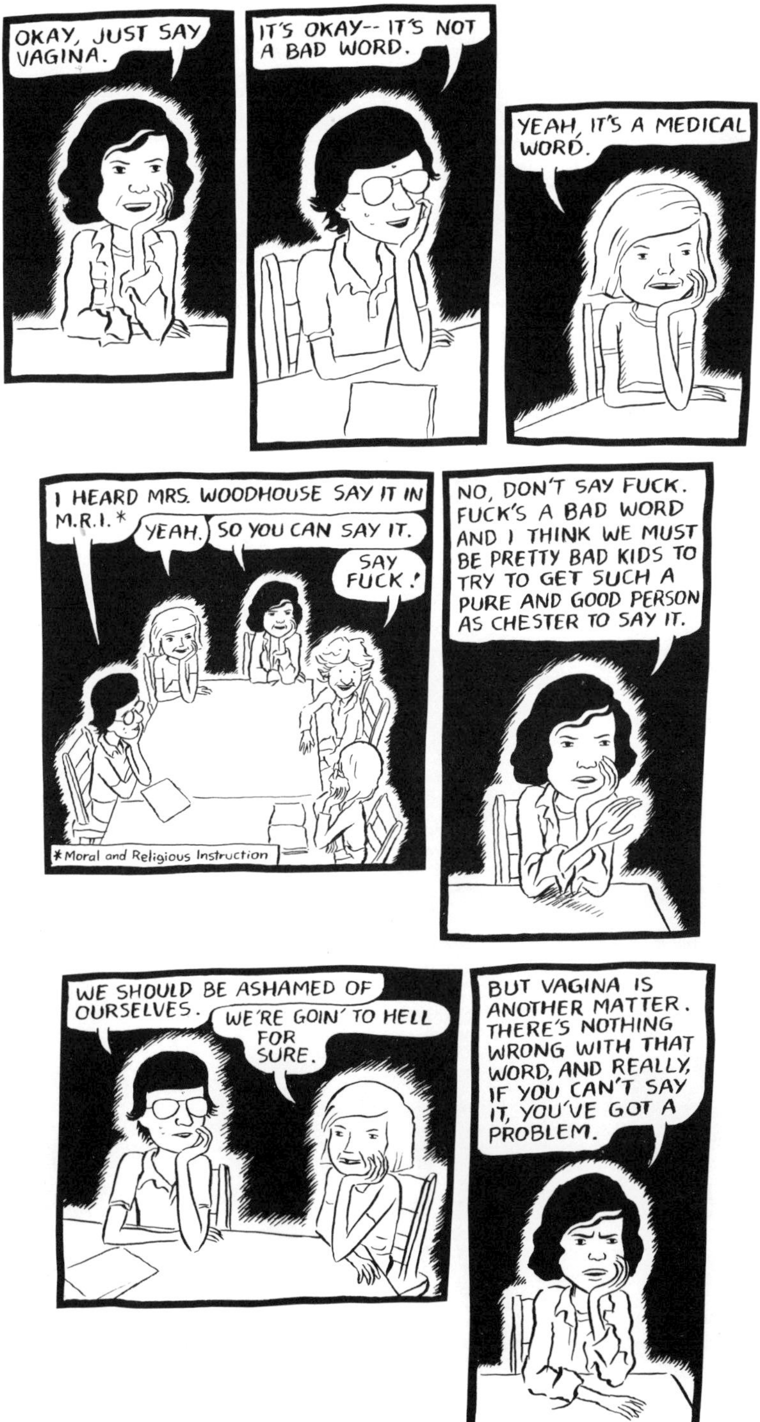
OKAY, JUST SAY VAGINA.
IT'S OKAY-- IT'S NOT A BAD WORD.
YEAH, IT'S A MEDICAL WORD.
I HEARD MRS. WOODHOUSE SAY IT IN M.R.I.*
YEAH.
SO YOU CAN SAY IT.
SAY FUCK!
*Moral and Religious Instruction
NO, DON'T SAY FUCK. FUCK'S A BAD WORD AND I THINK WE MUST BE PRETTY BAD KIDS TO TRY TO GET SUCH A PURE AND GOOD PERSON AS CHESTER TO SAY IT.
WE SHOULD BE ASHAMED OF OURSELVES.
WE'RE GOIN' TO HELL FOR SURE.
BUT VAGINA IS ANOTHER MATTER. THERE'S NOTHING WRONG WITH THAT WORD, AND REALLY, IF YOU CAN'T SAY IT, YOU'VE GOT A PROBLEM.

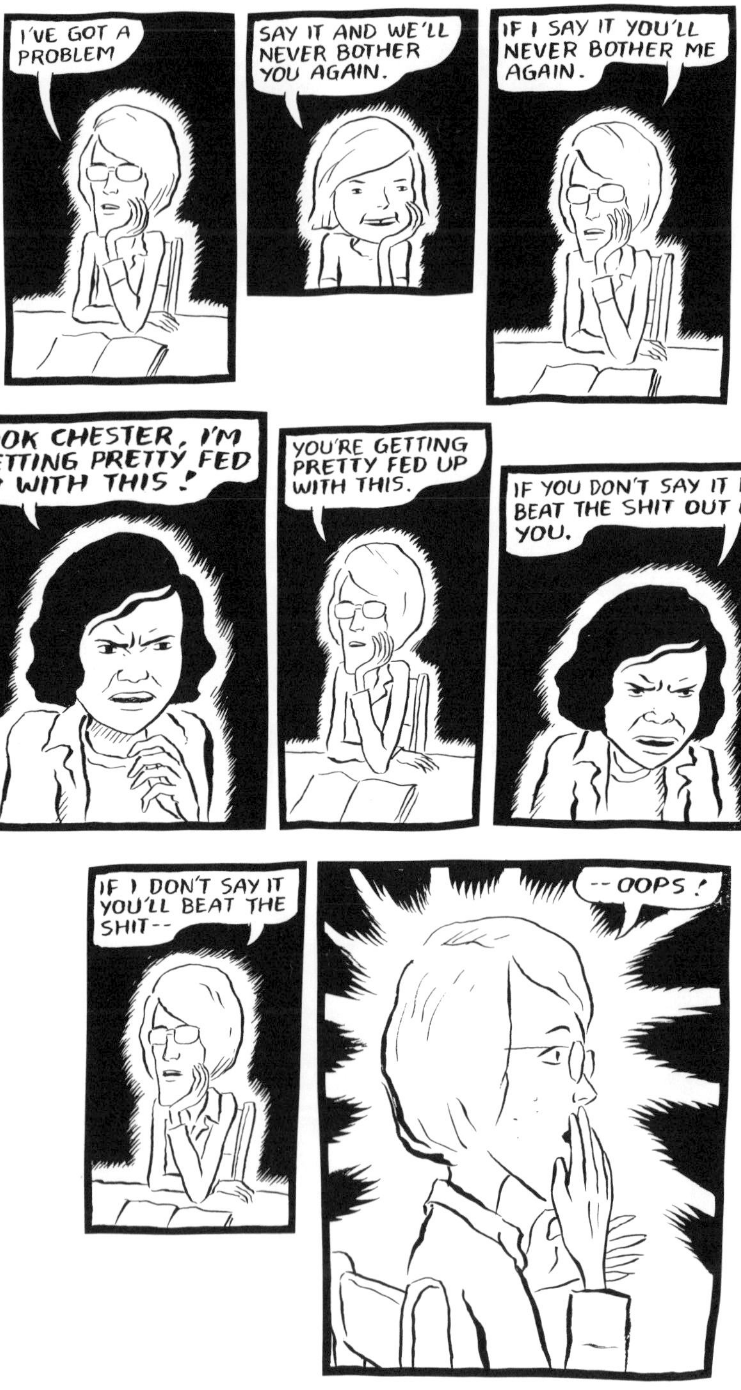
I'VE GOT A PROBLEM
SAY IT AND WE'LL NEVER BOTHER YOU AGAIN.
IF I SAY IT YOU'LL NEVER BOTHER ME AGAIN.
LOOK CHESTER, I'M GETTING PRETTY FED UP WITH THIS!
YOU'RE GETTING PRETTY FED UP WITH THIS.
IF YOU DON'T SAY IT I'LL BEAT THE SHIT OUT OF YOU.
IF I DON'T SAY IT YOU'LL BEAT THE SHIT--
--OOPS!

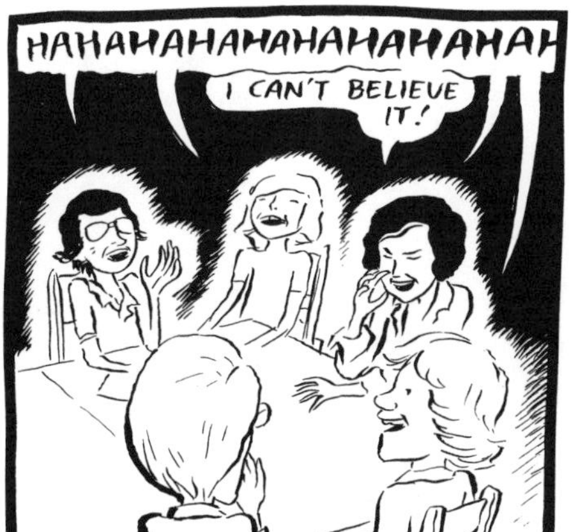
HAHAHAHAHAHAHAHAHAH
I CAN'T BELIEVE IT!

YOUR FACE HAS CHANGED A LOT IN THE LAST YEAR. YOUR JAW'S BECOME MORE DOMINANT. YOU'RE REALLY BECOMING QUITE HANDSOME.

UH-HUH?

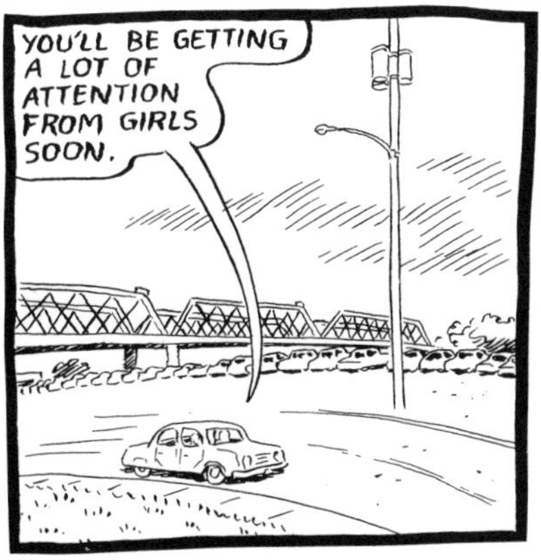
YOU'LL BE GETTING A LOT OF ATTENTION FROM GIRLS SOON.

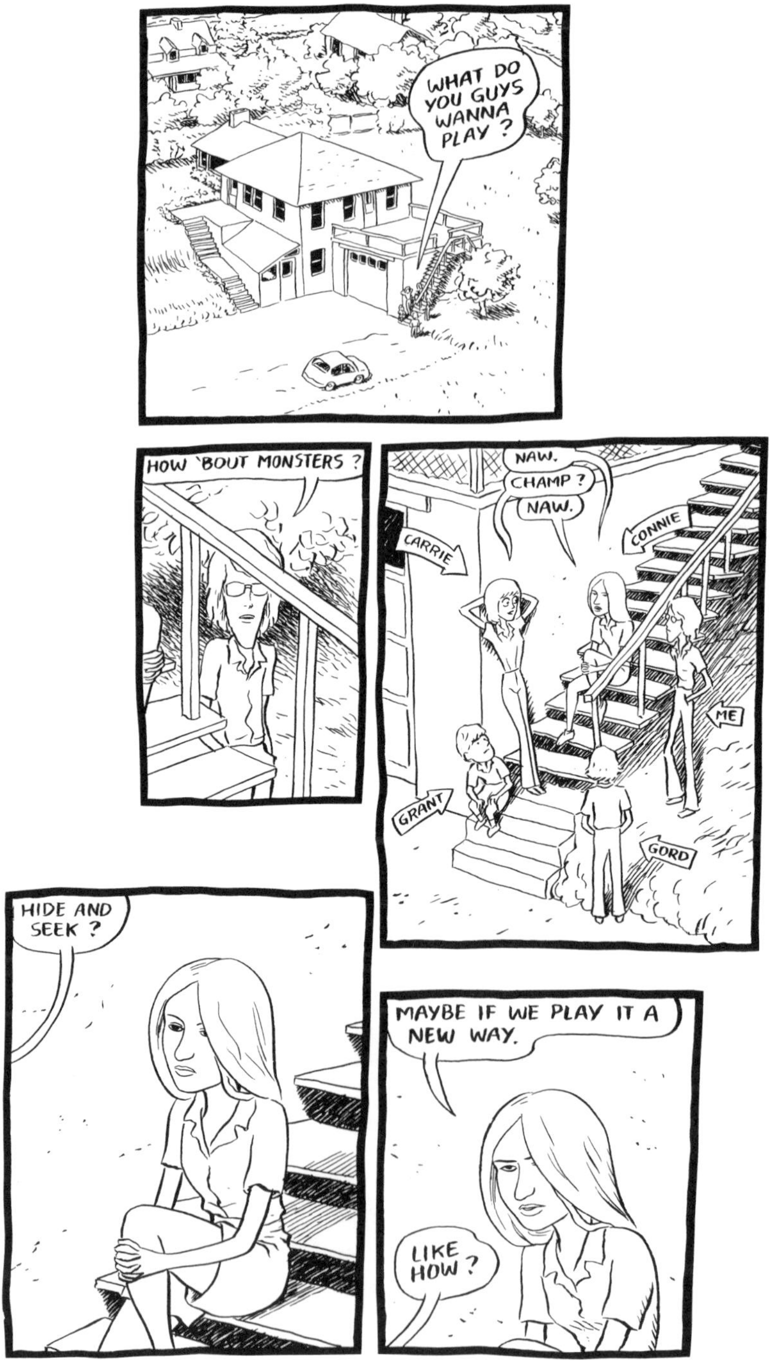
WHAT DO YOU GUYS WANNA PLAY ?
HOW 'BOUT MONSTERS ?
NAW.
CHAMP ?
NAW.
CARRIE
CONNIE
ME
GRANT
GORD
HIDE AND SEEK ?
MAYBE IF WE PLAY IT A NEW WAY.
LIKE HOW ?

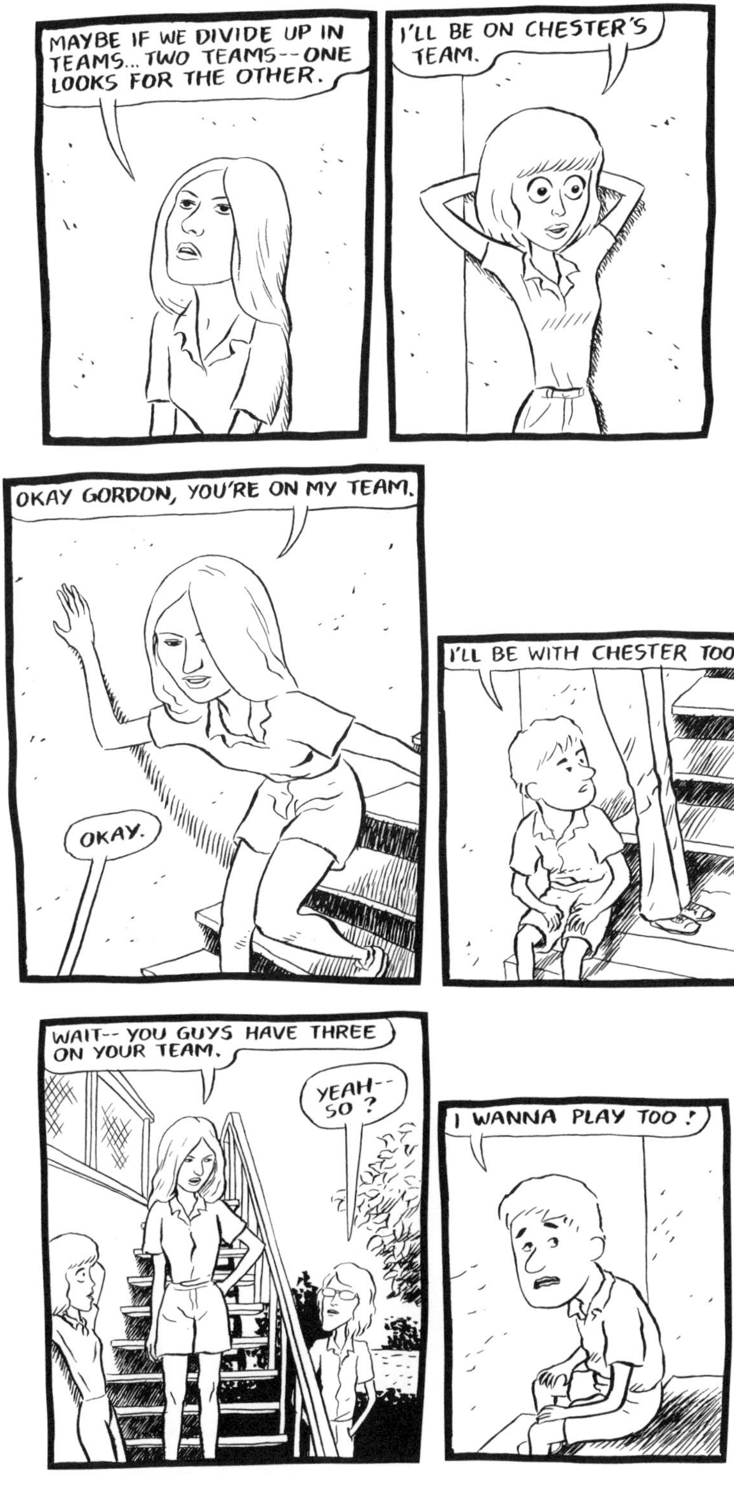
MAYBE IF WE DIVIDE UP IN TEAMS... TWO TEAMS--ONE LOOKS FOR THE OTHER.
I'LL BE ON CHESTER'S TEAM.
OKAY GORDON, YOU'RE ON MY TEAM.
OKAY.
I'LL BE WITH CHESTER TOO.
WAIT-- YOU GUYS HAVE THREE ON YOUR TEAM.
YEAH-- SO?
I WANNA PLAY TOO!

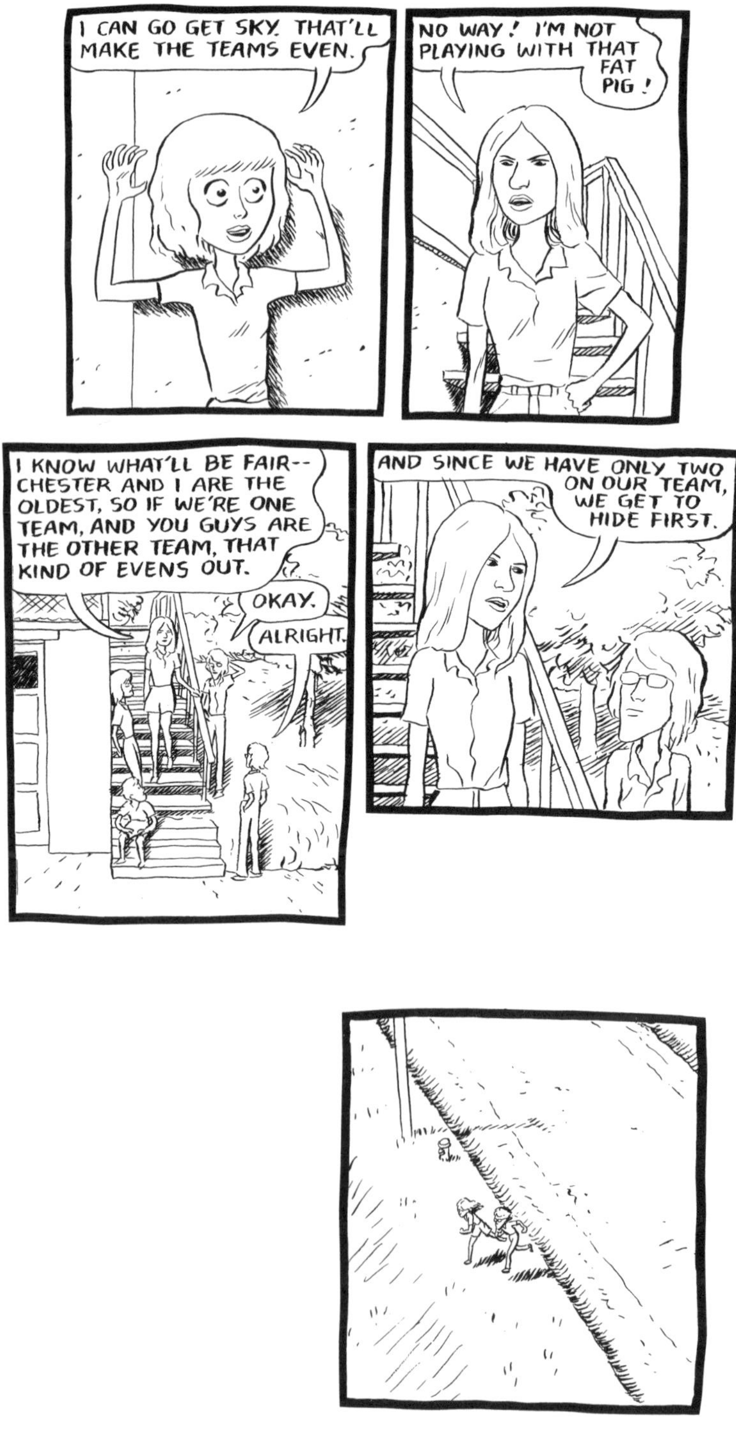
I CAN GO GET SKY. THAT'LL MAKE THE TEAMS EVEN.
NO WAY! I'M NOT PLAYING WITH THAT FAT PIG!
I KNOW WHAT'LL BE FAIR-- CHESTER AND I ARE THE OLDEST, SO IF WE'RE ONE TEAM, AND YOU GUYS ARE THE OTHER TEAM, THAT KIND OF EVENS OUT.
OKAY.
ALRIGHT.
AND SINCE WE HAVE ONLY TWO ON OUR TEAM, WE GET TO HIDE FIRST.

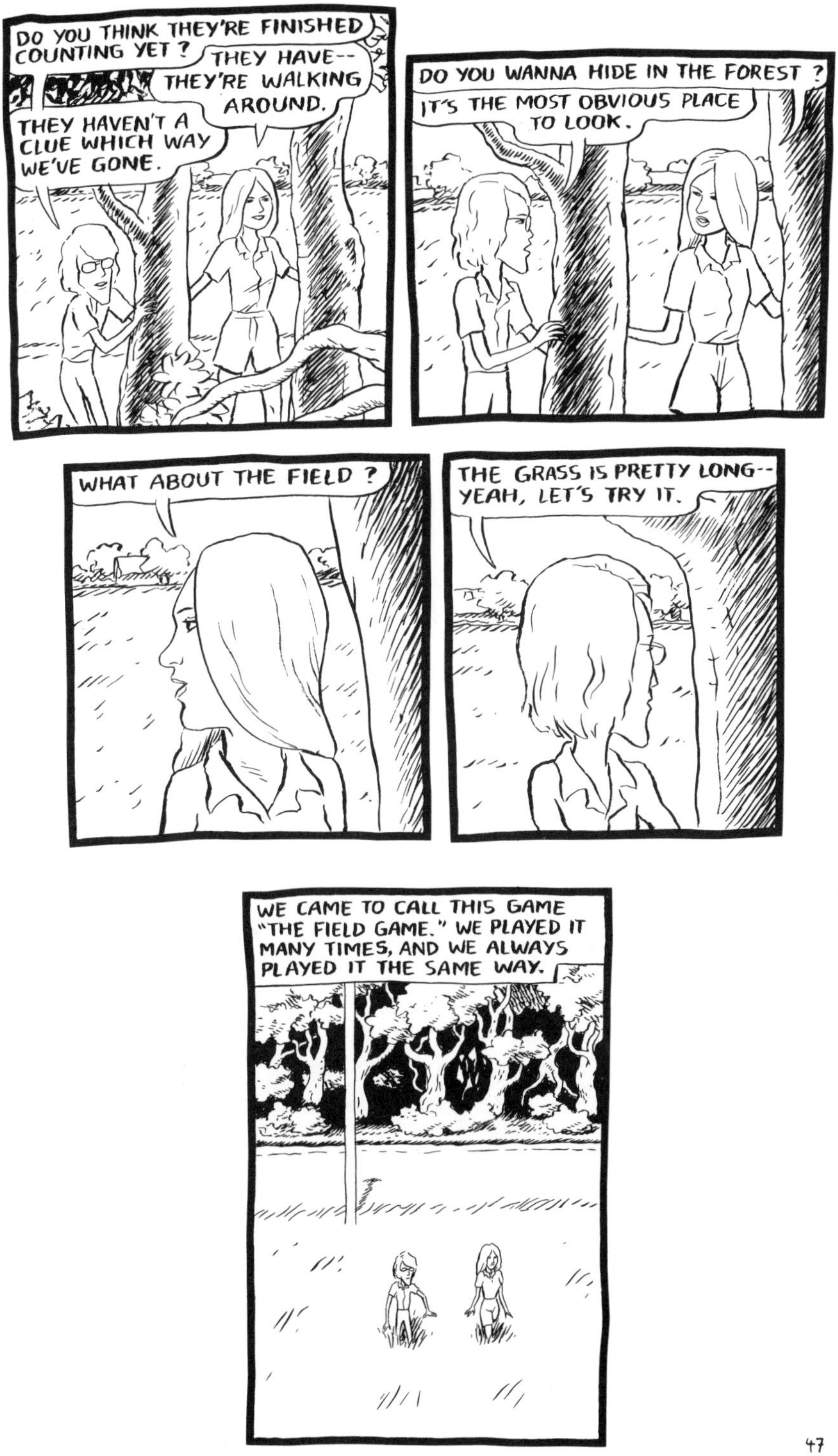
DO YOU THINK THEY'RE FINISHED COUNTING YET ?
THEY HAVE-- THEY'RE WALKING AROUND.
THEY HAVEN'T A CLUE WHICH WAY WE'VE GONE.
DO YOU WANNA HIDE IN THE FOREST ?
IT'S THE MOST OBVIOUS PLACE TO LOOK.
WHAT ABOUT THE FIELD ?
THE GRASS IS PRETTY LONG-- YEAH, LET'S TRY IT.
WE CAME TO CALL THIS GAME "THE FIELD GAME." WE PLAYED IT MANY TIMES, AND WE ALWAYS PLAYED IT THE SAME WAY.

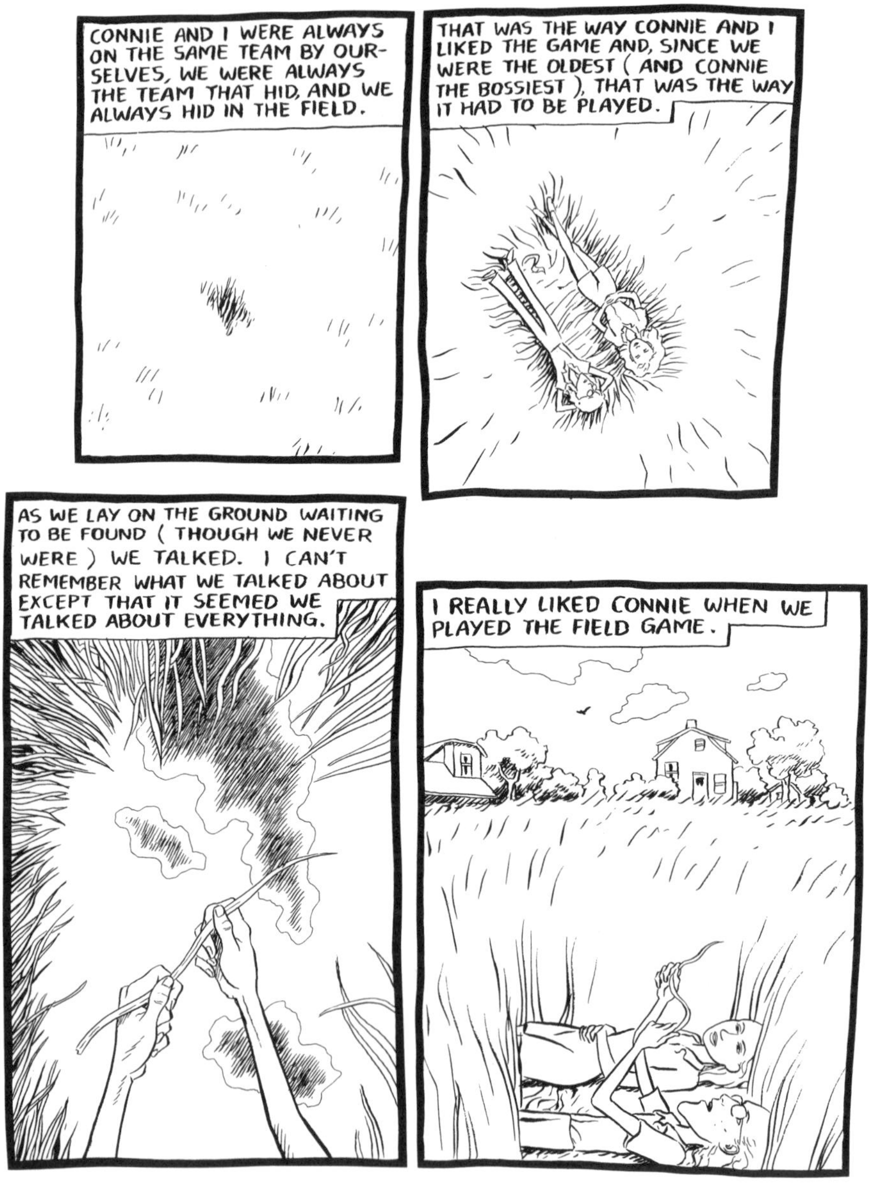
CONNIE AND I WERE ALWAYS ON THE SAME TEAM BY OURSELVES, WE WERE ALWAYS THE TEAM THAT HID, AND WE ALWAYS HID IN THE FIELD.
THAT WAS THE WAY CONNIE AND I LIKED THE GAME AND, SINCE WE WERE THE OLDEST (AND CONNIE THE BOSSIEST), THAT WAS THE WAY IT HAD TO BE PLAYED.
AS WE LAY ON THE GROUND WAITING TO BE FOUND (THOUGH WE NEVER WERE) WE TALKED. I CAN'T REMEMBER WHAT WE TALKED ABOUT EXCEPT THAT IT SEEMED WE TALKED ABOUT EVERYTHING.
I REALLY LIKED CONNIE WHEN WE PLAYED THE FIELD GAME.

WHENEVER WE WEREN'T PLAYING IT I DIDN'T LIKE HER MUCH AT ALL.

AND I WAS SURE SHE FELT THE SAME WAY ABOUT ME.

THEY'RE IN THE FOREST.

THEY'RE NOT IN THE FOREST. WE LOOKED ALL THROUGH THE FOREST.

THEY WOULDN'T BE OUT HERE.

49

I'M TIRED OF LOOKING. WHEN IS IT GOING TO BE OUR TURN TO HIDE ?
WHEN WE FIND THEM, SO SHUT UP AND KEEP LOOKING.
THIS IS HOPELESS. THEY'RE BACK IN THE FORT.
WE LOOKED THERE.
SNICKER
THEY WERE THIS CLOSE !

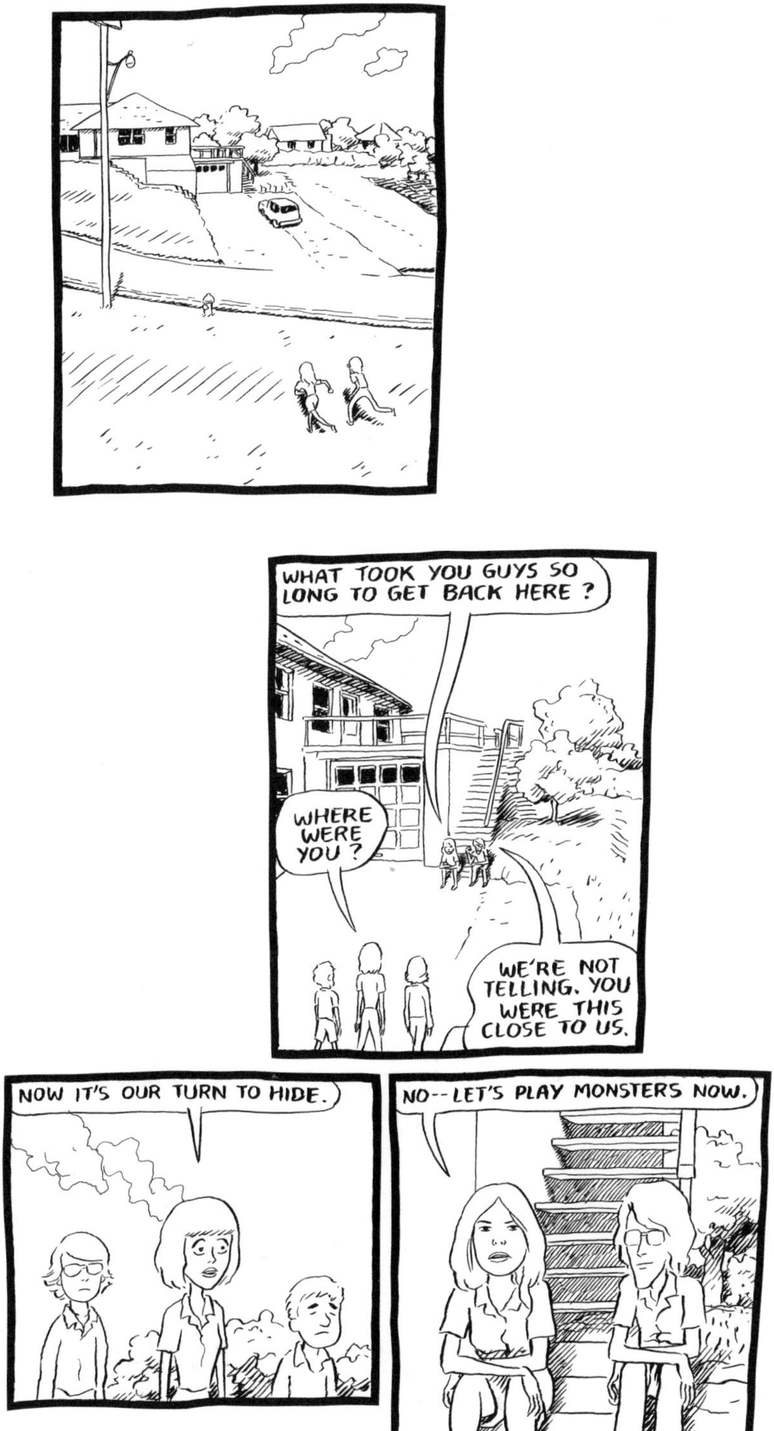
WHAT TOOK YOU GUYS SO LONG TO GET BACK HERE ?
WHERE WERE YOU ?
WE'RE NOT TELLING. YOU WERE THIS CLOSE TO US.
NOW IT'S OUR TURN TO HIDE.
NO--LET'S PLAY MONSTERS NOW.

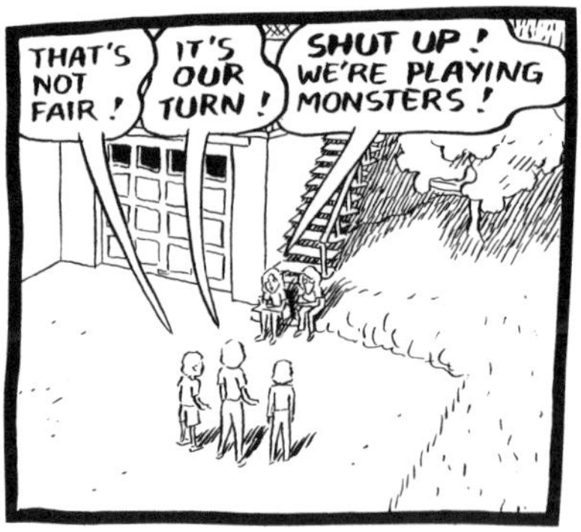
THAT'S NOT FAIR!
IT'S OUR TURN!
SHUT UP! WE'RE PLAYING MONSTERS!

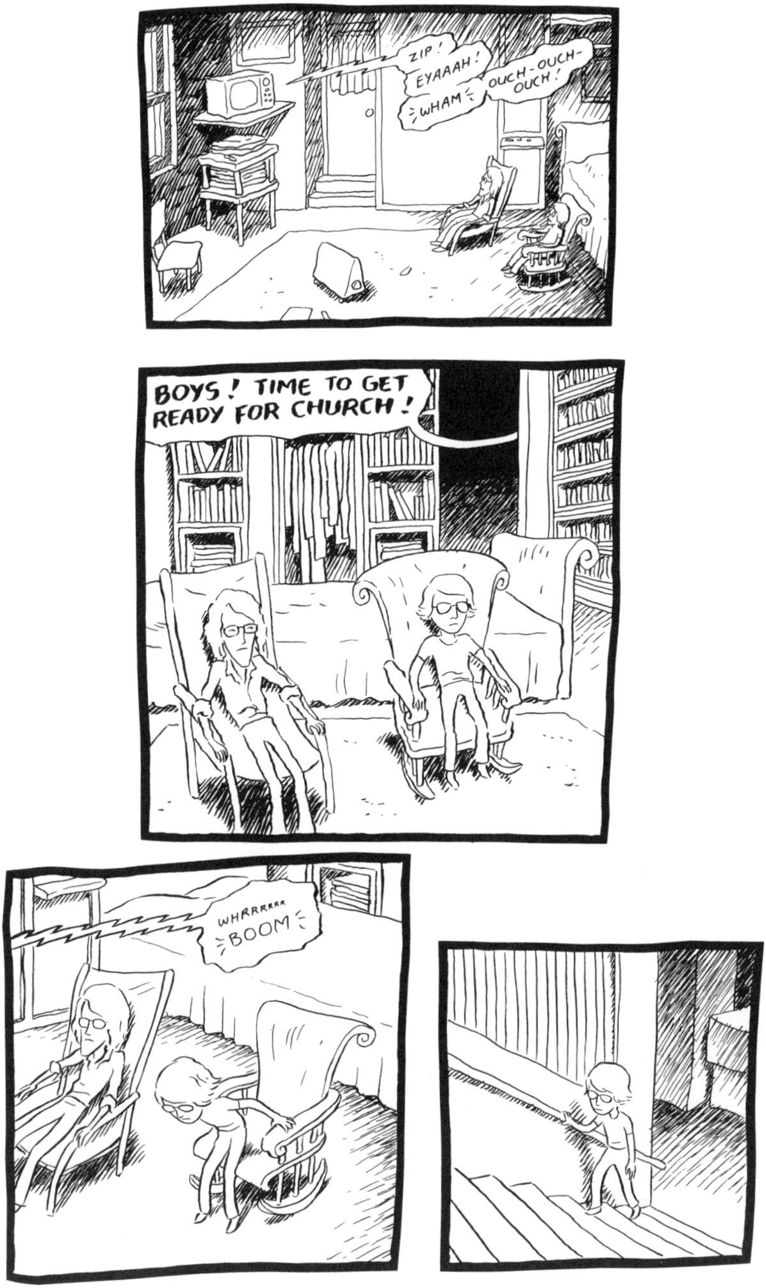
ZIP!
EYAAAH!
WHAM
OUCH-OUCH-OUCH!
BOYS! TIME TO GET READY FOR CHURCH!
WHRRRRRR
BOOM

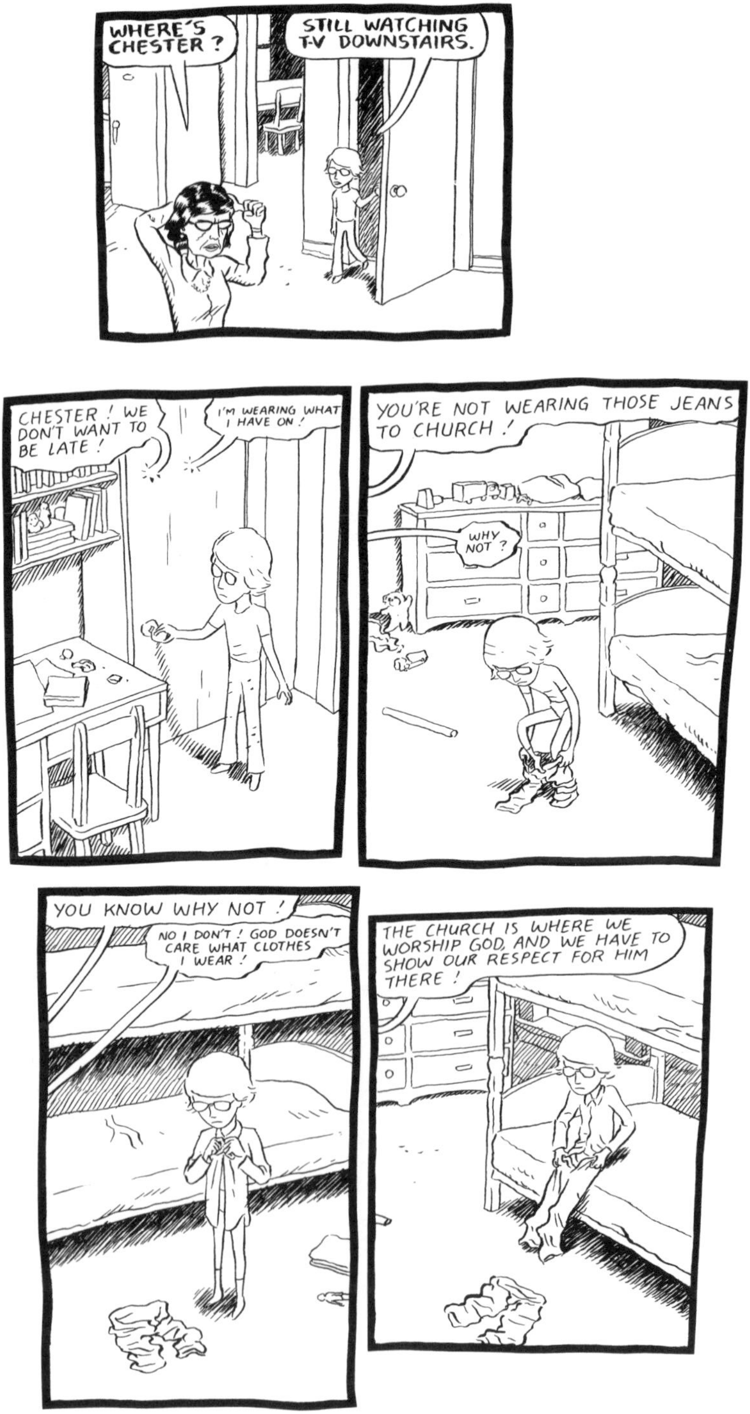
WHERE'S CHESTER?
STILL WATCHING T-V DOWNSTAIRS.
CHESTER! WE DON'T WANT TO BE LATE!
I'M WEARING WHAT I HAVE ON!
YOU'RE NOT WEARING THOSE JEANS TO CHURCH!
WHY NOT?
YOU KNOW WHY NOT!
NO I DON'T! GOD DOESN'T CARE WHAT CLOTHES I WEAR!
THE CHURCH IS WHERE WE WORSHIP GOD, AND WE HAVE TO SHOW OUR RESPECT FOR HIM THERE!

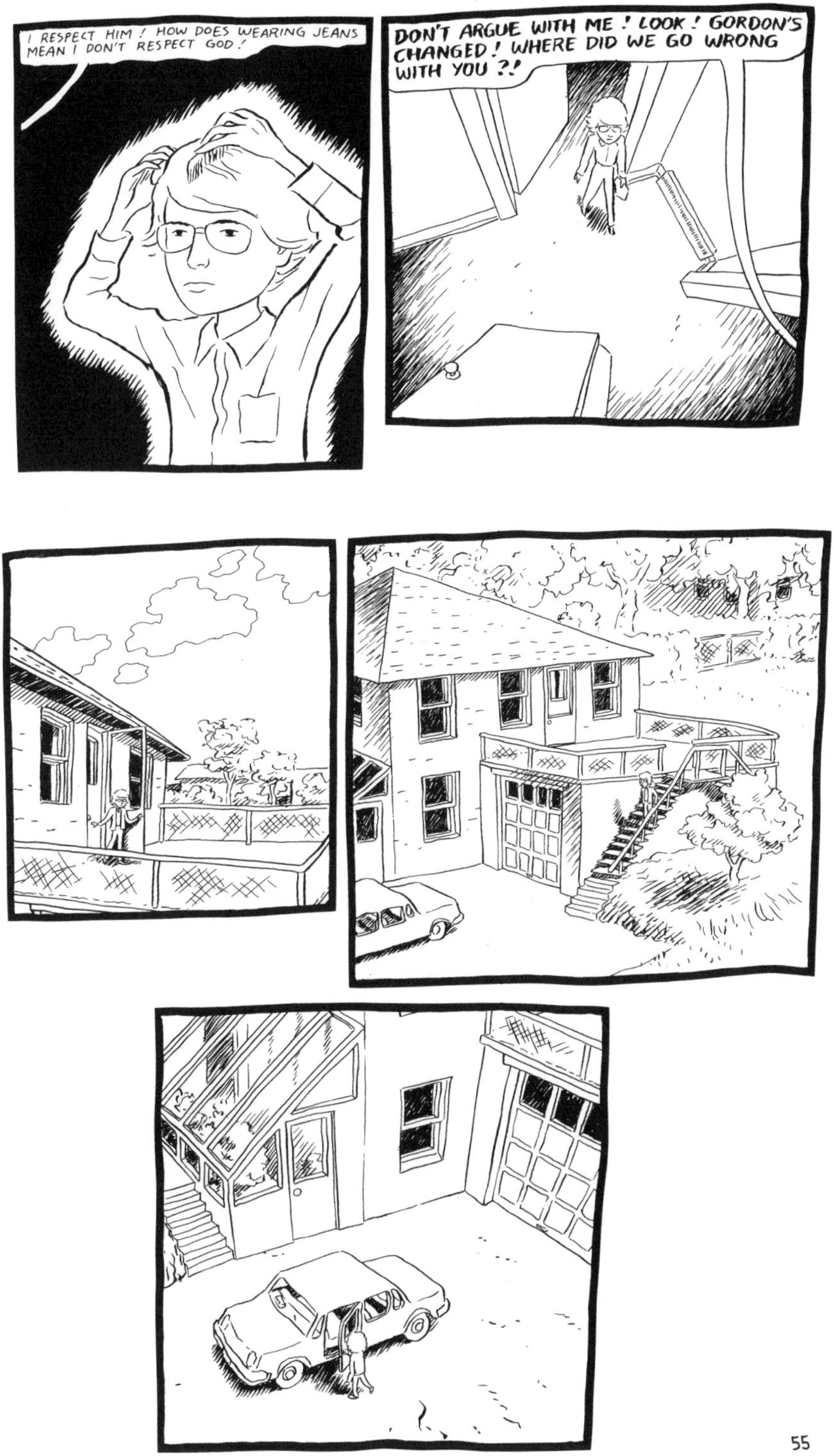
I RESPECT HIM! HOW DOES WEARING JEANS MEAN I DON'T RESPECT GOD!
DON'T ARGUE WITH ME! LOOK! GORDON'S CHANGED! WHERE DID WE GO WRONG WITH YOU?!

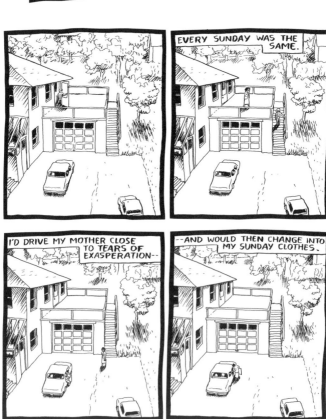

EVERY SUNDAY WAS THE SAME.

I'D DRIVE MY MOTHER CLOSE TO TEARS OF EXASPERATION--

--AND WOULD THEN CHANGE INTO MY SUNDAY CLOTHES.

HI CHESTER.

HI SKY.

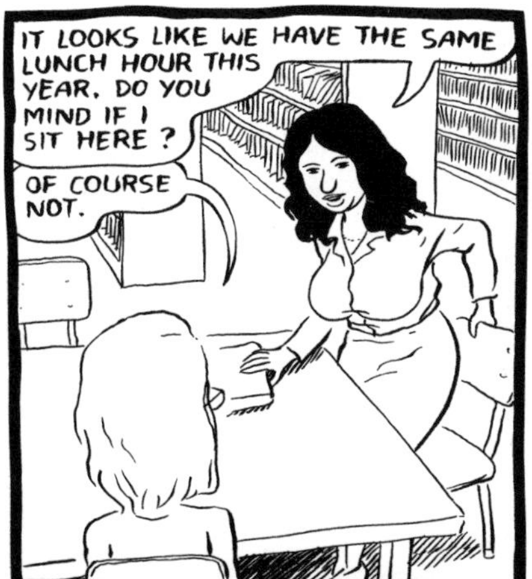
IT LOOKS LIKE WE HAVE THE SAME LUNCH HOUR THIS YEAR. DO YOU MIND IF I SIT HERE ?
OF COURSE NOT.

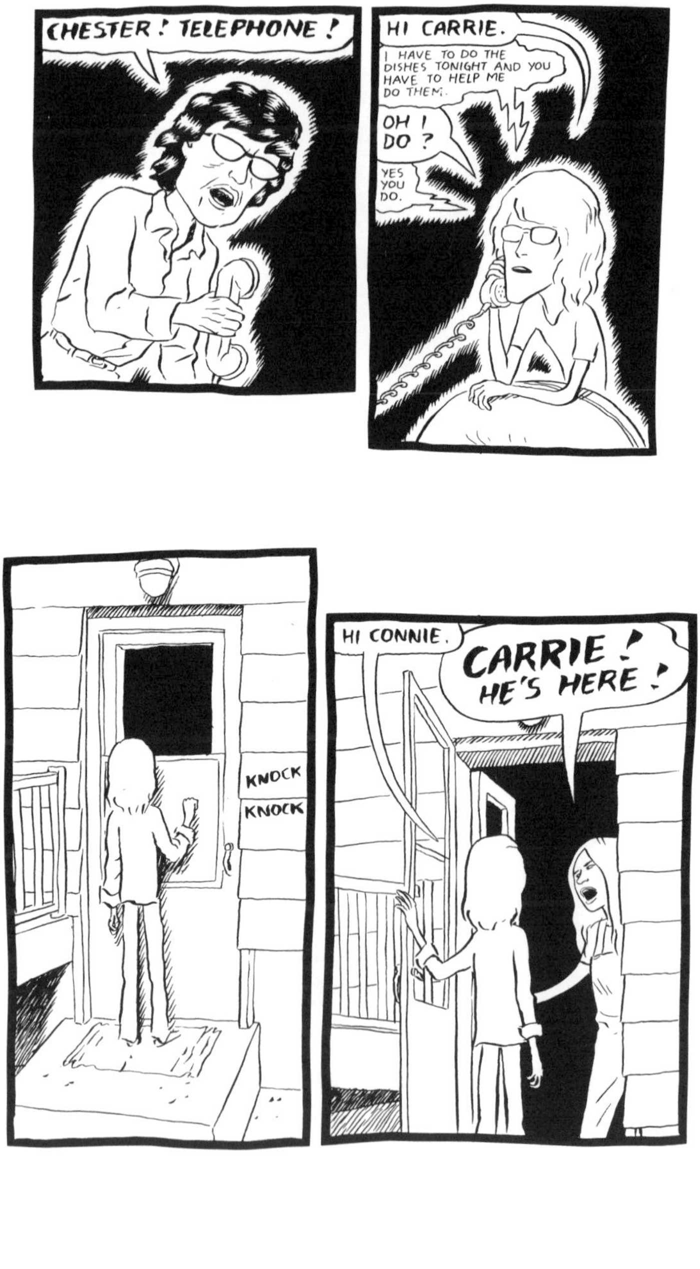
CHESTER ! TELEPHONE !
HI CARRIE.
I HAVE TO DO THE DISHES TONIGHT AND YOU HAVE TO HELP ME DO THEM.
OH I DO ?
YES YOU DO.
KNOCK
KNOCK
HI CONNIE.
CARRIE ! HE'S HERE !

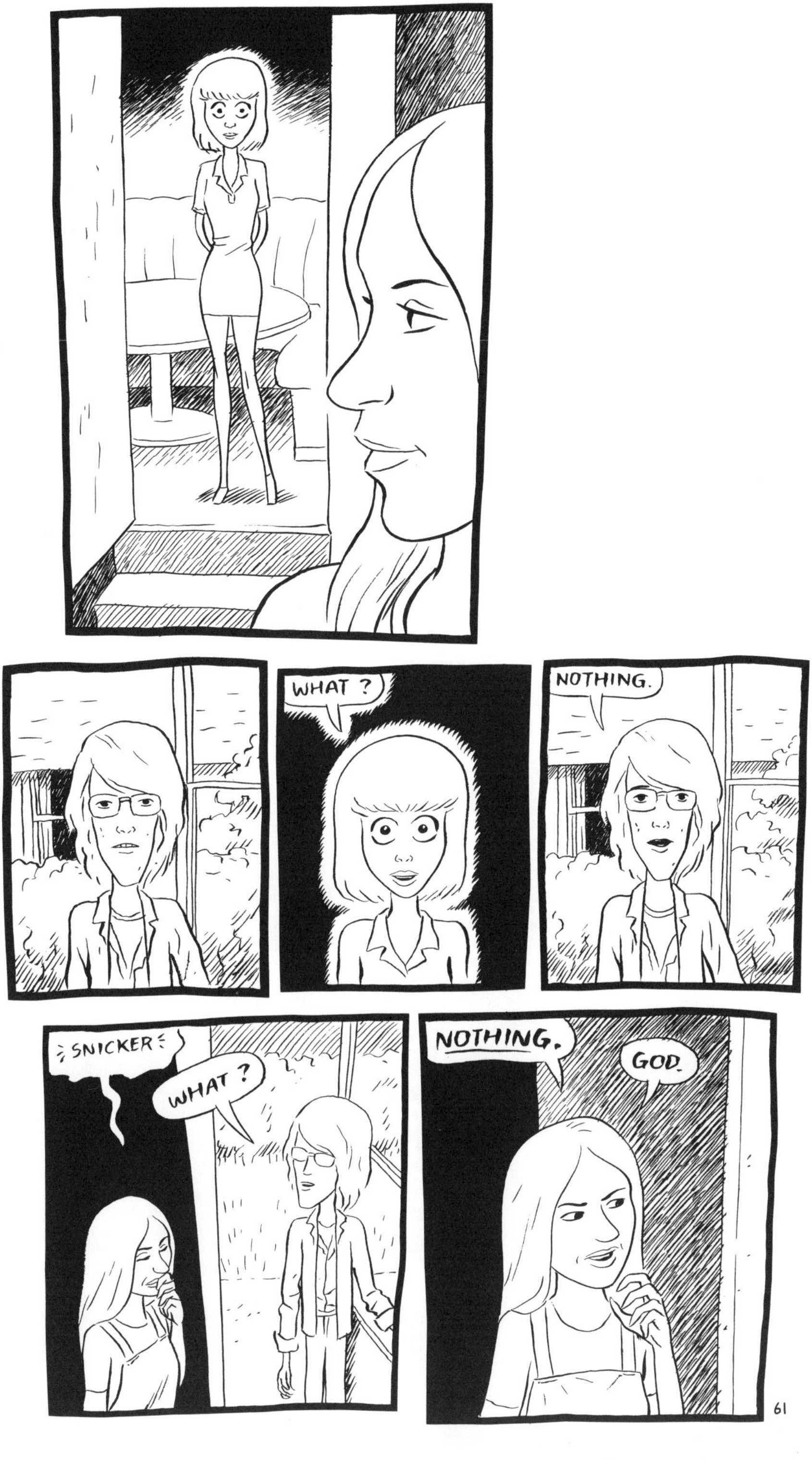
WHAT ?
NOTHING.
SNICKER
WHAT ?
NOTHING.
GOD.

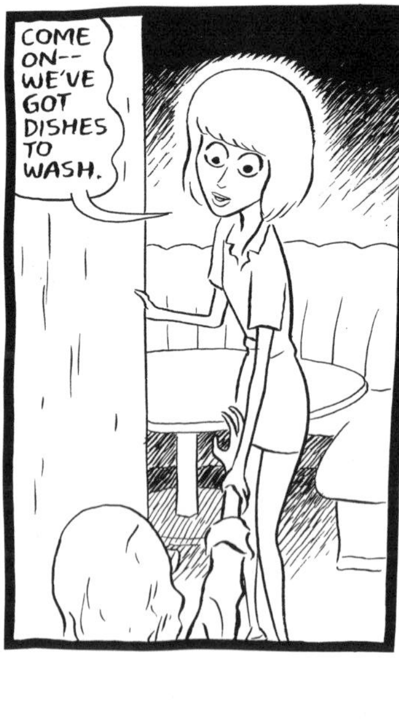
COME ON-- WE'VE GOT DISHES TO WASH.

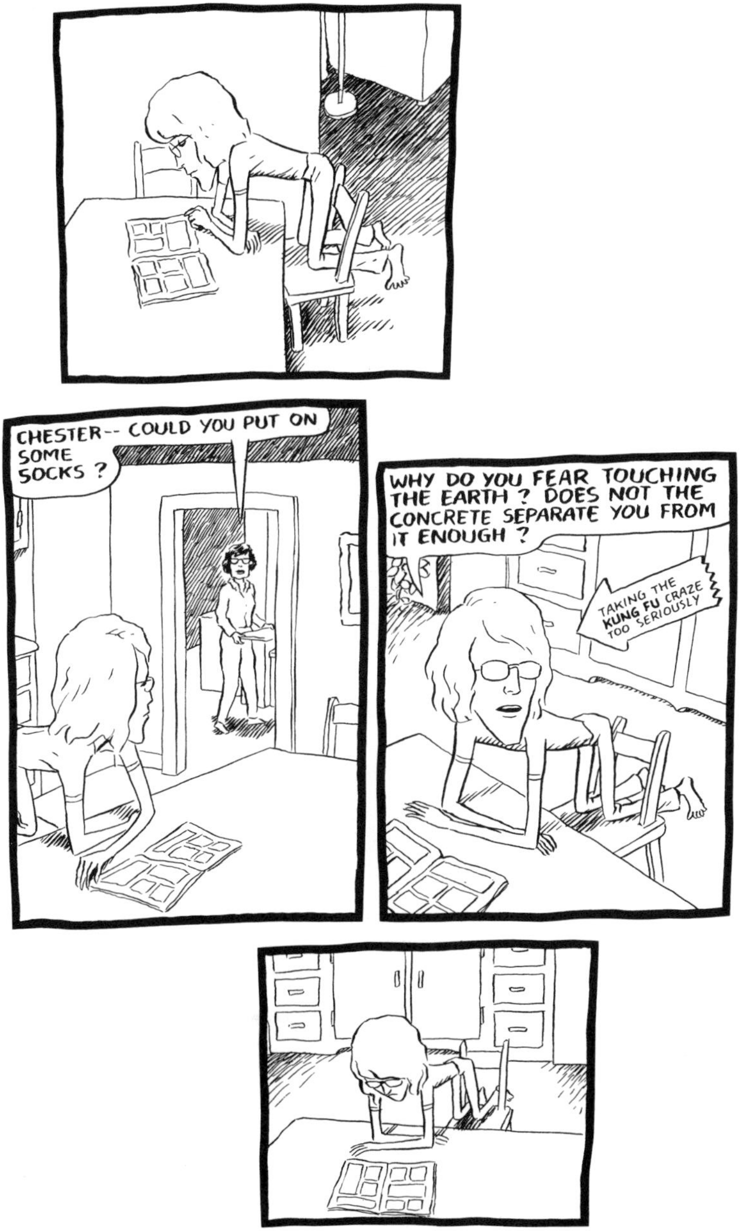
CHESTER-- COULD YOU PUT ON SOME SOCKS ?
WHY DO YOU FEAR TOUCHING THE EARTH ? DOES NOT THE CONCRETE SEPARATE YOU FROM IT ENOUGH ?
TAKING THE KUNG FU CRAZE TOO SERIOUSLY

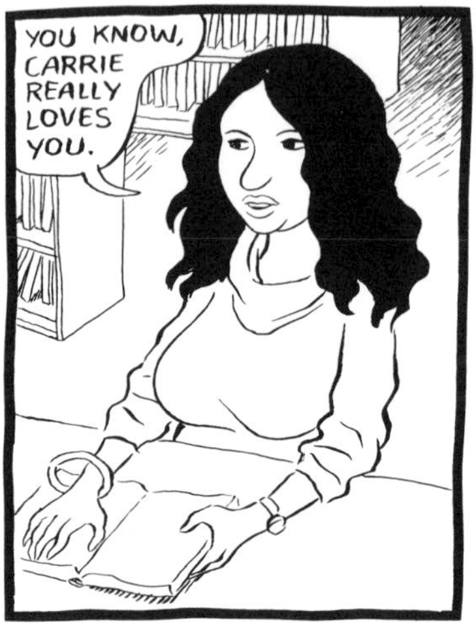
YOU KNOW, CARRIE REALLY LOVES YOU.

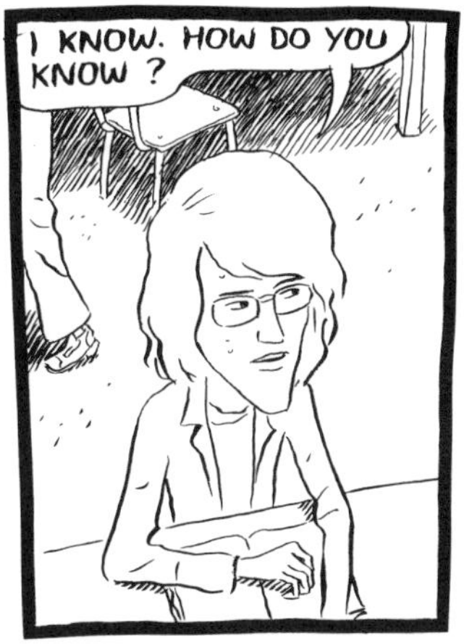
I KNOW. HOW DO YOU KNOW ?

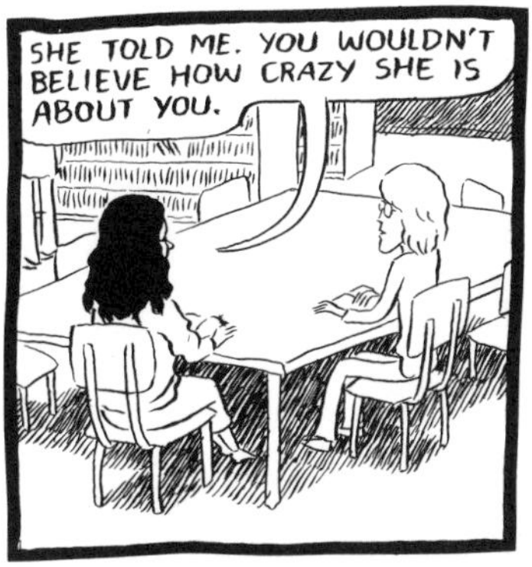
SHE TOLD ME. YOU WOULDN'T BELIEVE HOW CRAZY SHE IS ABOUT YOU.

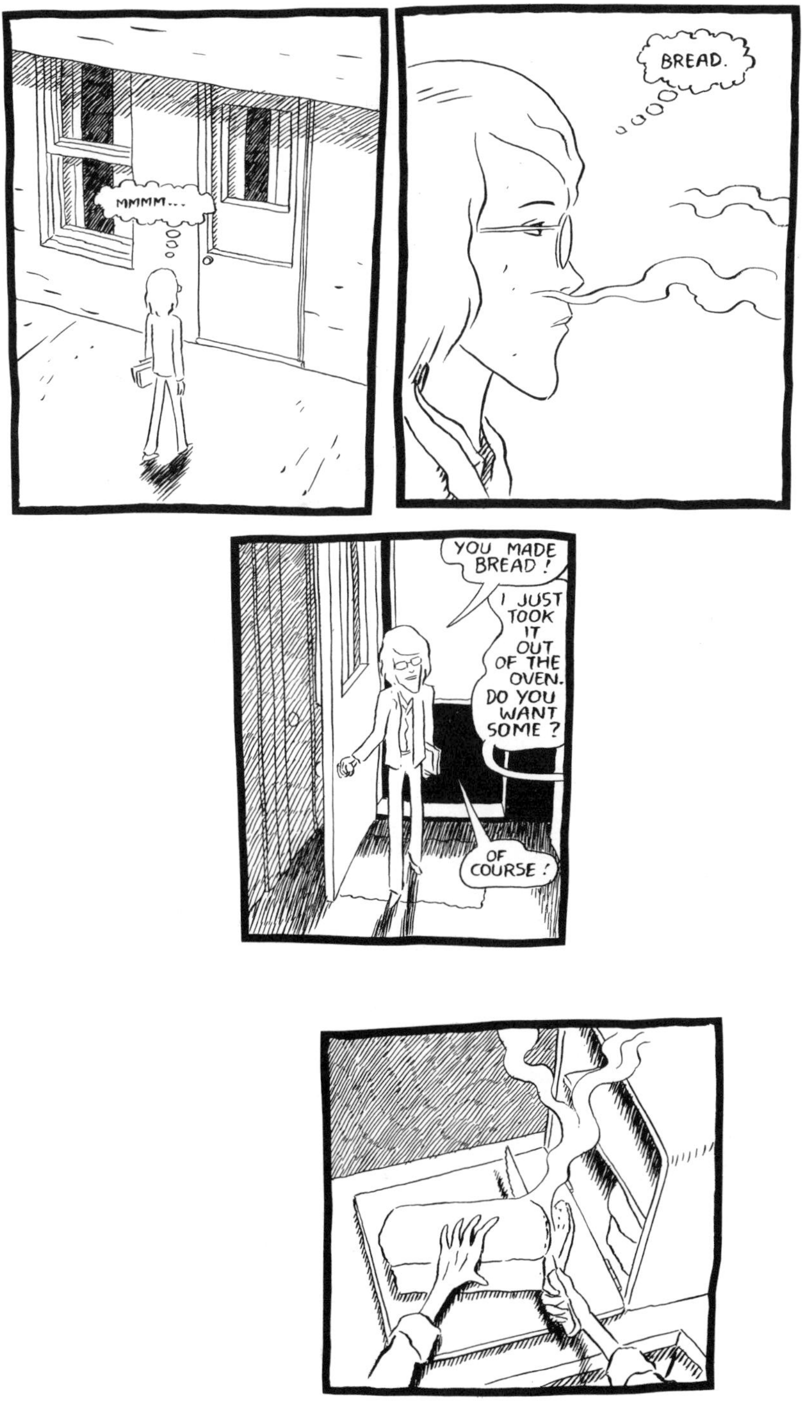
MMMM...
BREAD.
YOU MADE BREAD!
I JUST TOOK IT OUT OF THE OVEN. DO YOU WANT SOME?
OF COURSE!

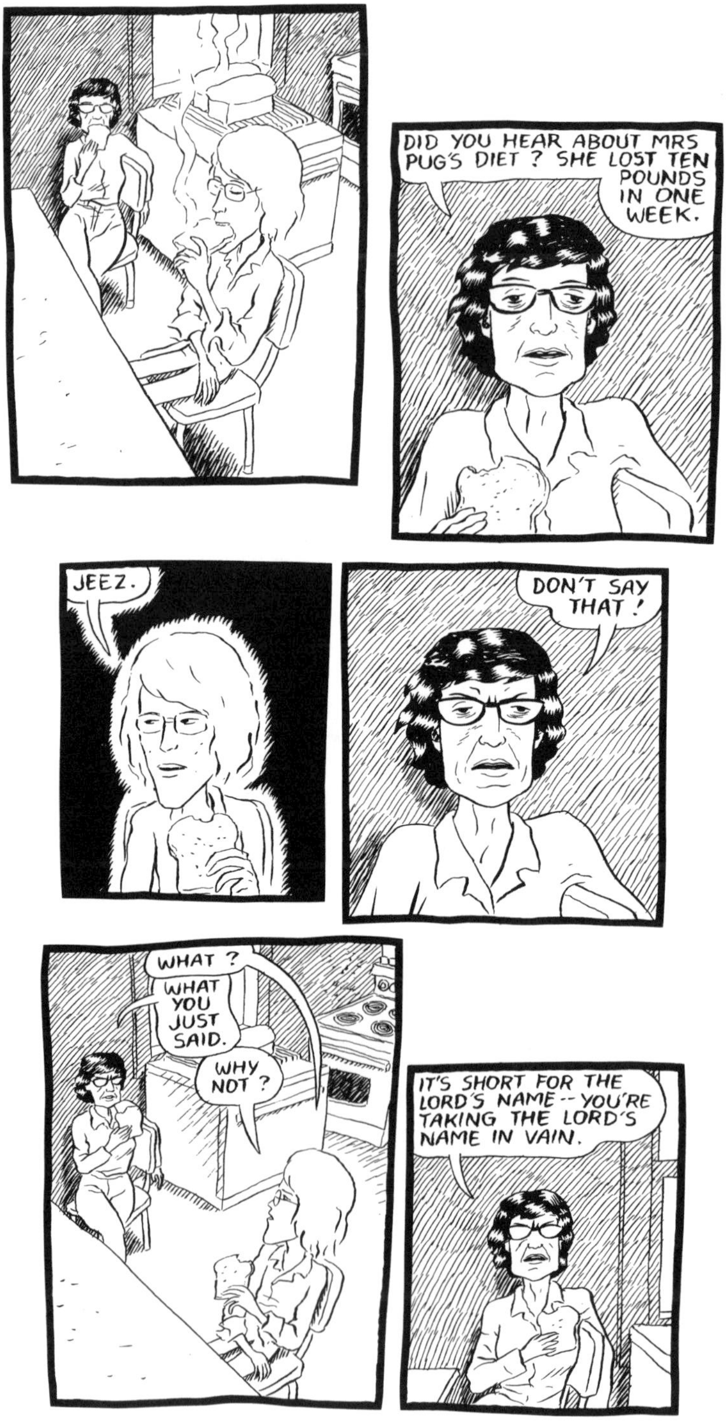
DID YOU HEAR ABOUT MRS PUG'S DIET ? SHE LOST TEN POUNDS IN ONE WEEK.
JEEZ.
DON'T SAY THAT !
WHAT ?
WHAT YOU JUST SAID.
WHY NOT ?
IT'S SHORT FOR THE LORD'S NAME -- YOU'RE TAKING THE LORD'S NAME IN VAIN.

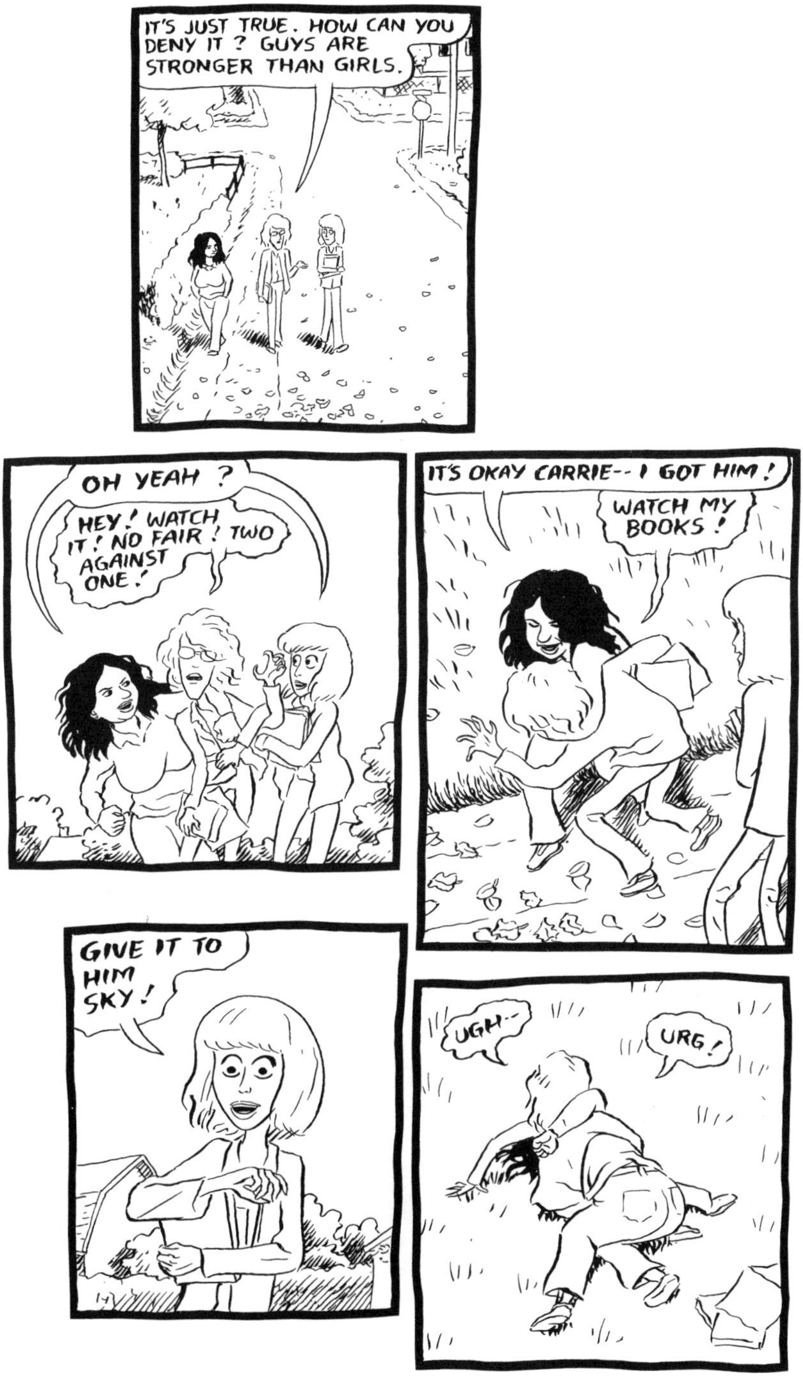
IT'S JUST TRUE. HOW CAN YOU DENY IT ? GUYS ARE STRONGER THAN GIRLS.
OH YEAH ?
HEY! WATCH IT! NO FAIR! TWO AGAINST ONE!
IT'S OKAY CARRIE-- I GOT HIM!
WATCH MY BOOKS!
GIVE IT TO HIM SKY!
UGH--
URG!

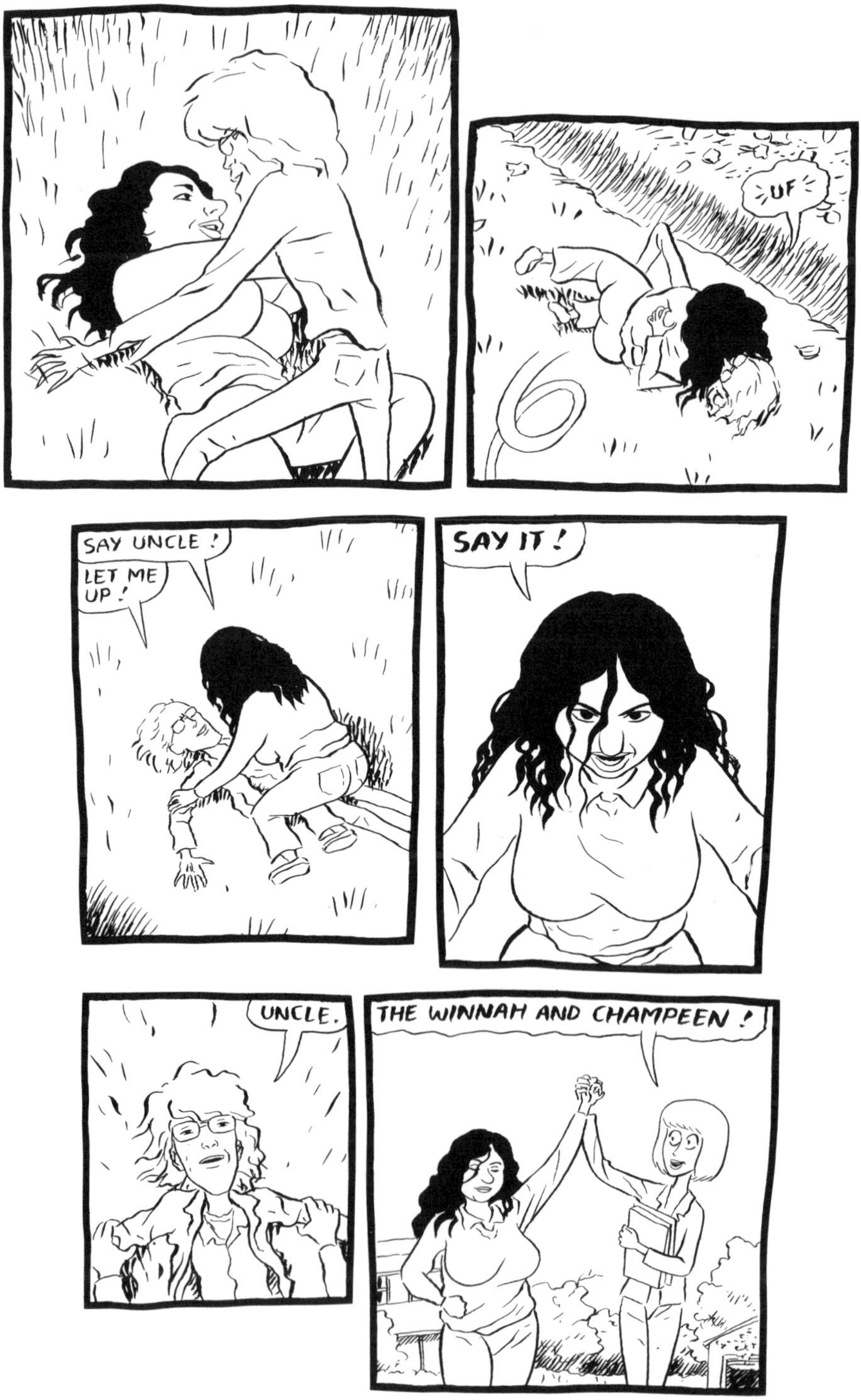
UF
SAY UNCLE!
LET ME UP!
SAY IT!
UNCLE.
THE WINNAH AND CHAMPEEN!

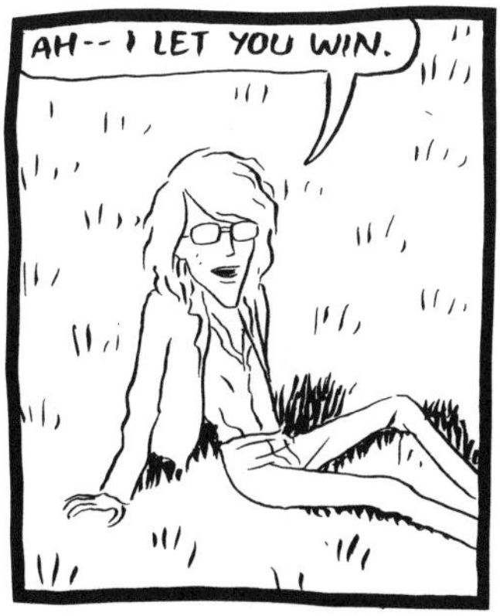
AH-- I LET YOU WIN.

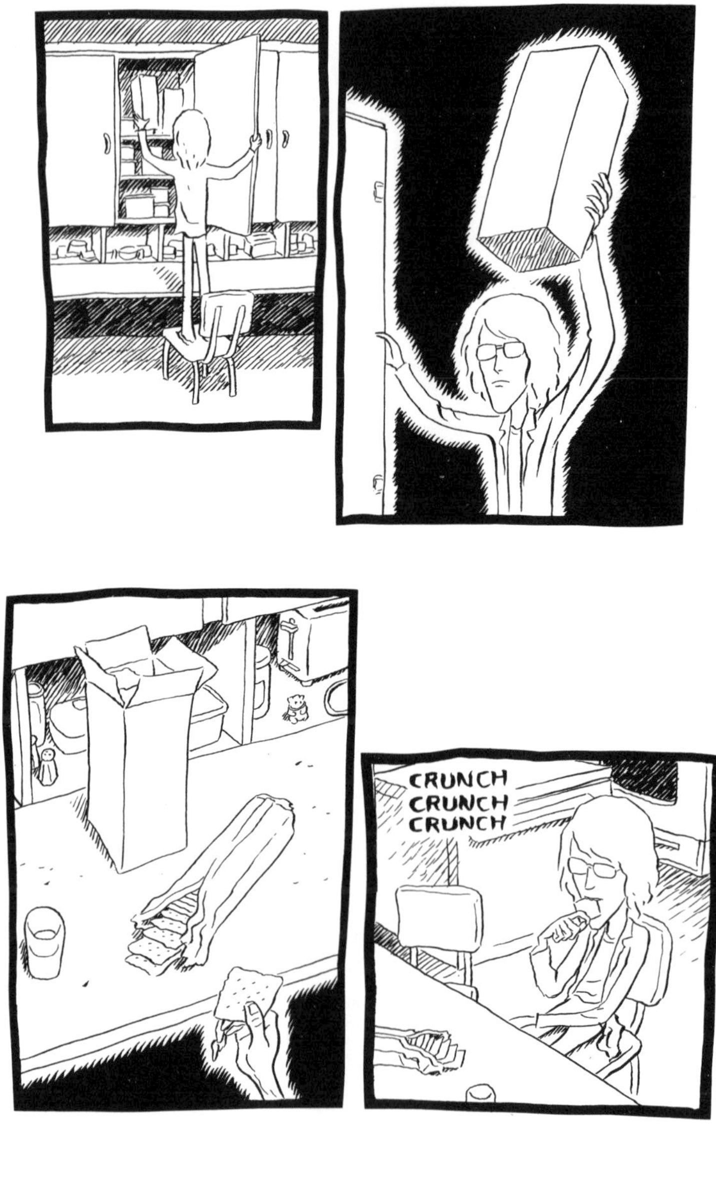
CRUNCH
CRUNCH
CRUNCH

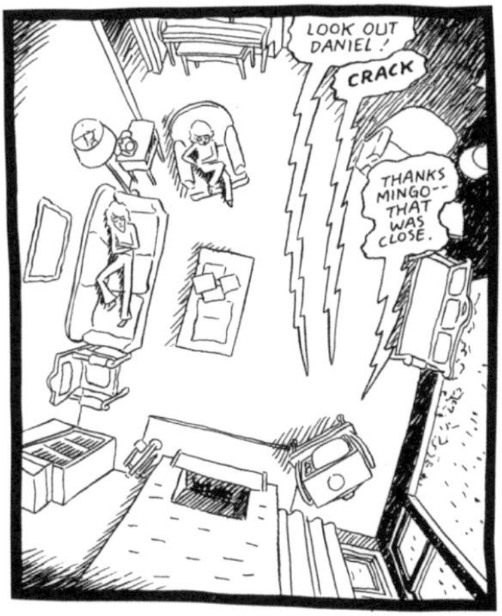
LOOK OUT DANIEL!
CRACK
THANKS MINGO-- THAT WAS CLOSE.

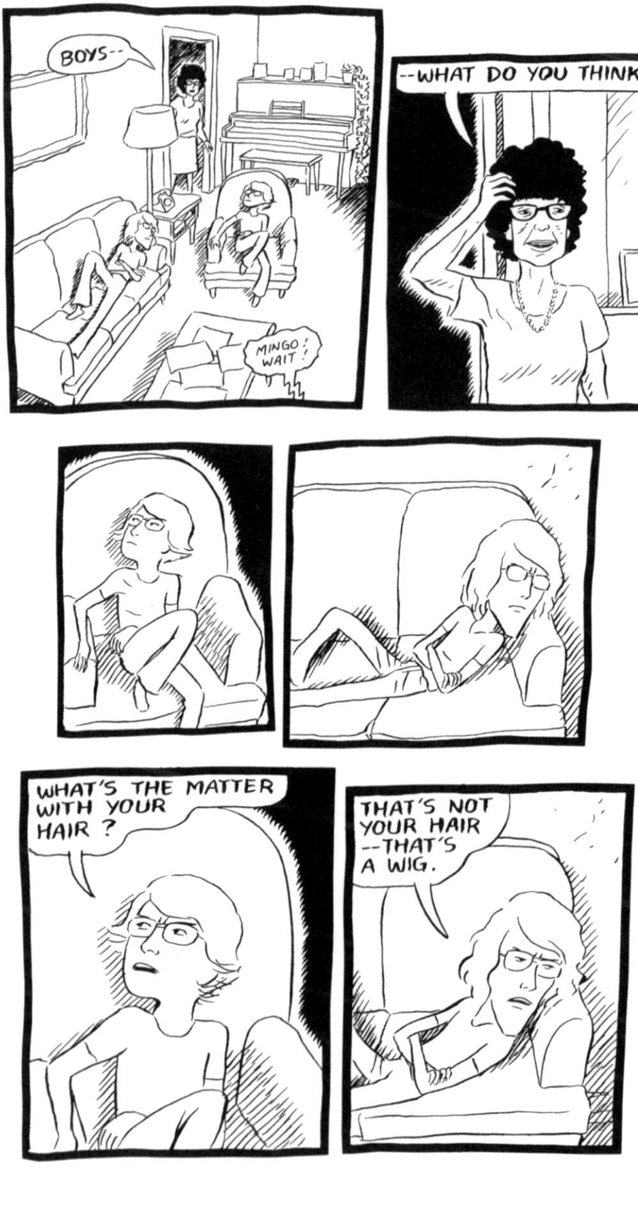
BOYS--
MINGO! WAIT!
--WHAT DO YOU THINK ?
WHAT'S THE MATTER WITH YOUR HAIR ?
THAT'S NOT YOUR HAIR --THAT'S A WIG.

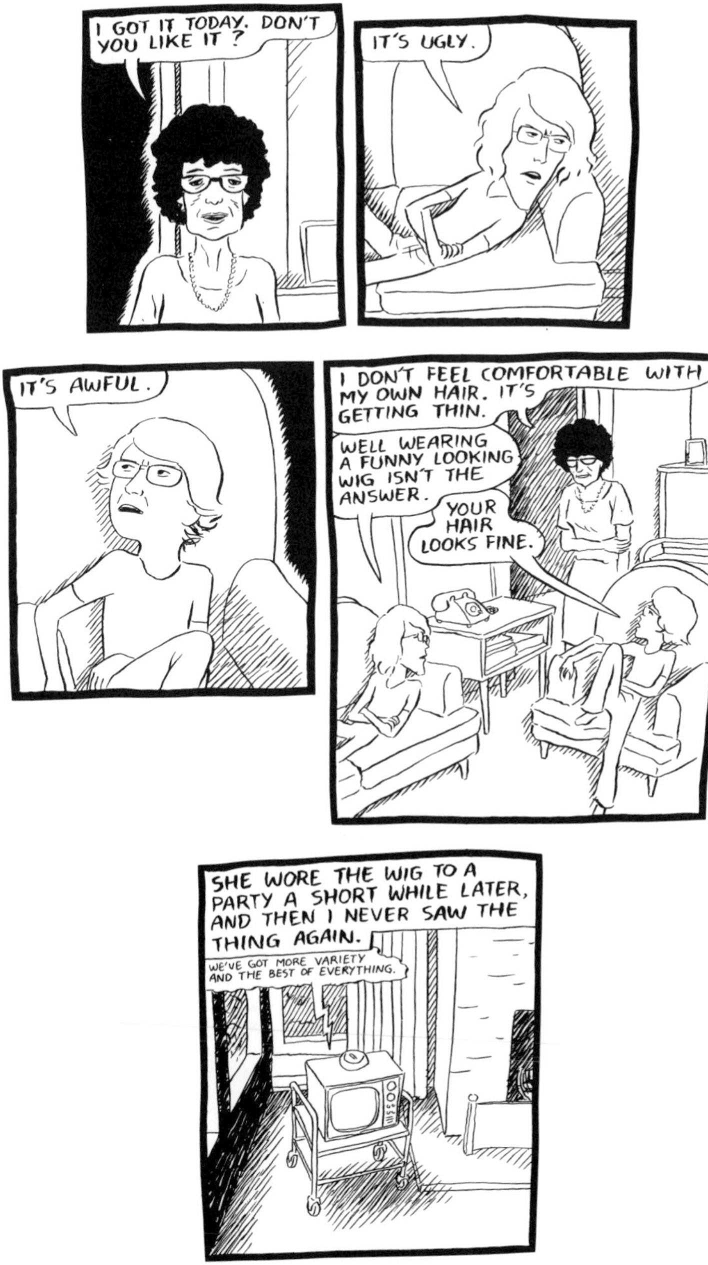
I GOT IT TODAY. DON'T YOU LIKE IT ?
IT'S UGLY.
IT'S AWFUL.
I DON'T FEEL COMFORTABLE WITH MY OWN HAIR. IT'S GETTING THIN.
WELL WEARING A FUNNY LOOKING WIG ISN'T THE ANSWER.
YOUR HAIR LOOKS FINE.
SHE WORE THE WIG TO A PARTY A SHORT WHILE LATER, AND THEN I NEVER SAW THE THING AGAIN.
WE'VE GOT MORE VARIETY AND THE BEST OF EVERYTHING.

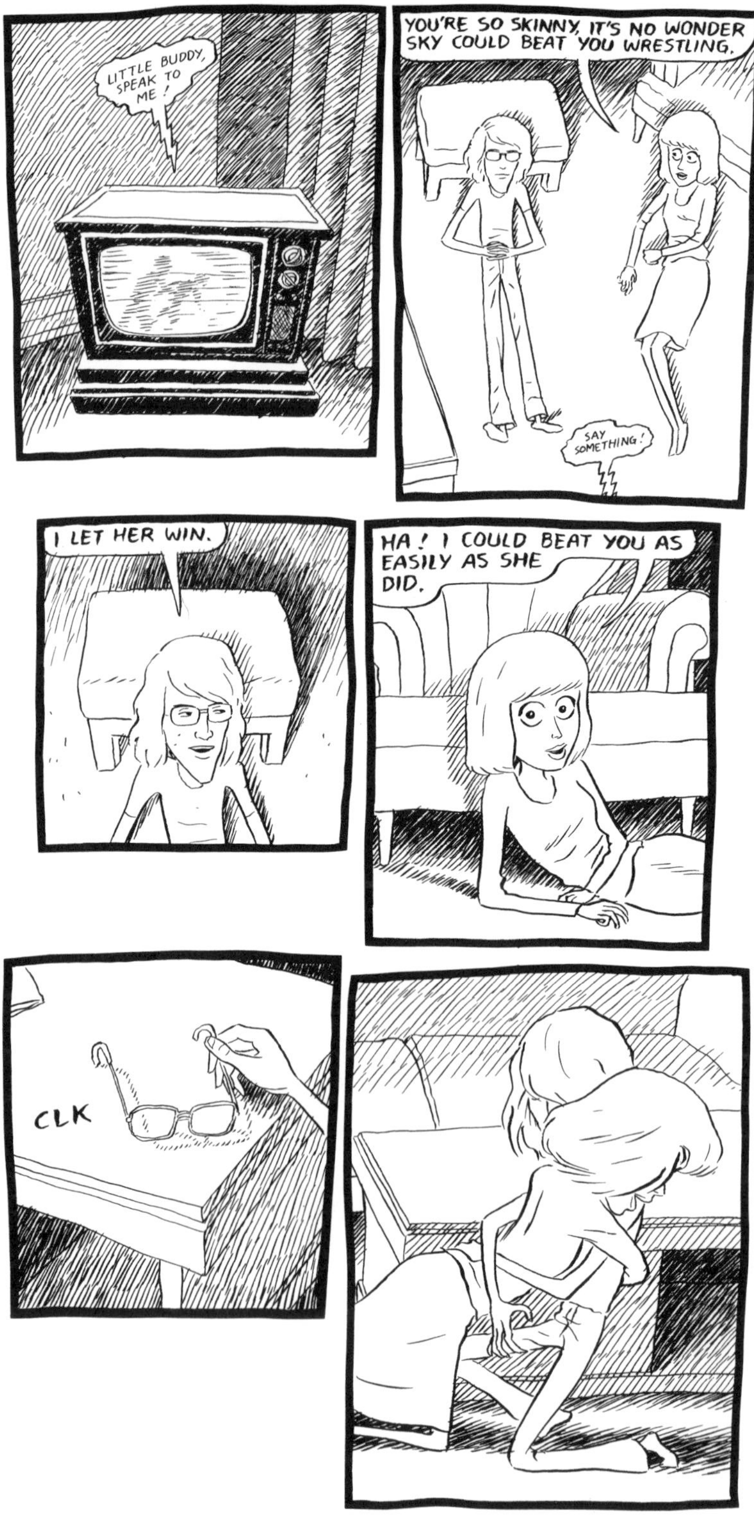
LITTLE BUDDY, SPEAK TO ME!
YOU'RE SO SKINNY, IT'S NO WONDER SKY COULD BEAT YOU WRESTLING.
SAY SOMETHING!
I LET HER WIN.
HA! I COULD BEAT YOU AS EASILY AS SHE DID.
CLK

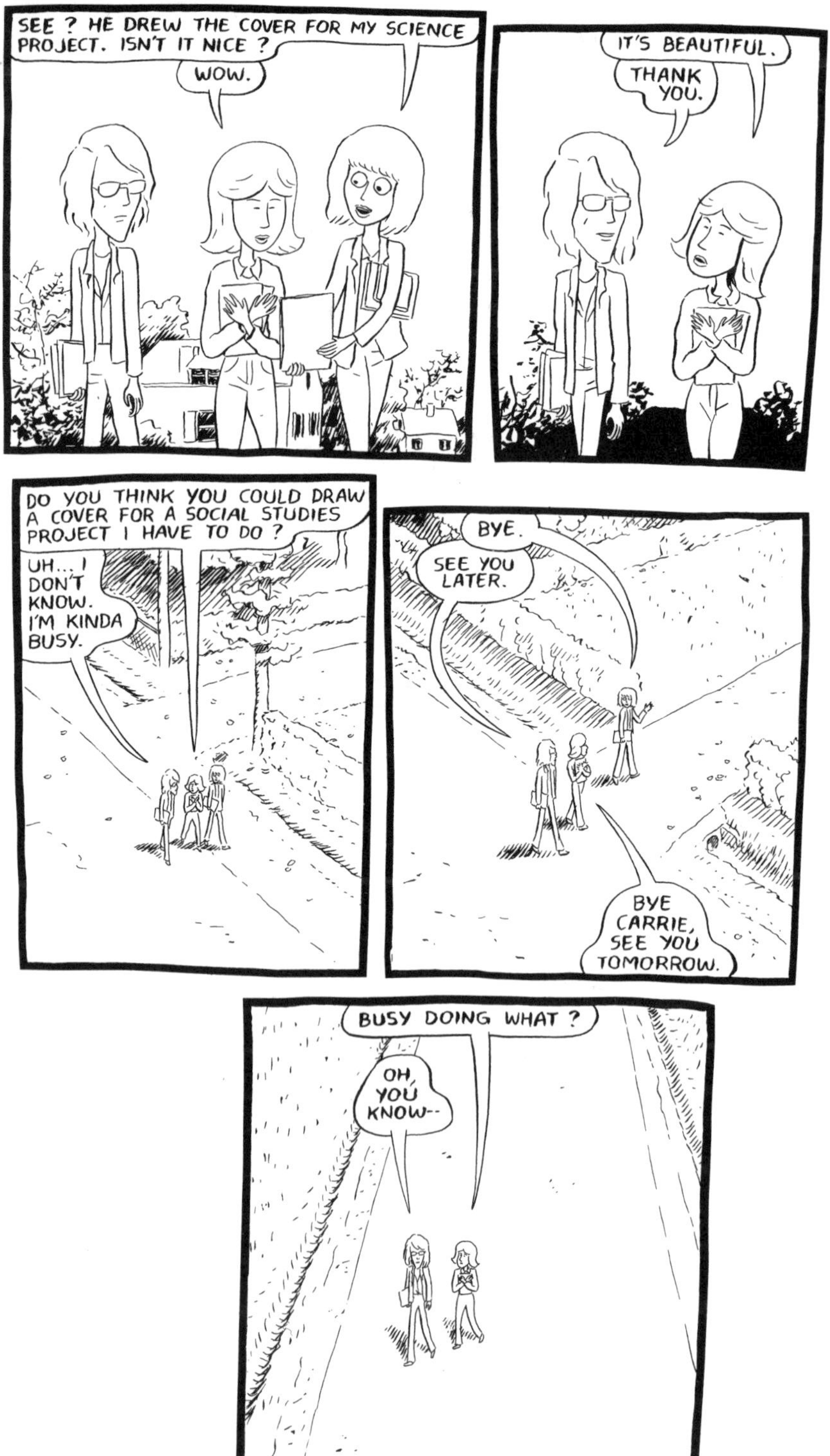
SEE ? HE DREW THE COVER FOR MY SCIENCE PROJECT. ISN'T IT NICE ?
WOW.
IT'S BEAUTIFUL.
THANK YOU.
DO YOU THINK YOU COULD DRAW A COVER FOR A SOCIAL STUDIES PROJECT I HAVE TO DO ?
UH... I DON'T KNOW. I'M KINDA BUSY.
BYE.
SEE YOU LATER.
BYE CARRIE, SEE YOU TOMORROW.
BUSY DOING WHAT ?
OH, YOU KNOW--

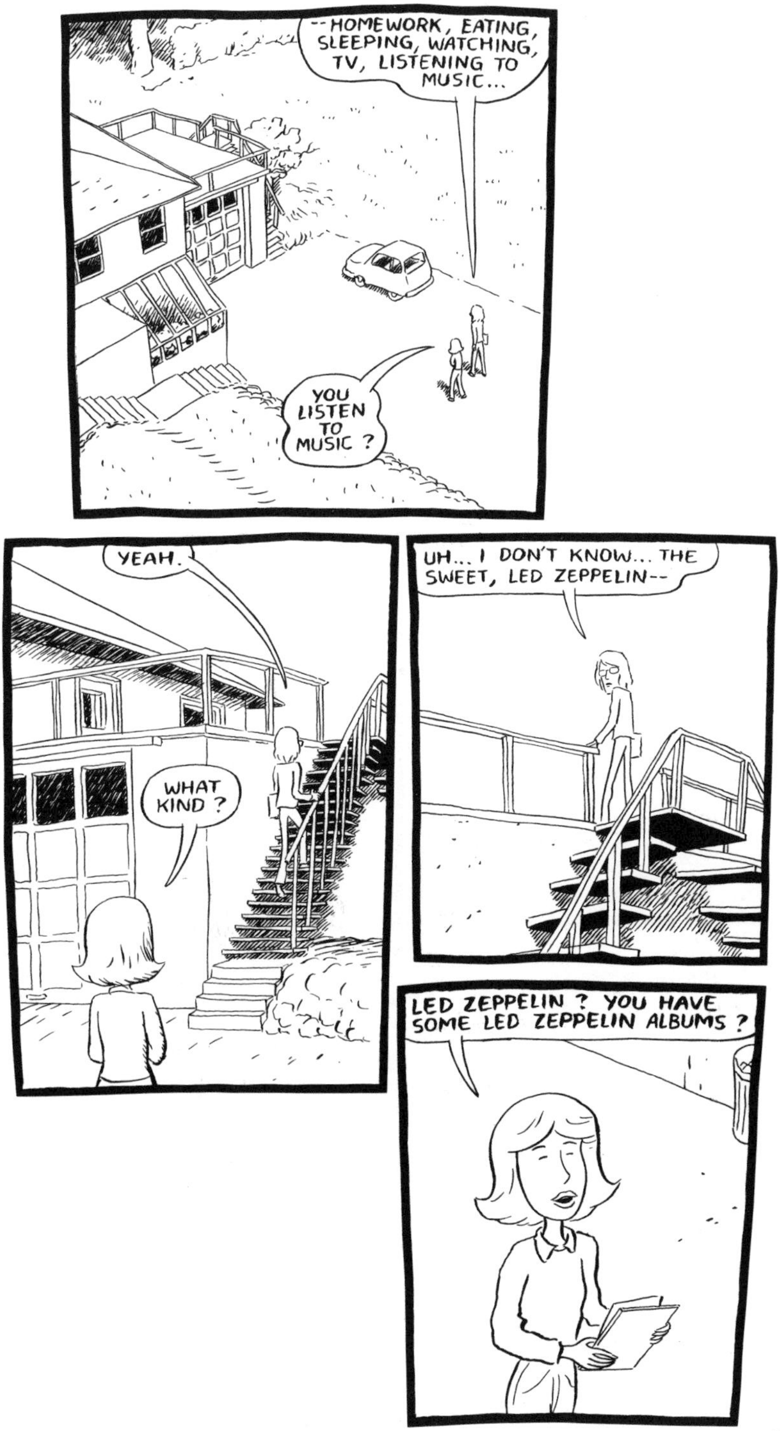
--HOMEWORK, EATING, SLEEPING, WATCHING, TV, LISTENING TO MUSIC...
YOU LISTEN TO MUSIC ?
YEAH.
WHAT KIND ?
UH... I DON'T KNOW... THE SWEET, LED ZEPPELIN--
LED ZEPPELIN ? YOU HAVE SOME LED ZEPPELIN ALBUMS ?

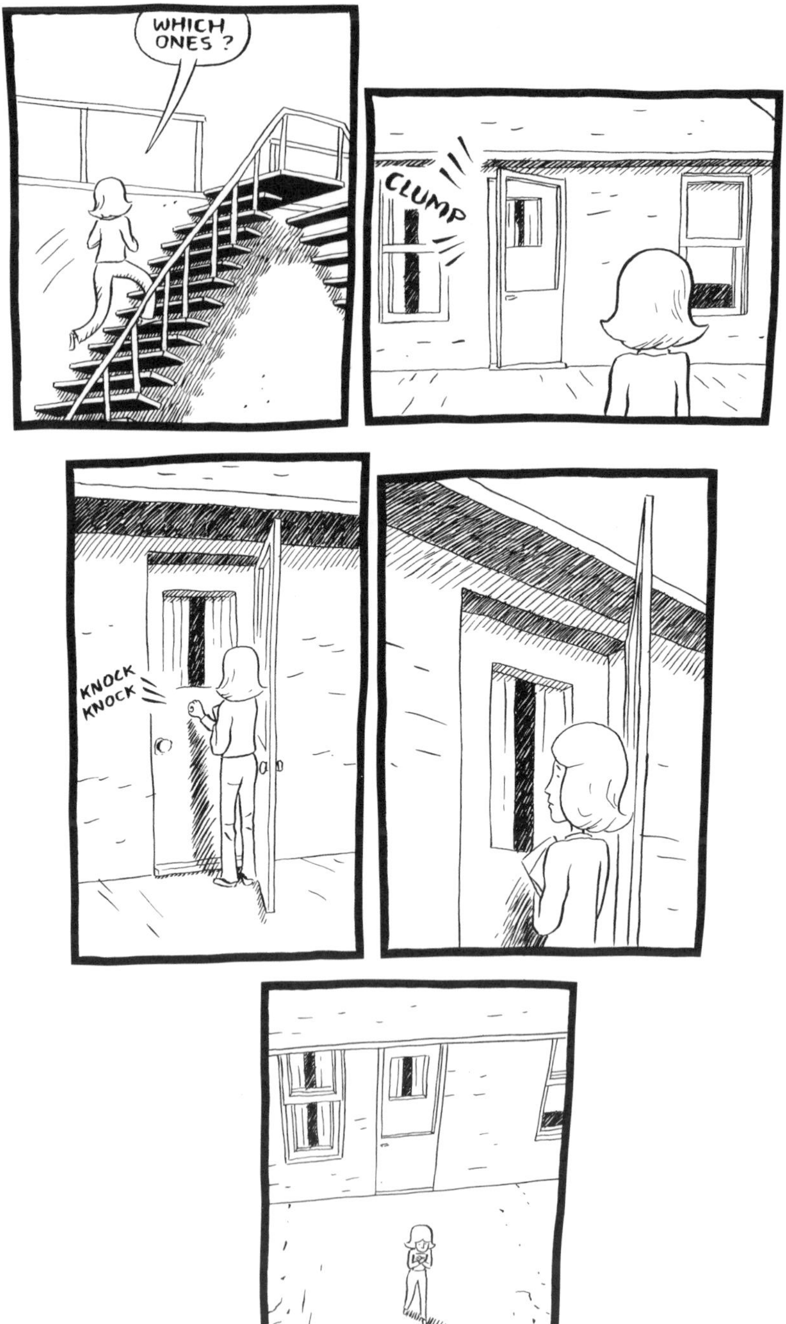
WHICH ONES ?
CLUMP
KNOCK KNOCK

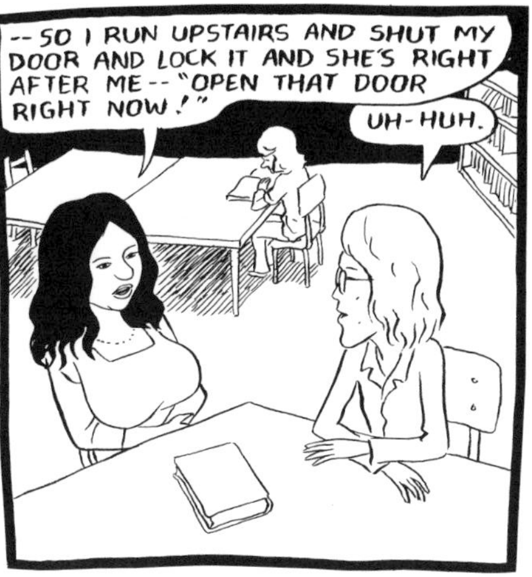
--SO I RUN UPSTAIRS AND SHUT MY DOOR AND LOCK IT AND SHE'S RIGHT AFTER ME--"OPEN THAT DOOR RIGHT NOW!"
UH-HUH.

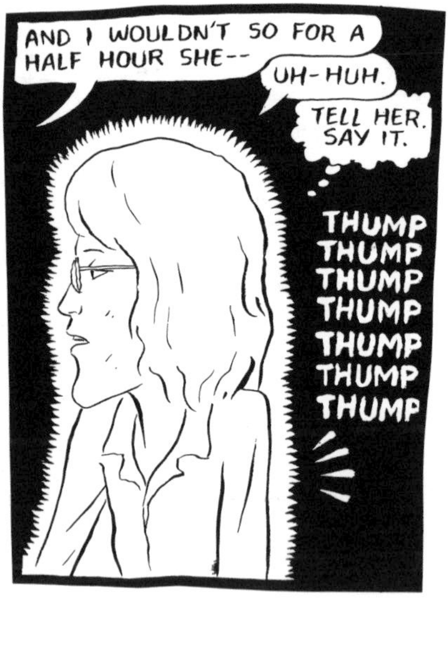
AND I WOULDN'T SO FOR A HALF HOUR SHE--
UH-HUH.
TELL HER. SAY IT.
THUMP
THUMP
THUMP
THUMP
THUMP
THUMP
THUMP

--SO STICK AROUND, YOU'RE GONNA HEAR ELECTRIC MUSIC--
--SOLID WALLS OF SOUND, SAY CANDY AND RONNIE--
YOU'RE A REALLY GOOD SINGER.

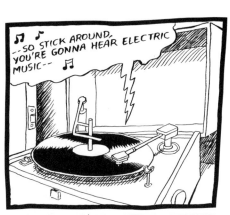

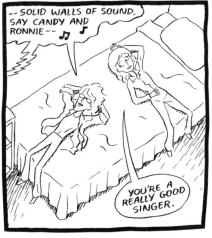

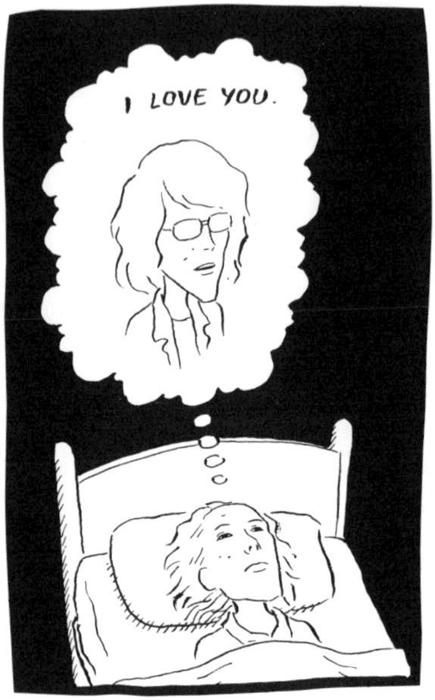
I LOVE YOU.

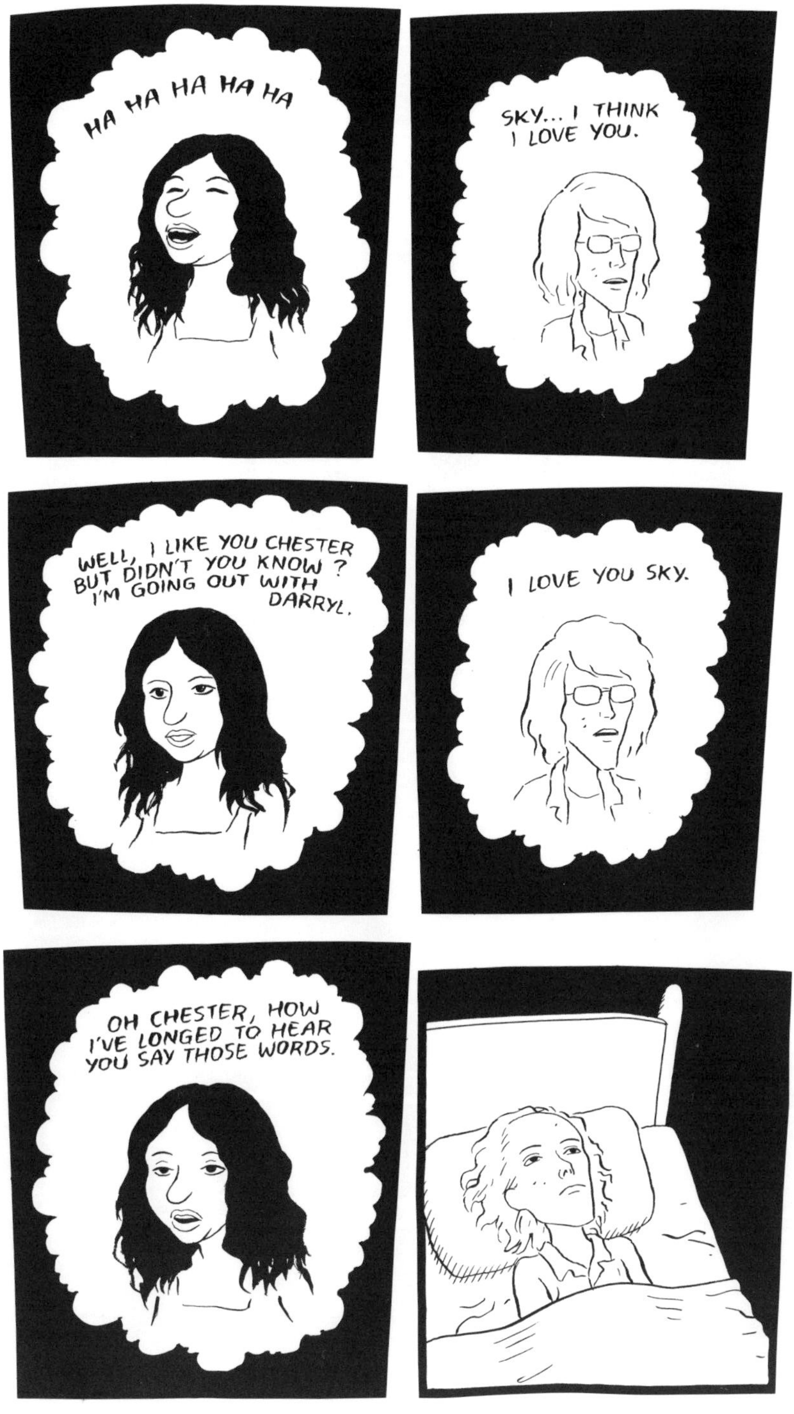
HA HA HA HA HA
SKY... I THINK I LOVE YOU.
WELL, I LIKE YOU CHESTER BUT DIDN'T YOU KNOW? I'M GOING OUT WITH DARRYL.
I LOVE YOU SKY.
OH CHESTER, HOW I'VE LONGED TO HEAR YOU SAY THOSE WORDS.

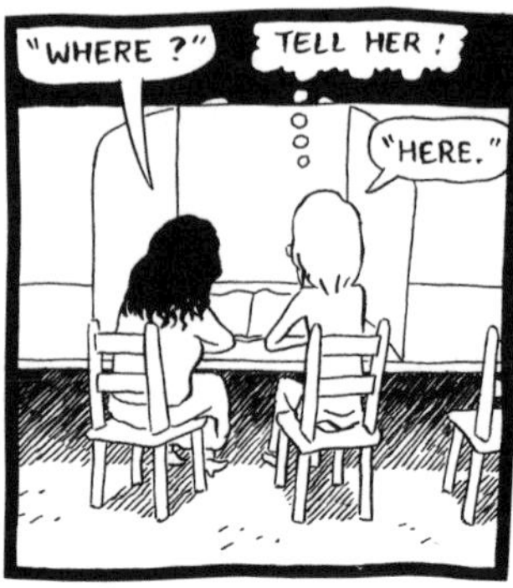
"WHERE ?"
TELL HER !
"HERE."

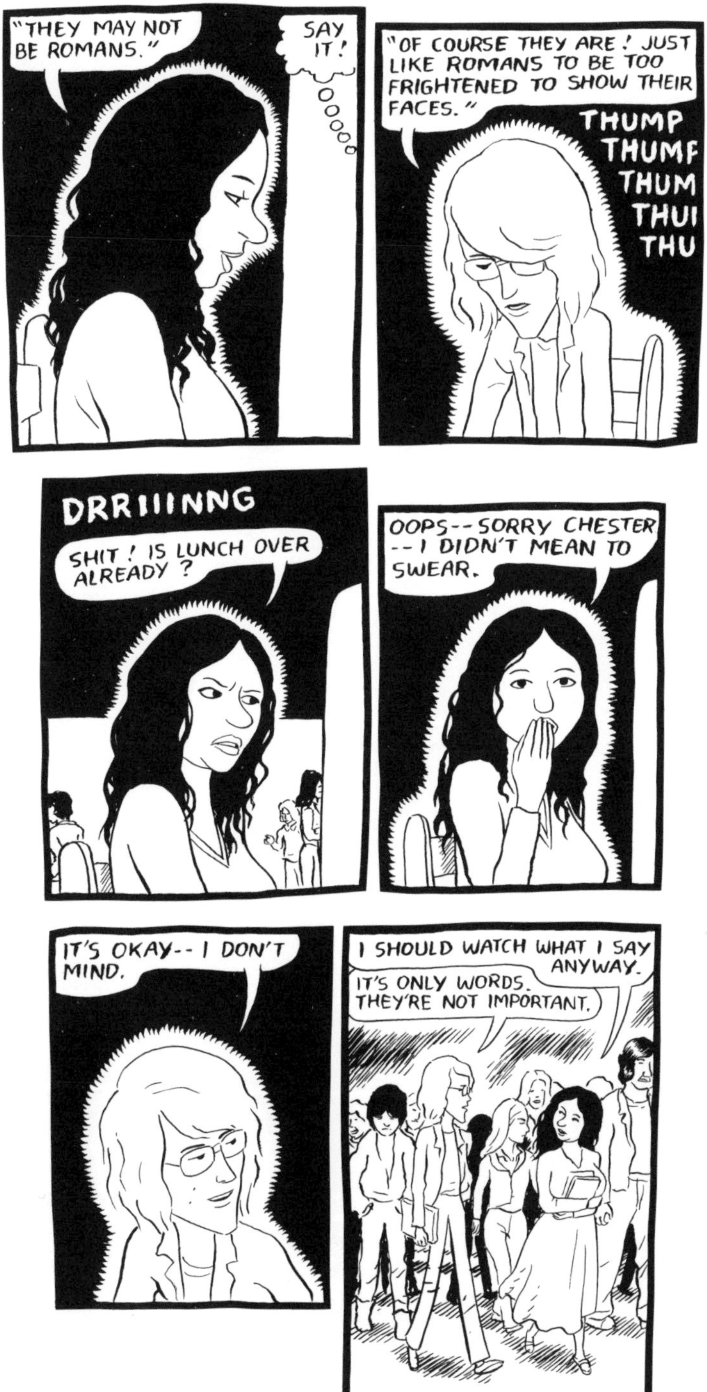
"THEY MAY NOT BE ROMANS."
SAY IT!
"OF COURSE THEY ARE! JUST LIKE ROMANS TO BE TOO FRIGHTENED TO SHOW THEIR FACES."
THUMP
THUMP
THUM
THUI
THU
DRRIIINNG
SHIT! IS LUNCH OVER ALREADY?
OOPS--SORRY CHESTER --I DIDN'T MEAN TO SWEAR.
IT'S OKAY-- I DON'T MIND.
I SHOULD WATCH WHAT I SAY ANYWAY.
IT'S ONLY WORDS. THEY'RE NOT IMPORTANT.

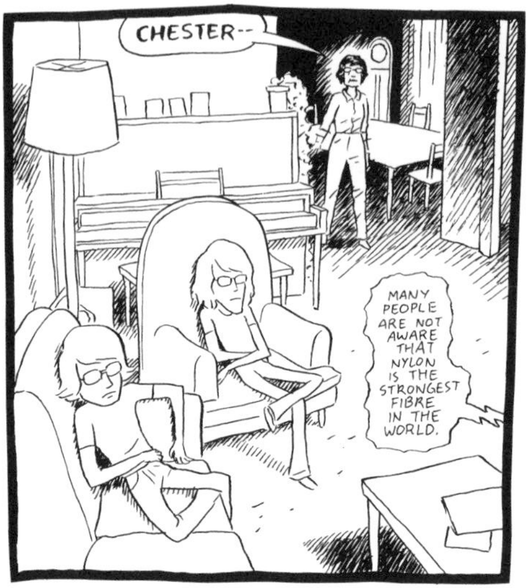
CHESTER--
MANY PEOPLE ARE NOT AWARE THAT NYLON IS THE STRONGEST FIBRE IN THE WORLD.

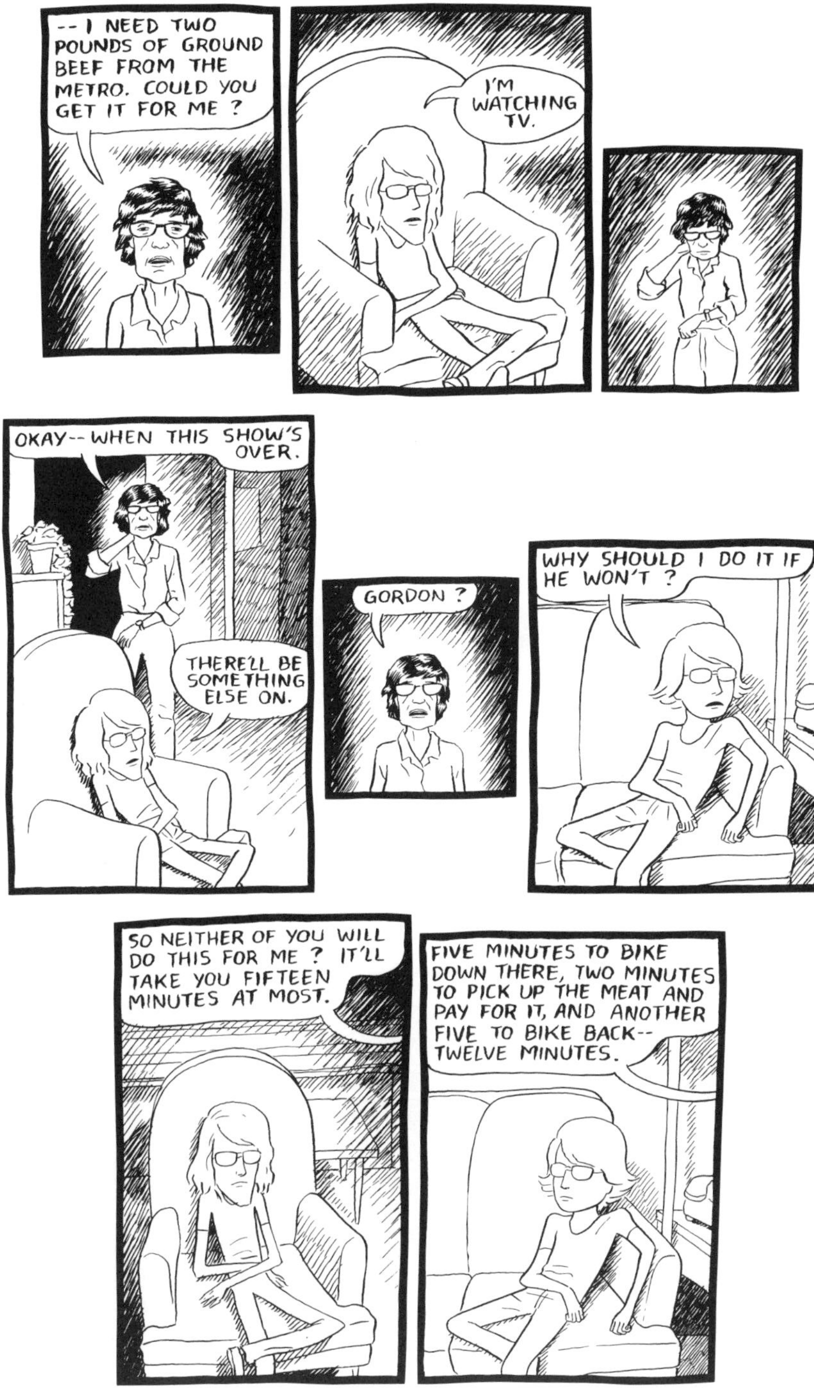
--I NEED TWO POUNDS OF GROUND BEEF FROM THE METRO. COULD YOU GET IT FOR ME ?
I'M WATCHING TV.
OKAY--WHEN THIS SHOW'S OVER.
THERE'LL BE SOMETHING ELSE ON.
GORDON ?
WHY SHOULD I DO IT IF HE WON'T ?
SO NEITHER OF YOU WILL DO THIS FOR ME ? IT'LL TAKE YOU FIFTEEN MINUTES AT MOST.
FIVE MINUTES TO BIKE DOWN THERE, TWO MINUTES TO PICK UP THE MEAT AND PAY FOR IT, AND ANOTHER FIVE TO BIKE BACK-- TWELVE MINUTES.

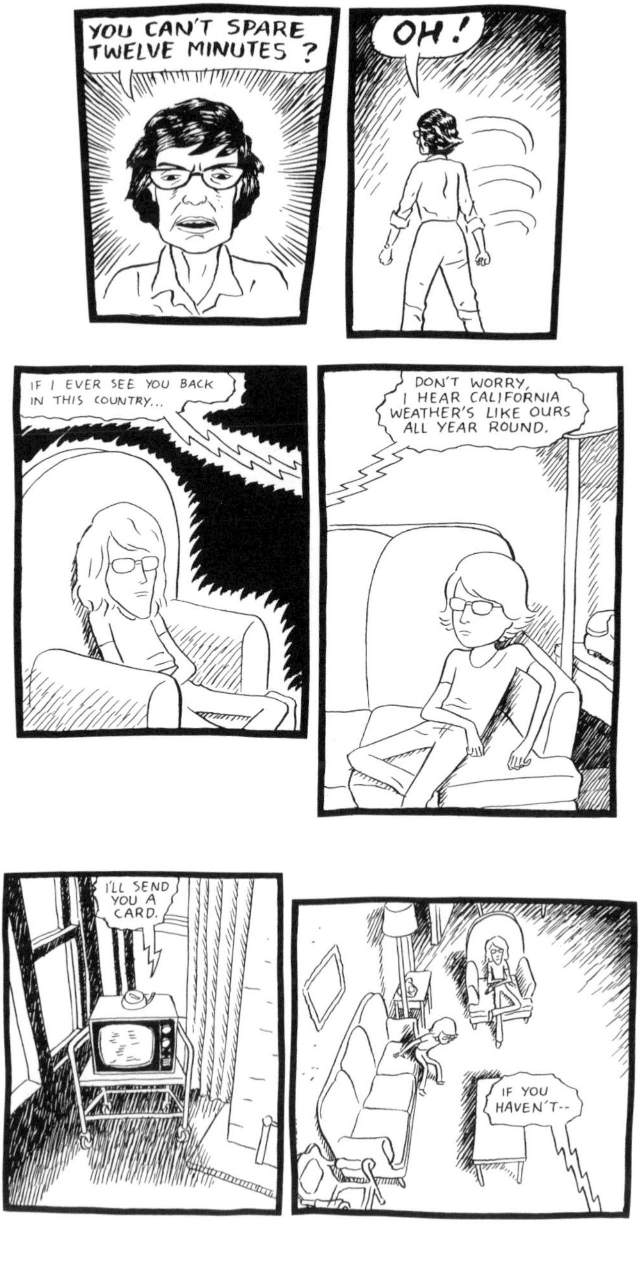
YOU CAN'T SPARE TWELVE MINUTES ?
OH !
IF I EVER SEE YOU BACK IN THIS COUNTRY...
DON'T WORRY, I HEAR CALIFORNIA WEATHER'S LIKE OURS ALL YEAR ROUND.
I'LL SEND YOU A CARD.
IF YOU HAVEN'T--

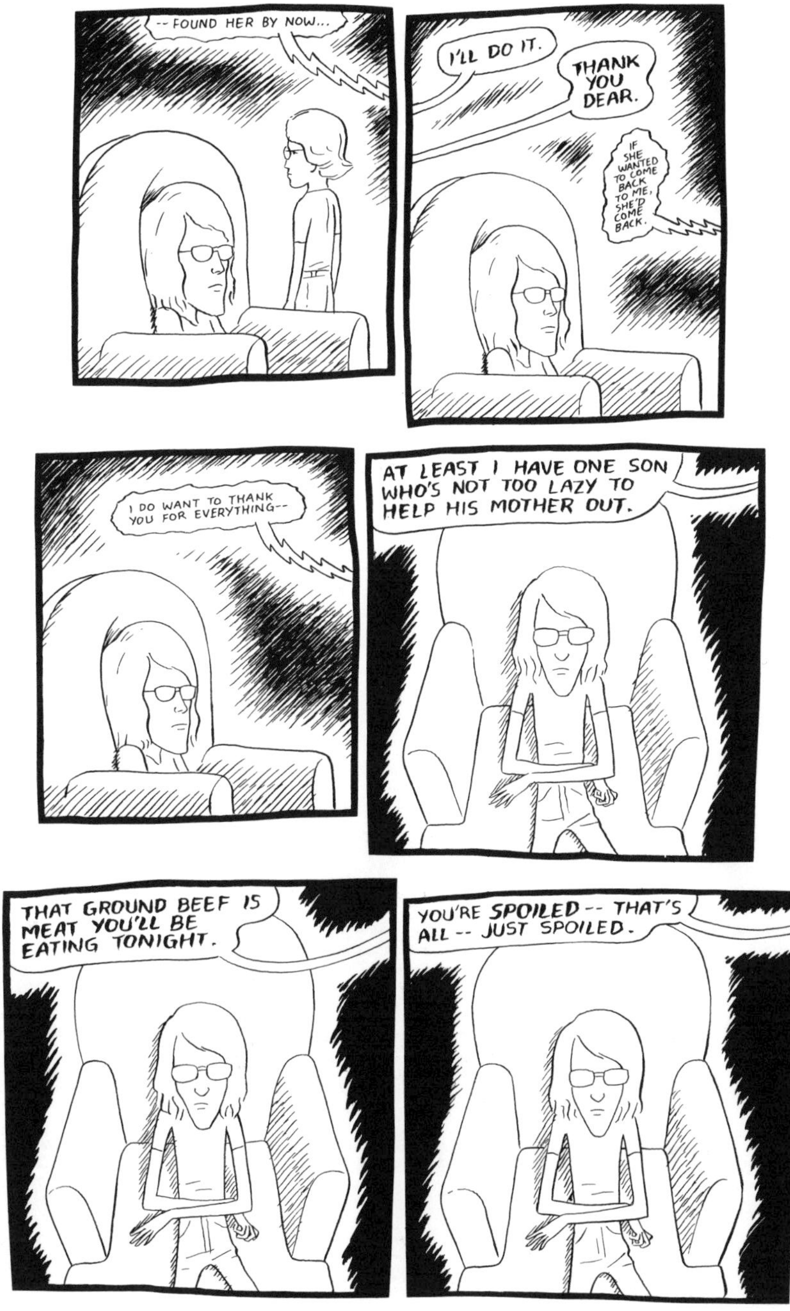
--FOUND HER BY NOW...
I'LL DO IT.
THANK YOU DEAR.
IF SHE WANTED TO COME BACK TO ME, SHE'D COME BACK.
I DO WANT TO THANK YOU FOR EVERYTHING--
AT LEAST I HAVE ONE SON WHO'S NOT TOO LAZY TO HELP HIS MOTHER OUT.
THAT GROUND BEEF IS MEAT YOU'LL BE EATING TONIGHT.
YOU'RE SPOILED -- THAT'S ALL -- JUST SPOILED.

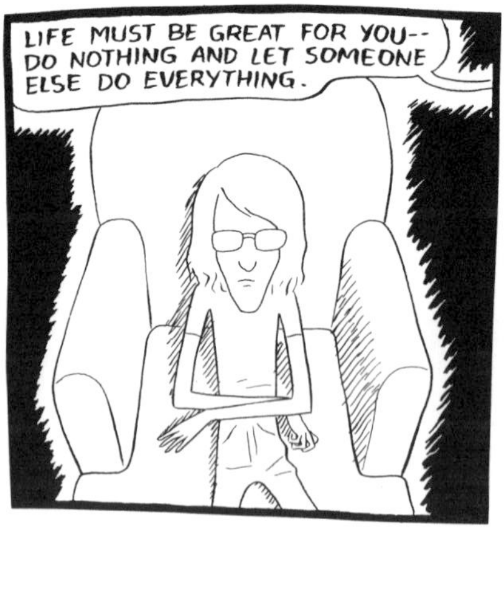
LIFE MUST BE GREAT FOR YOU--
DO NOTHING AND LET SOMEONE
ELSE DO EVERYTHING.

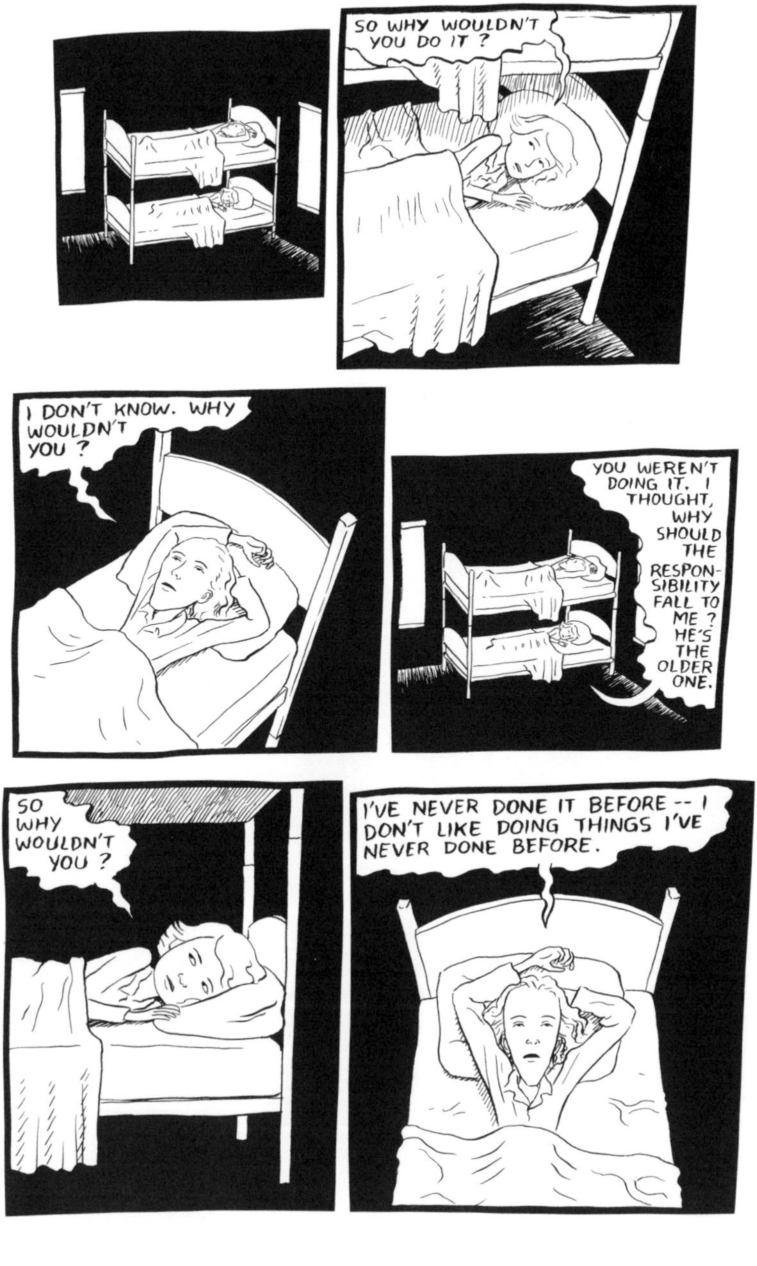
SO WHY WOULDN'T YOU DO IT ?
I DON'T KNOW. WHY WOULDN'T YOU ?
YOU WEREN'T DOING IT. I THOUGHT, WHY SHOULD THE RESPON-SIBILITY FALL TO ME ? HE'S THE OLDER ONE.
SO WHY WOULDN'T YOU ?
I'VE NEVER DONE IT BEFORE -- I DON'T LIKE DOING THINGS I'VE NEVER DONE BEFORE.

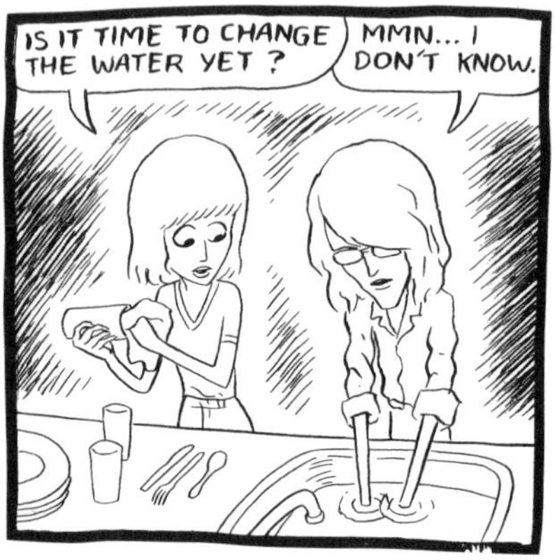
IS IT TIME TO CHANGE THE WATER YET?
MMN... I DON'T KNOW.

THUMP THUMP THUMP THUMP THUM
THUMP THUMP THUMP THUMP THUM
SAY IT.
HI SKY.
OH, HI.
CAN YOU ASK YOUR MOTHER TO BRING THOSE RECORDS OVER TO OUR PLACE ? MY DAD'S BEEN BUGGING ME ABOUT THEM.
HOW DOES BARRY KNOW SKY ? THEY CAN'T HAVE CLASSES TOGETHER. WHAT RECORDS ? HAVE THEY BEEN LISTENING TO MUSIC TOGETHER AT HER PLACE ?
OH SURE.

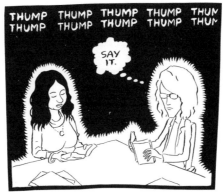

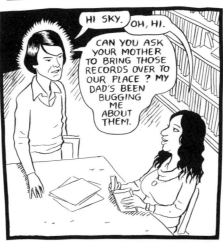

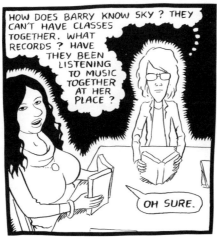

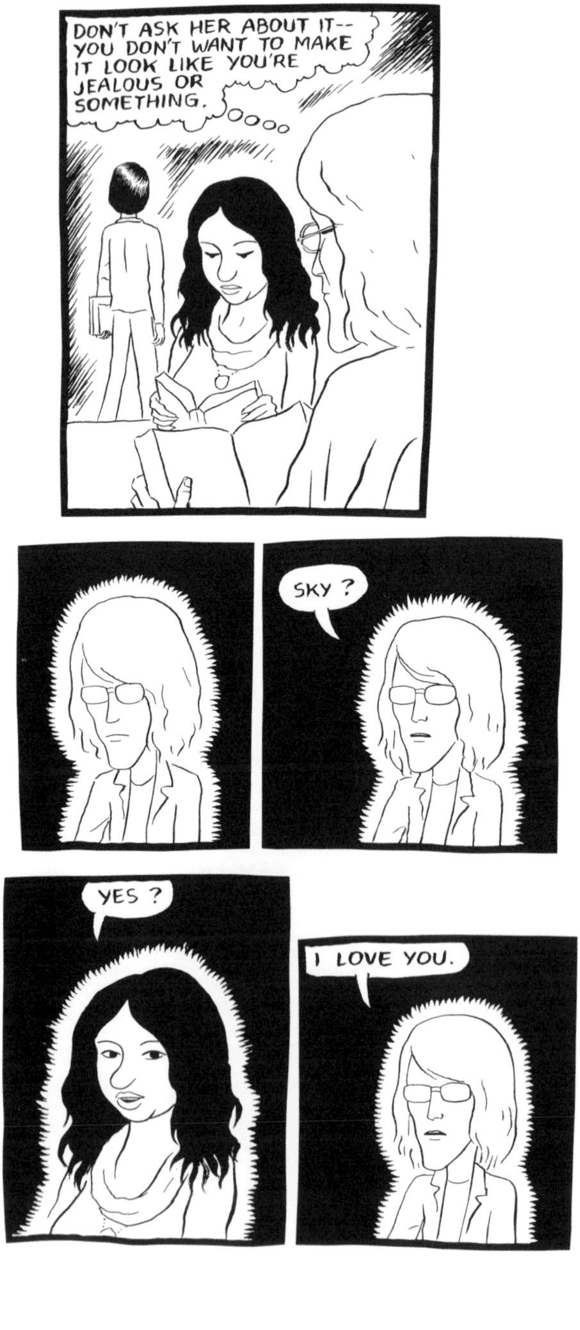
DON'T ASK HER ABOUT IT-- YOU DON'T WANT TO MAKE IT LOOK LIKE YOU'RE JEALOUS OR SOMETHING.
SKY ?
YES ?
I LOVE YOU.

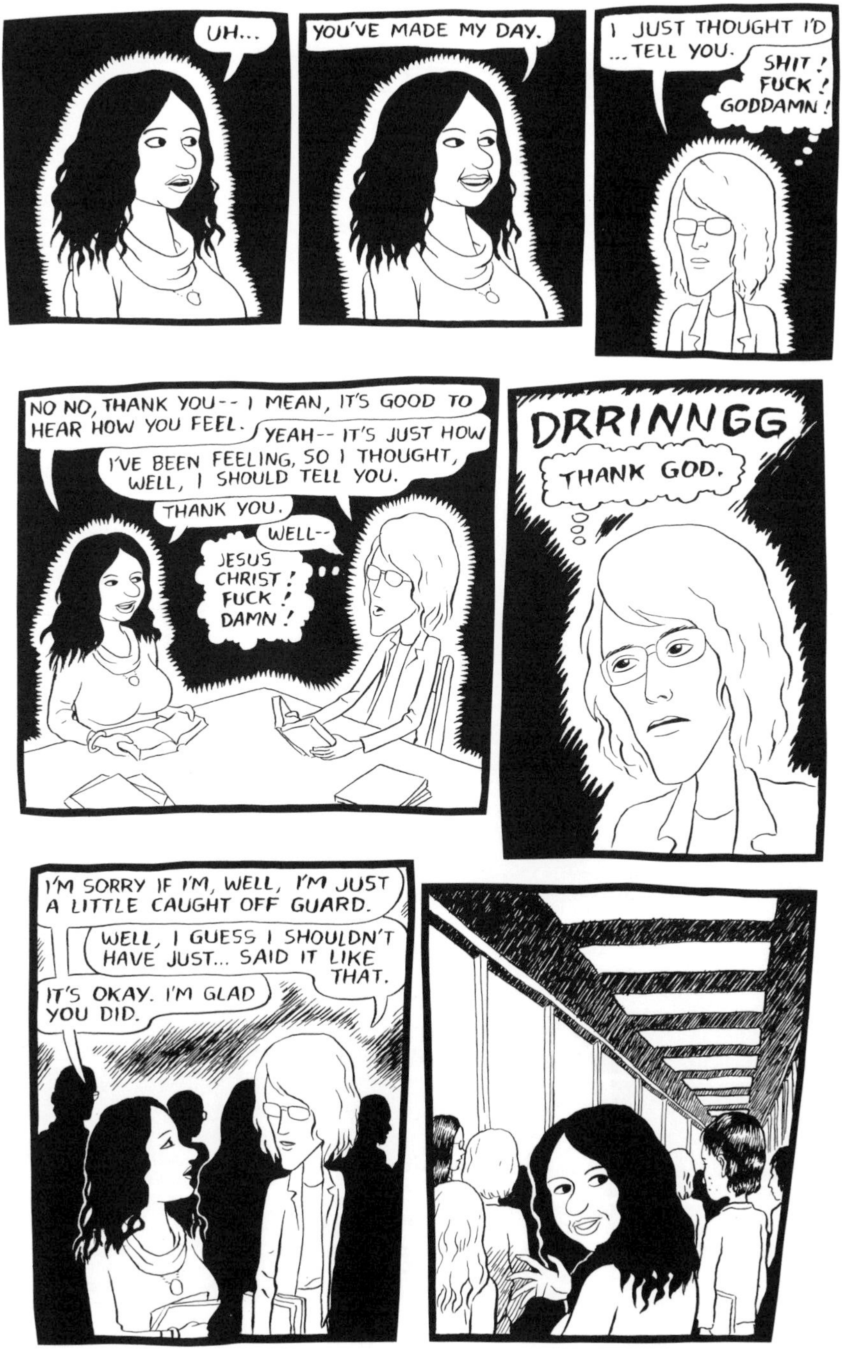
UH...
YOU'VE MADE MY DAY.
I JUST THOUGHT I'D ...TELL YOU.
SHIT! FUCK! GODDAMN!
NO NO, THANK YOU-- I MEAN, IT'S GOOD TO HEAR HOW YOU FEEL.
YEAH-- IT'S JUST HOW I'VE BEEN FEELING, SO I THOUGHT, WELL, I SHOULD TELL YOU.
THANK YOU.
WELL--
JESUS CHRIST! FUCK! DAMN!
DRRINNGG
THANK GOD.
I'M SORRY IF I'M, WELL, I'M JUST A LITTLE CAUGHT OFF GUARD.
WELL, I GUESS I SHOULDN'T HAVE JUST... SAID IT LIKE THAT.
IT'S OKAY. I'M GLAD YOU DID.

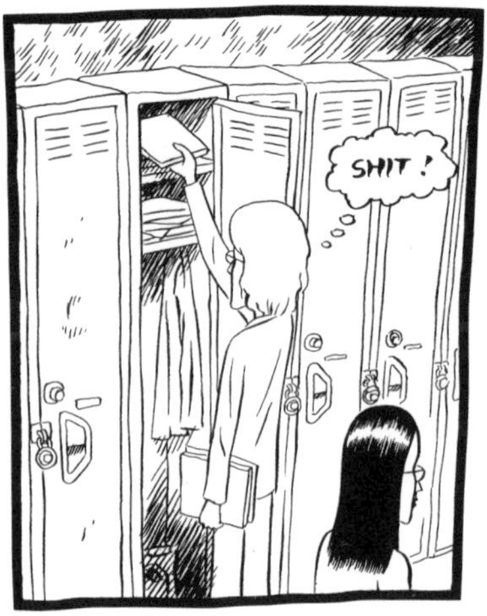
SHIT !

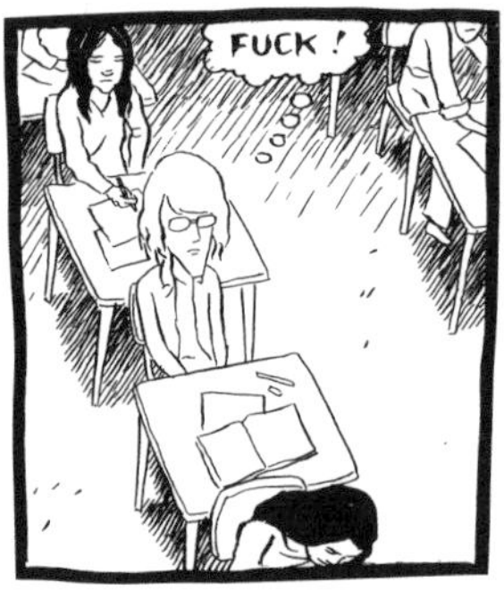
FUCK !

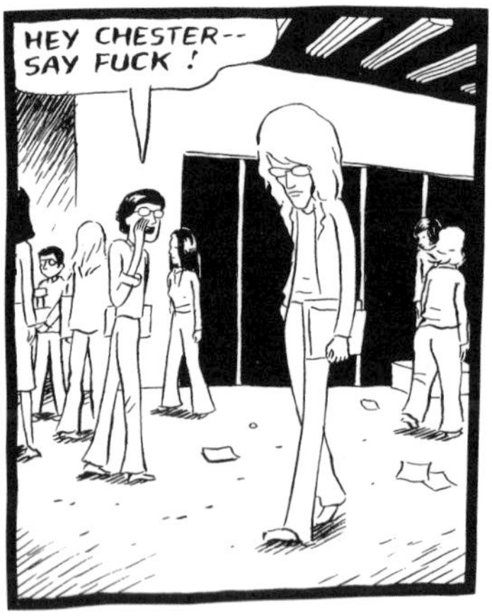
HEY CHESTER--
SAY FUCK !

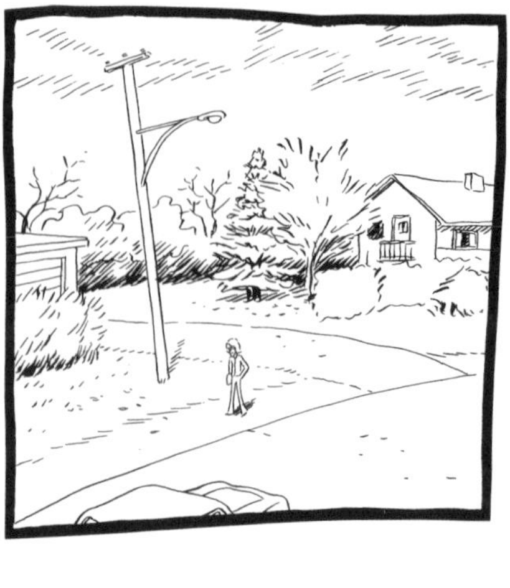

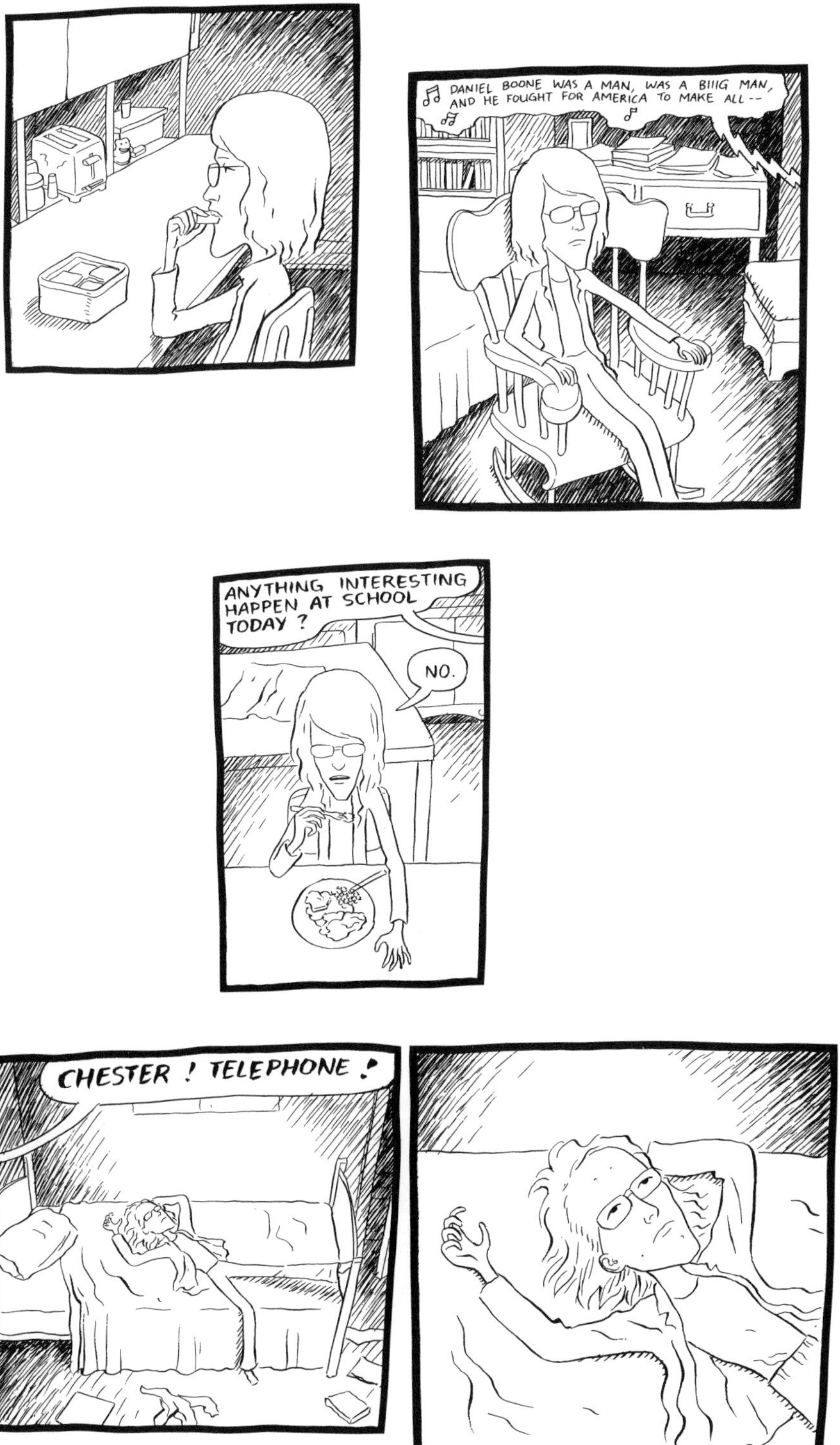
DANIEL BOONE WAS A MAN, WAS A BIIIG MAN, AND HE FOUGHT FOR AMERICA TO MAKE ALL --
ANYTHING INTERESTING HAPPEN AT SCHOOL TODAY ?
NO.
CHESTER ! TELEPHONE !

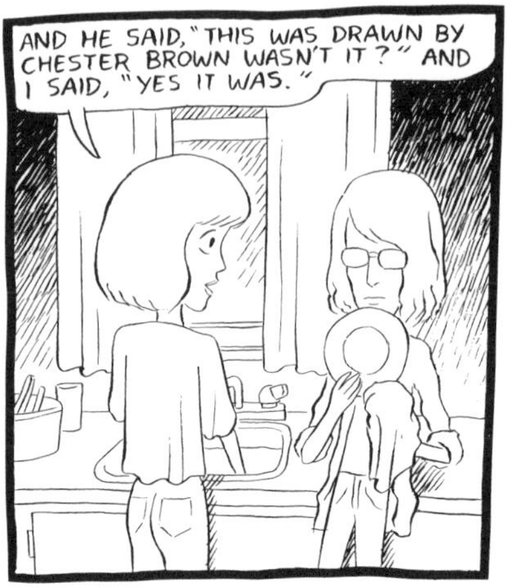
AND HE SAID, "THIS WAS DRAWN BY CHESTER BROWN WASN'T IT?" AND I SAID, "YES IT WAS."

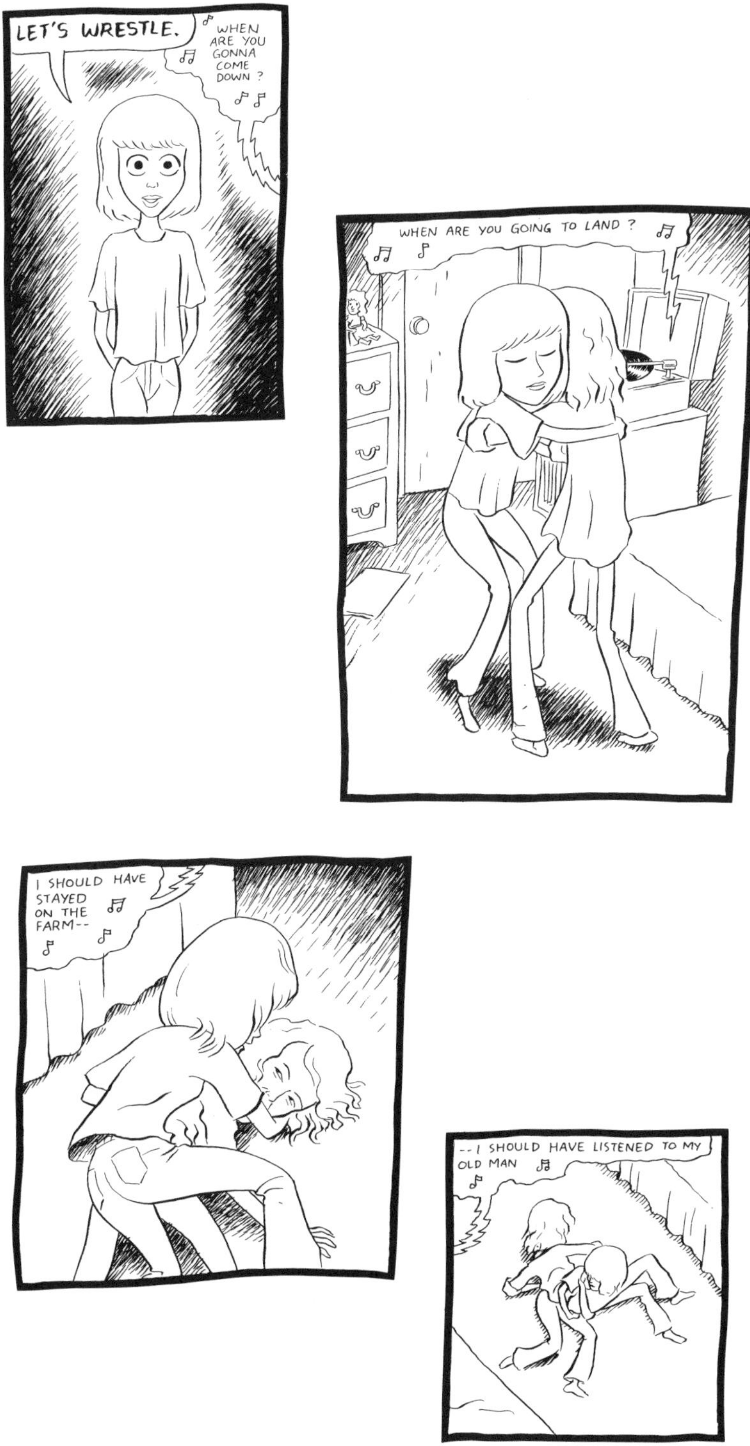
LET'S WRESTLE.
WHEN ARE YOU GONNA COME DOWN ?
WHEN ARE YOU GOING TO LAND ?
I SHOULD HAVE STAYED ON THE FARM--
--I SHOULD HAVE LISTENED TO MY OLD MAN

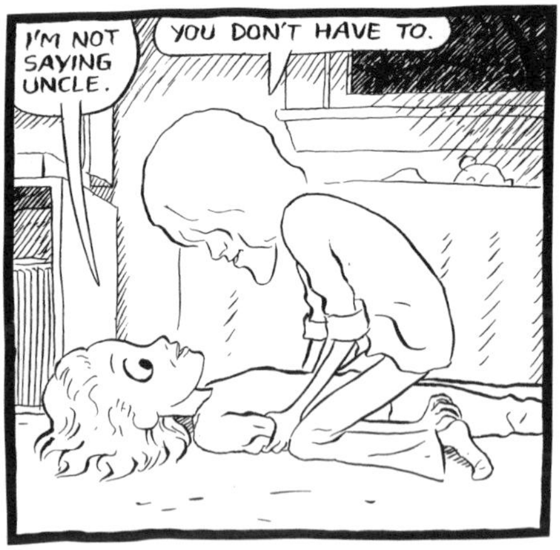
I'M NOT SAYING UNCLE.
YOU DON'T HAVE TO.

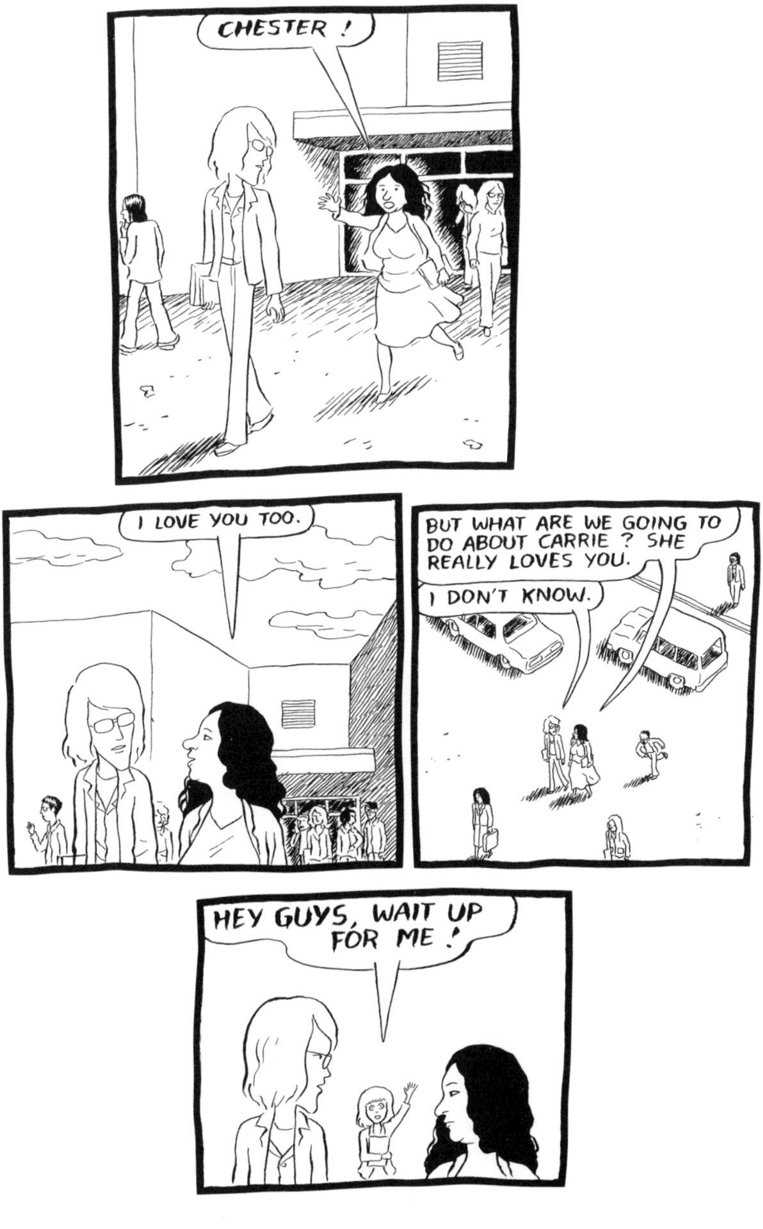
CHESTER !
I LOVE YOU TOO.
BUT WHAT ARE WE GOING TO DO ABOUT CARRIE ? SHE REALLY LOVES YOU.
I DON'T KNOW.
HEY GUYS, WAIT UP FOR ME !

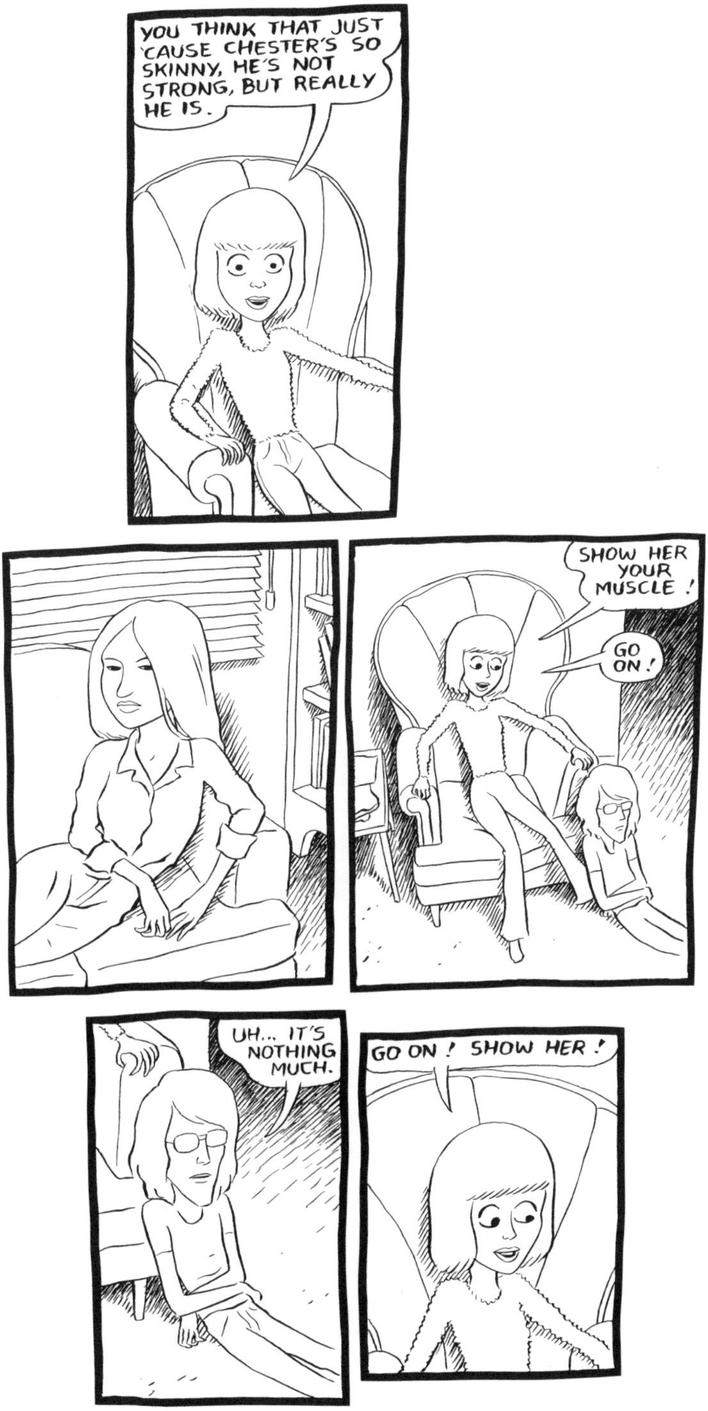
YOU THINK THAT JUST 'CAUSE CHESTER'S SO SKINNY, HE'S NOT STRONG, BUT REALLY HE IS.
SHOW HER YOUR MUSCLE!
GO ON!
UH... IT'S NOTHING MUCH.
GO ON! SHOW HER!

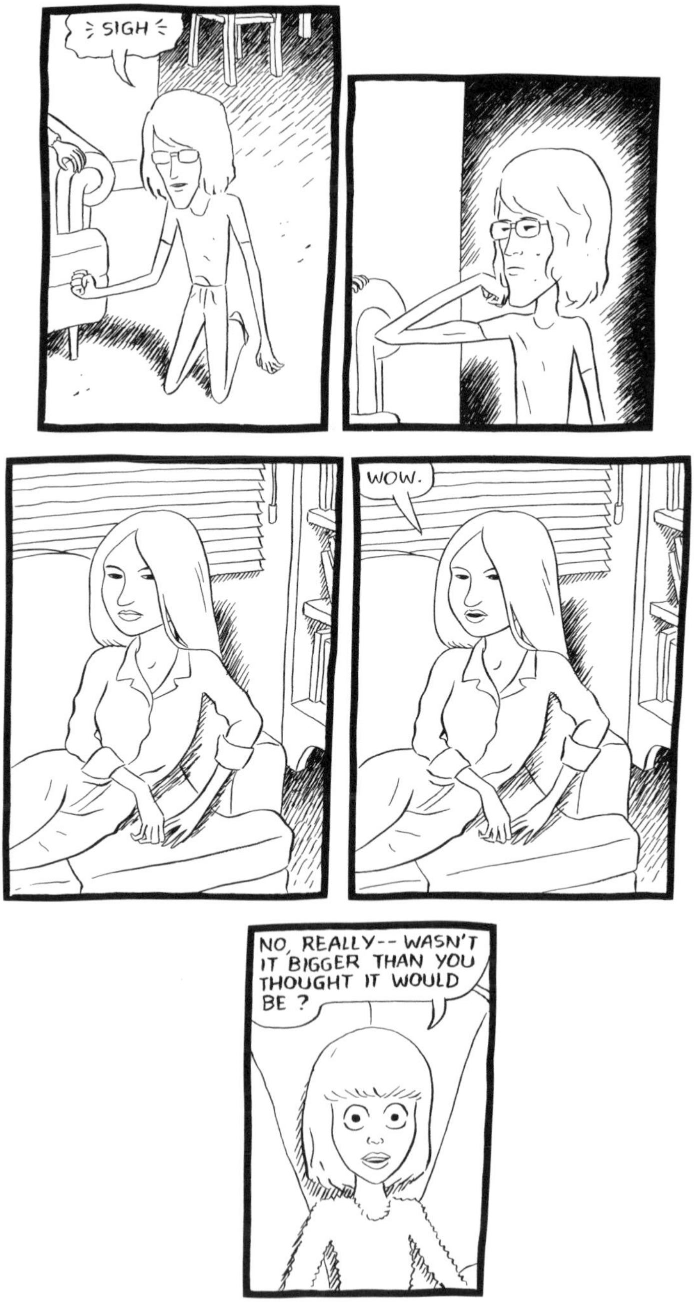
SIGH
WOW.
NO, REALLY-- WASN'T IT BIGGER THAN YOU THOUGHT IT WOULD BE ?

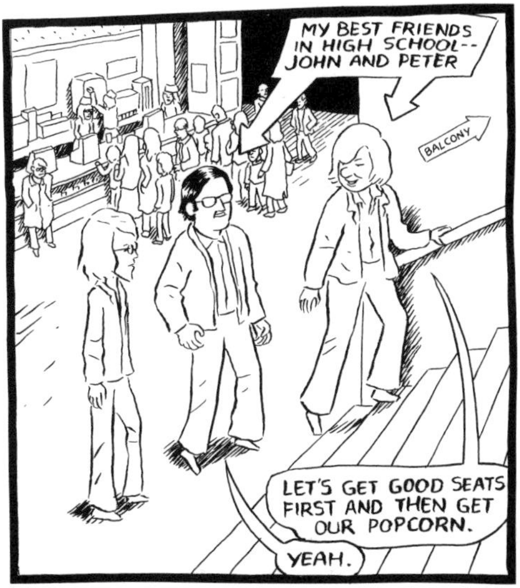
MY BEST FRIENDS IN HIGH SCHOOL-- JOHN AND PETER
BALCONY
LET'S GET GOOD SEATS FIRST AND THEN GET OUR POPCORN.
YEAH.

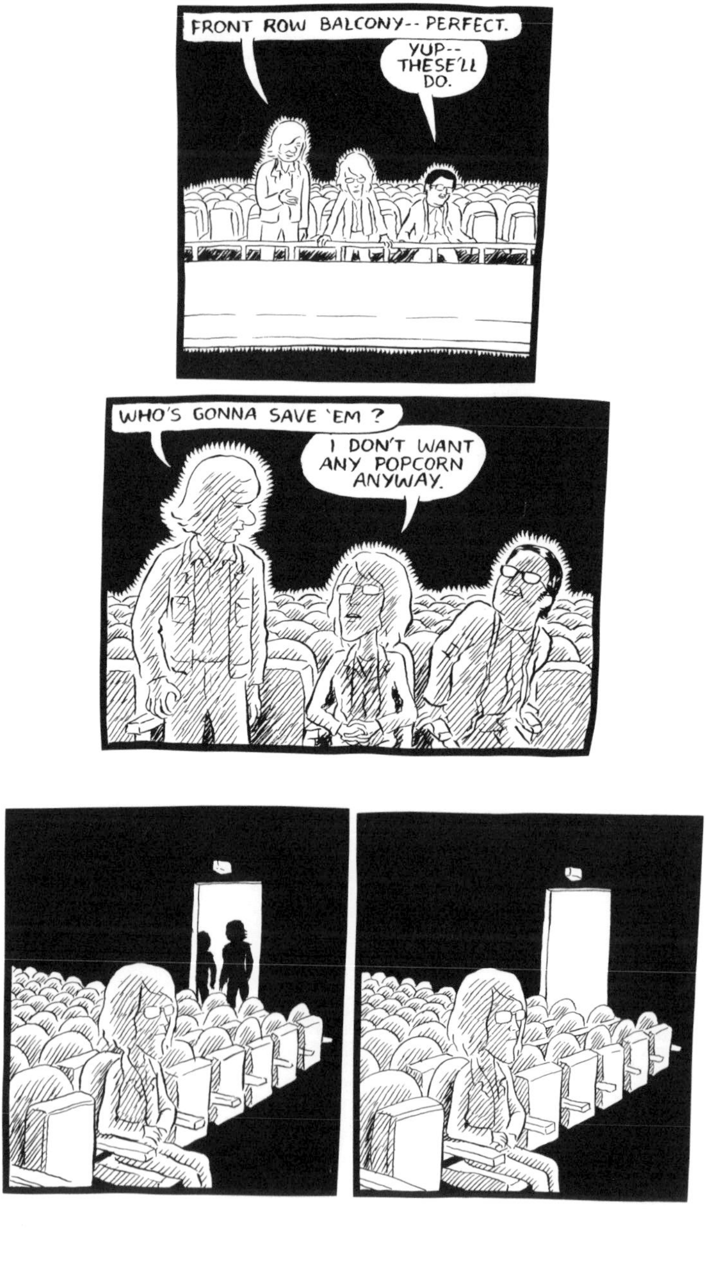
FRONT ROW BALCONY-- PERFECT.
YUP-- THESE'LL DO.
WHO'S GONNA SAVE 'EM ?
I DON'T WANT ANY POPCORN ANYWAY.

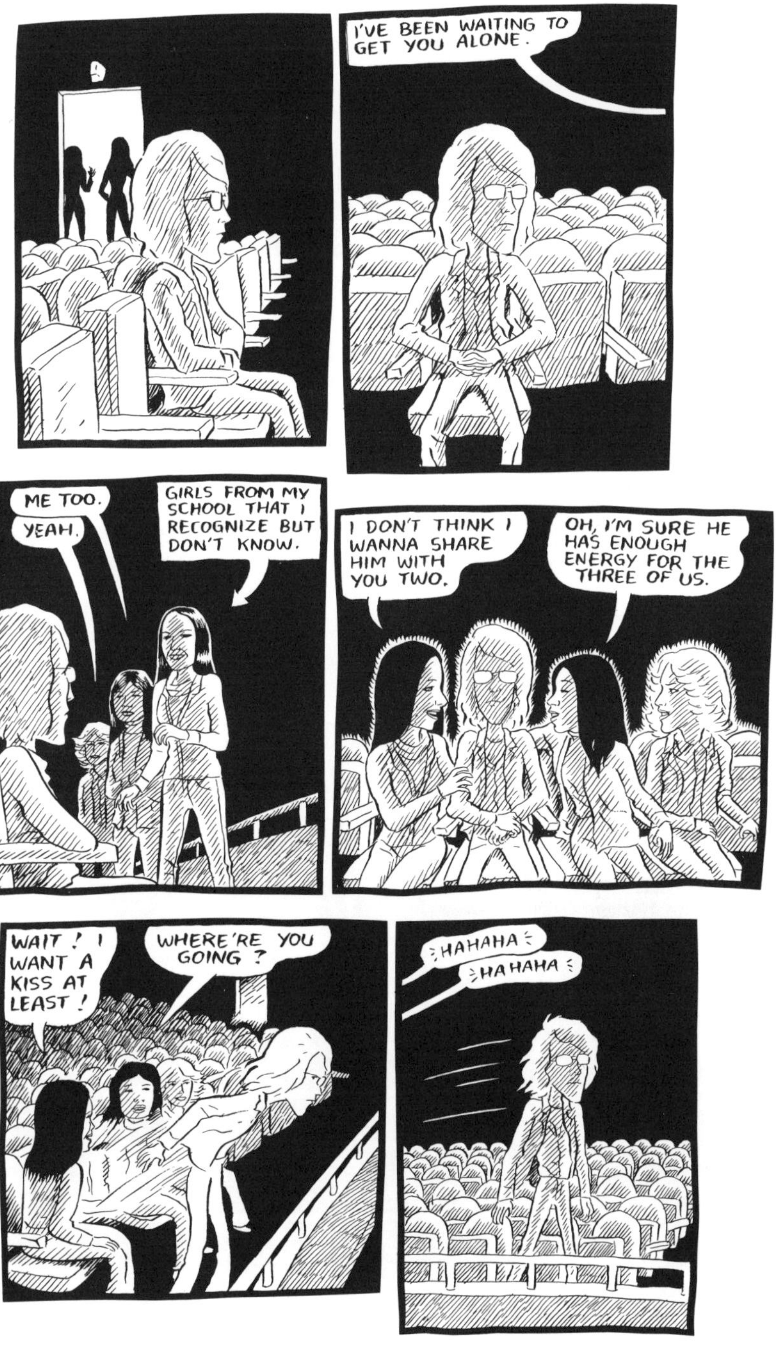
I'VE BEEN WAITING TO GET YOU ALONE.
ME TOO.
YEAH.
GIRLS FROM MY SCHOOL THAT I RECOGNIZE BUT DON'T KNOW.
I DON'T THINK I WANNA SHARE HIM WITH YOU TWO.
OH, I'M SURE HE HAS ENOUGH ENERGY FOR THE THREE OF US.
WAIT! I WANT A KISS AT LEAST!
WHERE'RE YOU GOING?
HAHAHA
HAHAHA

WHY AREN'T YOU HOLDING OUR SEATS?

I DECIDED I WANT A GINGER ALE. DON'T WORRY-- THERE'S NO ONE UP THERE. WE'LL STILL GET THOSE SEATS.

YOU SEE? WE'VE STILL GOT THE SEATS.

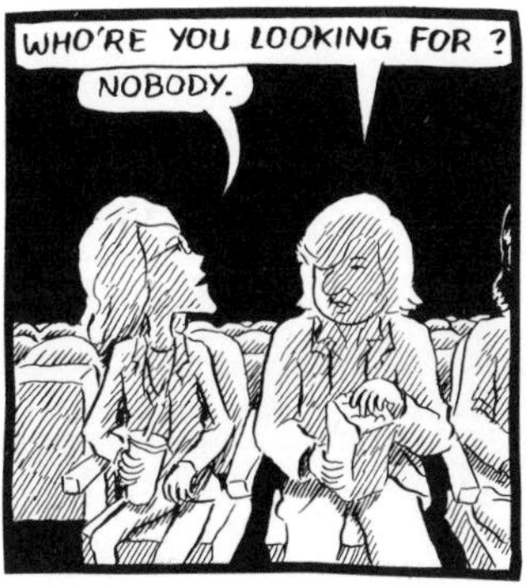
WHO'RE YOU LOOKING FOR?
NOBODY.

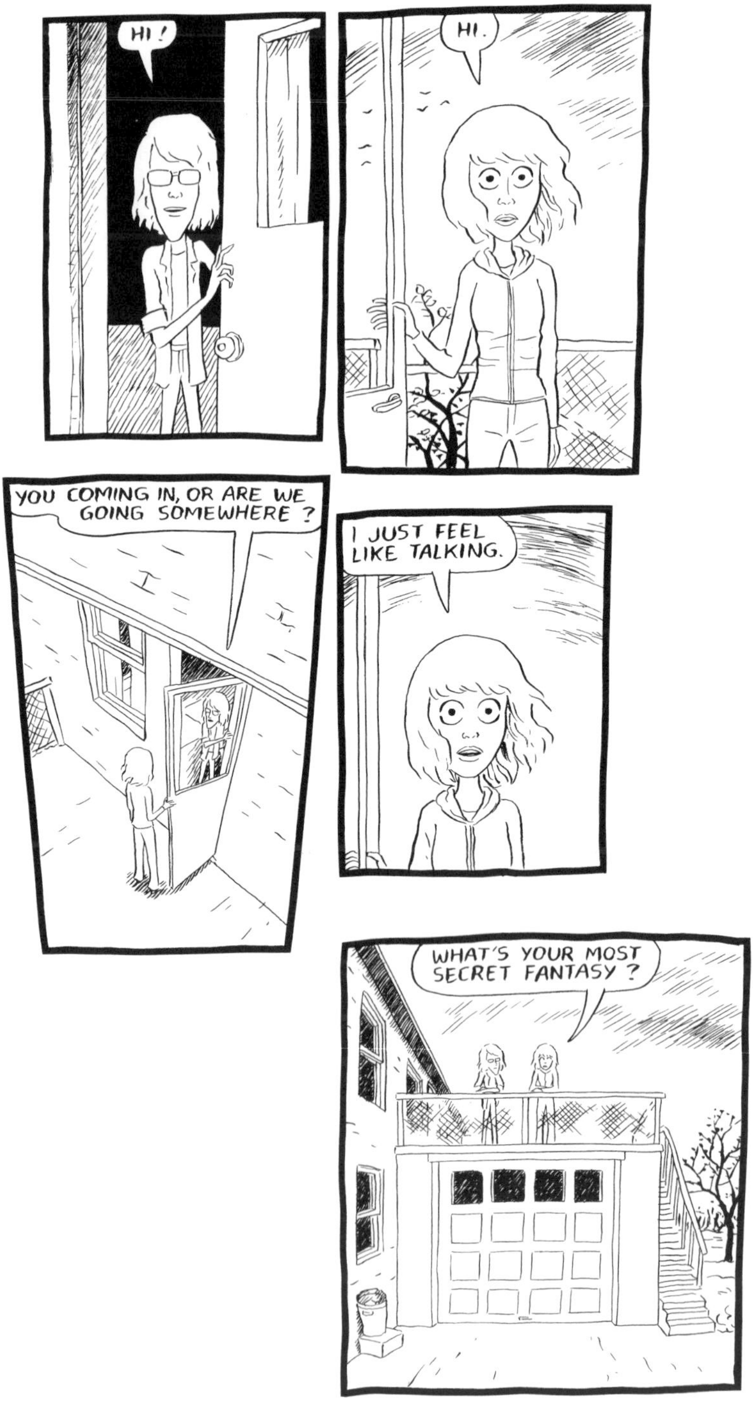
HI!
HI.
YOU COMING IN, OR ARE WE GOING SOMEWHERE?
I JUST FEEL LIKE TALKING.
WHAT'S YOUR MOST SECRET FANTASY?

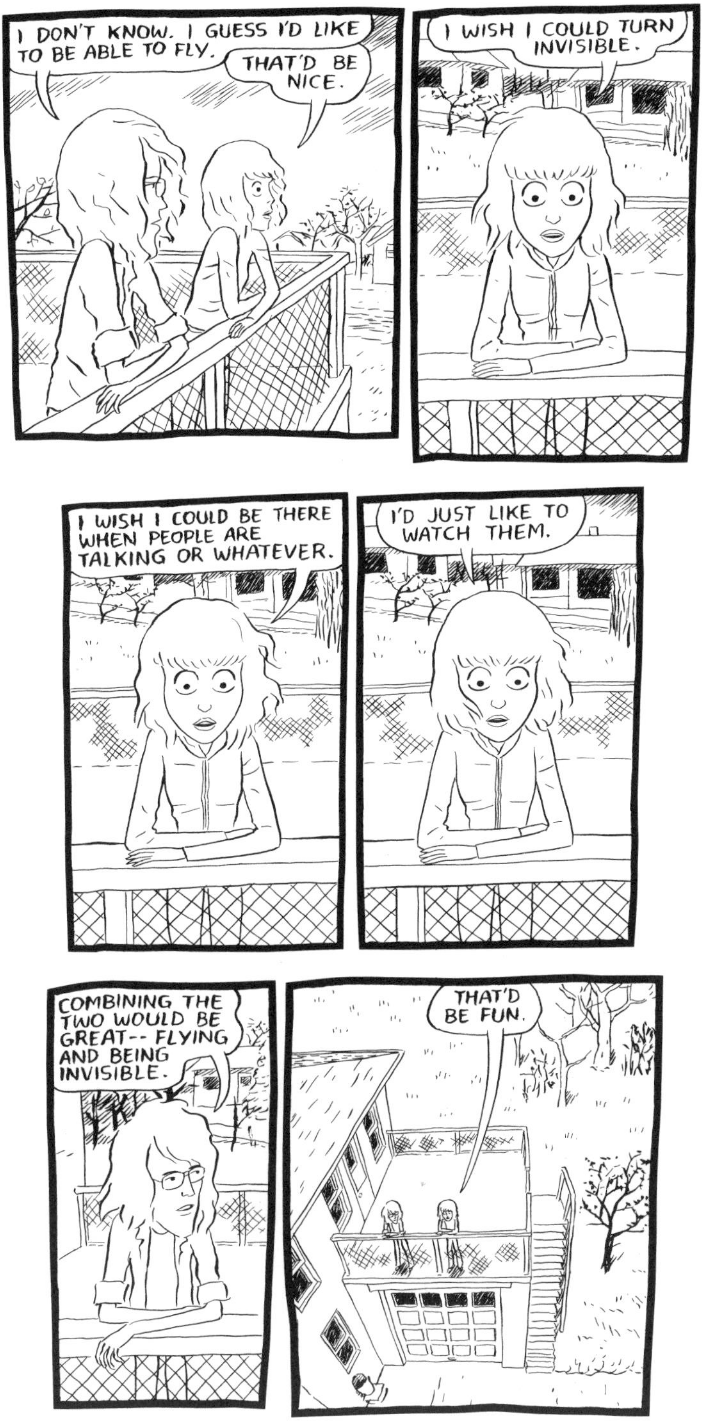
I DON'T KNOW. I GUESS I'D LIKE TO BE ABLE TO FLY.
THAT'D BE NICE.
I WISH I COULD TURN INVISIBLE.
I WISH I COULD BE THERE WHEN PEOPLE ARE TALKING OR WHATEVER.
I'D JUST LIKE TO WATCH THEM.
COMBINING THE TWO WOULD BE GREAT-- FLYING AND BEING INVISIBLE.
THAT'D BE FUN.

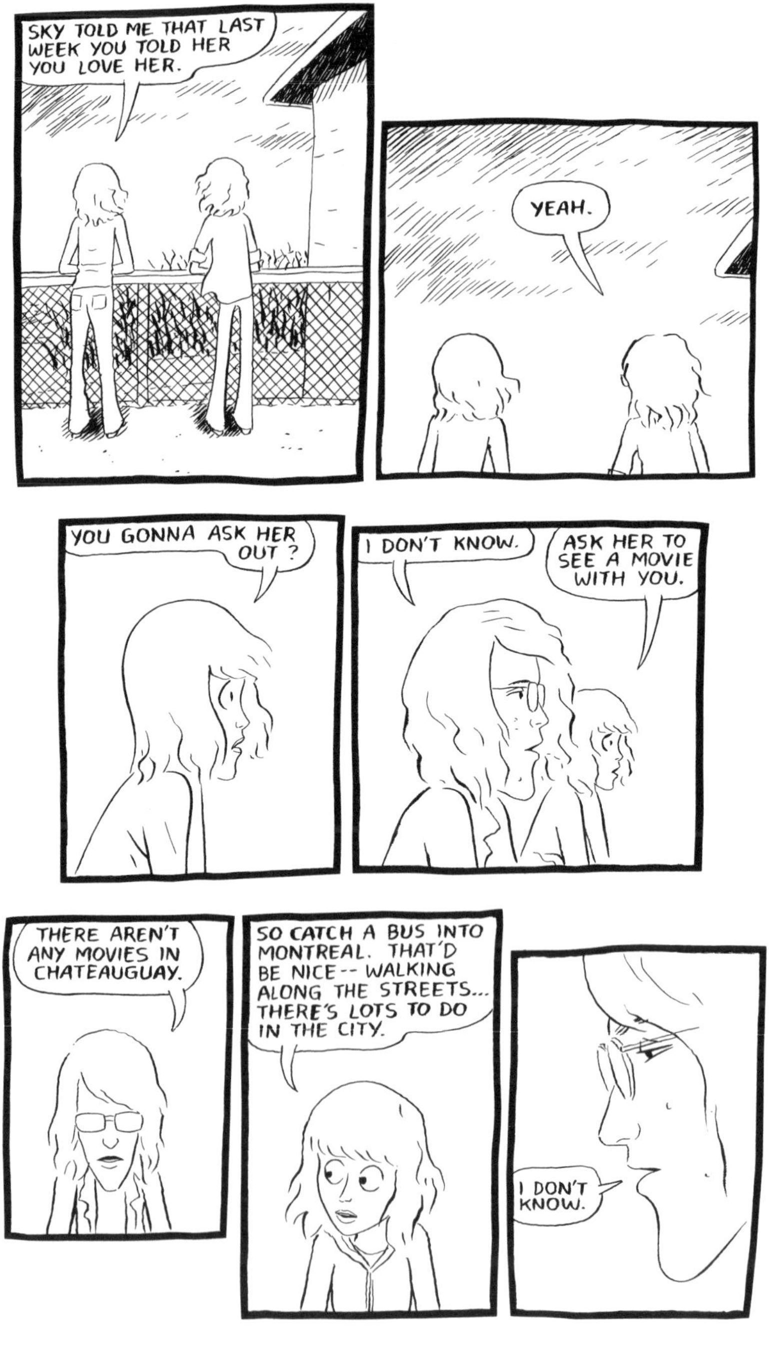
SKY TOLD ME THAT LAST WEEK YOU TOLD HER YOU LOVE HER.
YEAH.
YOU GONNA ASK HER OUT ?
I DON'T KNOW.
ASK HER TO SEE A MOVIE WITH YOU.
THERE AREN'T ANY MOVIES IN CHATEAUGUAY.
SO CATCH A BUS INTO MONTREAL. THAT'D BE NICE-- WALKING ALONG THE STREETS... THERE'S LOTS TO DO IN THE CITY.
I DON'T KNOW.

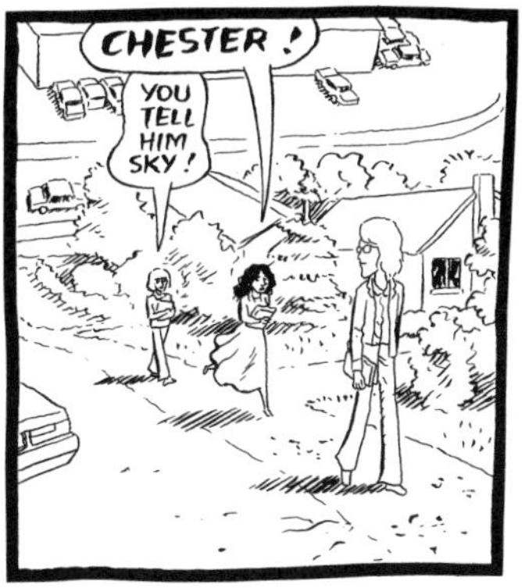
CHESTER!
YOU TELL HIM SKY!

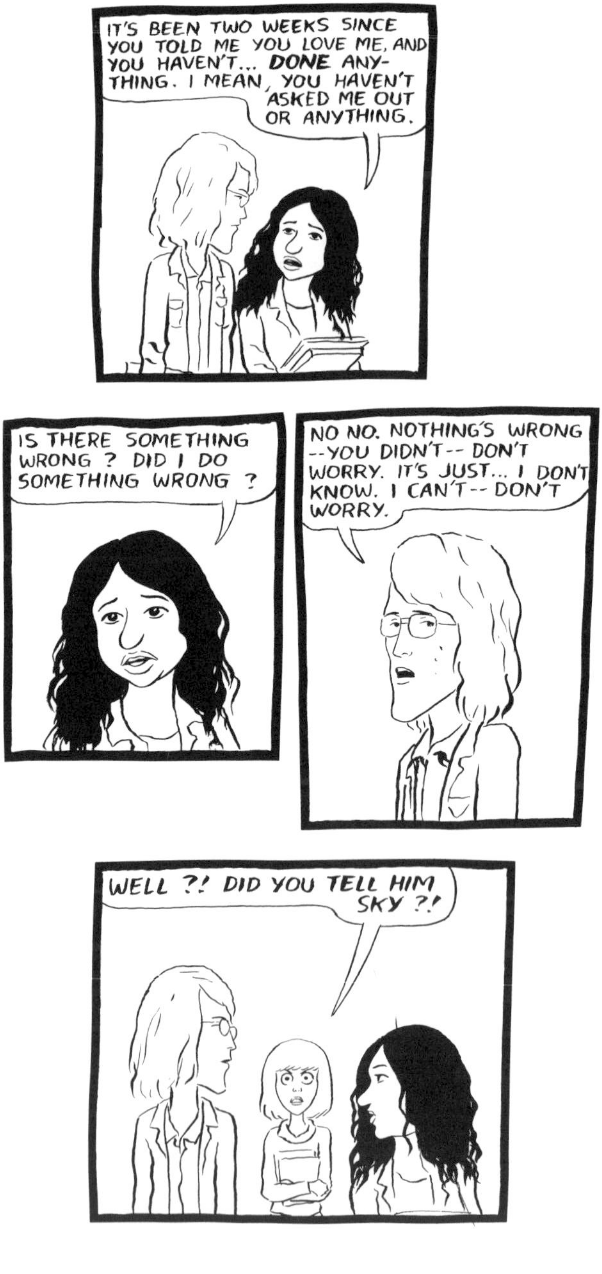
IT'S BEEN TWO WEEKS SINCE YOU TOLD ME YOU LOVE ME, AND YOU HAVEN'T... DONE ANYTHING. I MEAN, YOU HAVEN'T ASKED ME OUT OR ANYTHING.
IS THERE SOMETHING WRONG ? DID I DO SOMETHING WRONG ?
NO NO. NOTHING'S WRONG --YOU DIDN'T-- DON'T WORRY. IT'S JUST... I DON'T KNOW. I CAN'T-- DON'T WORRY.
WELL ?! DID YOU TELL HIM SKY ?!

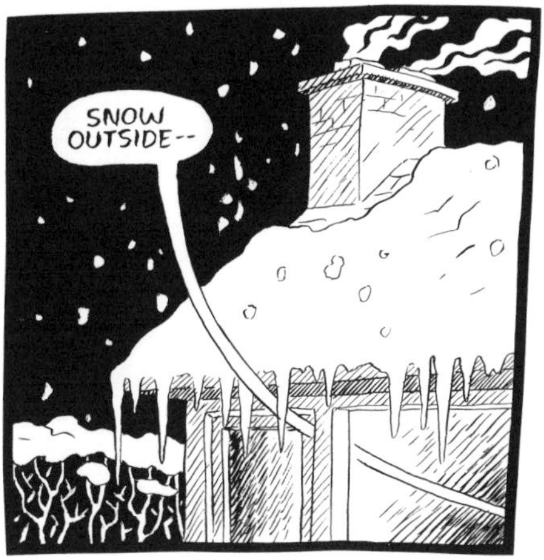
SNOW OUTSIDE--

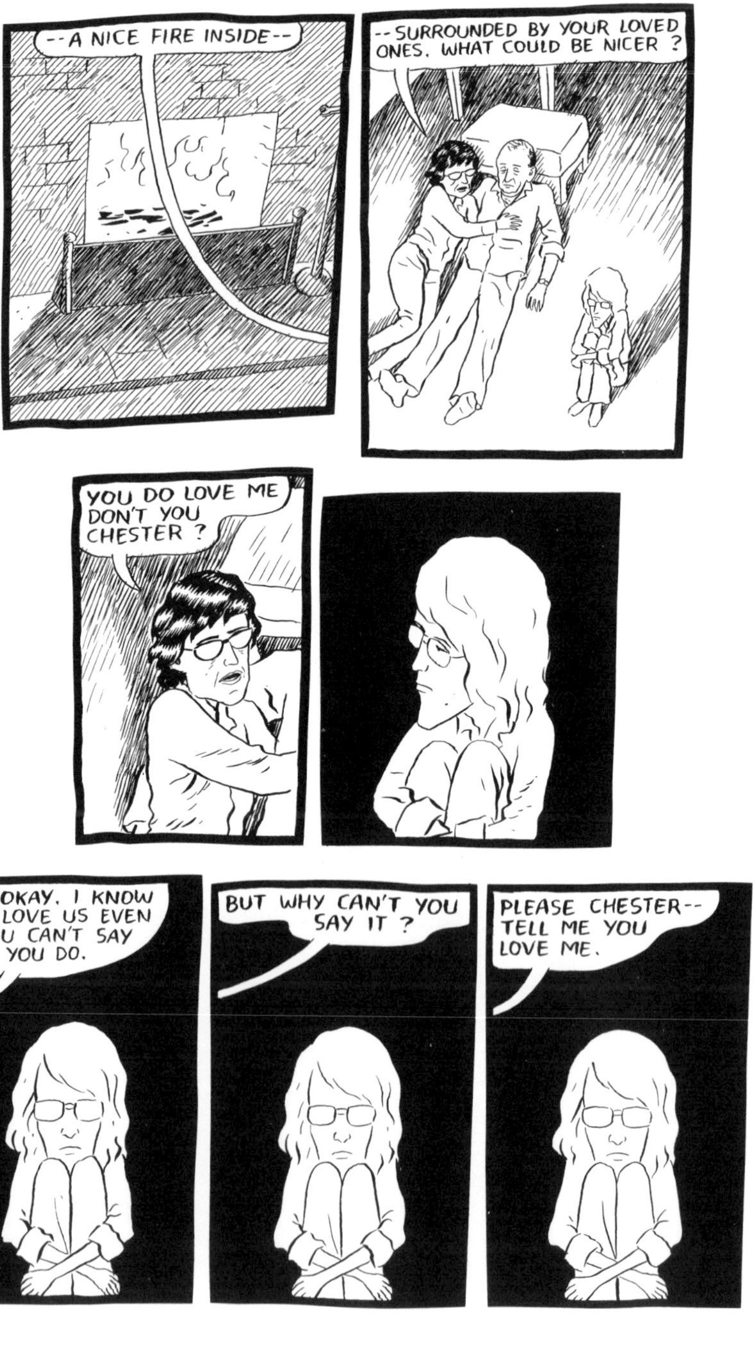
--A NICE FIRE INSIDE--
--SURROUNDED BY YOUR LOVED ONES. WHAT COULD BE NICER ?
YOU DO LOVE ME DON'T YOU CHESTER ?
IT'S OKAY. I KNOW YOU LOVE US EVEN IF YOU CAN'T SAY YOU DO.
BUT WHY CAN'T YOU SAY IT ?
PLEASE CHESTER-- TELL ME YOU LOVE ME.

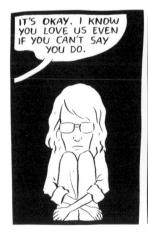

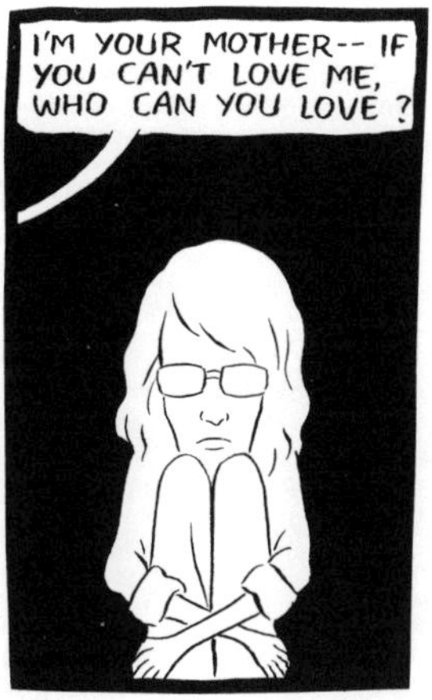
I'M YOUR MOTHER-- IF YOU CAN'T LOVE ME, WHO CAN YOU LOVE ?

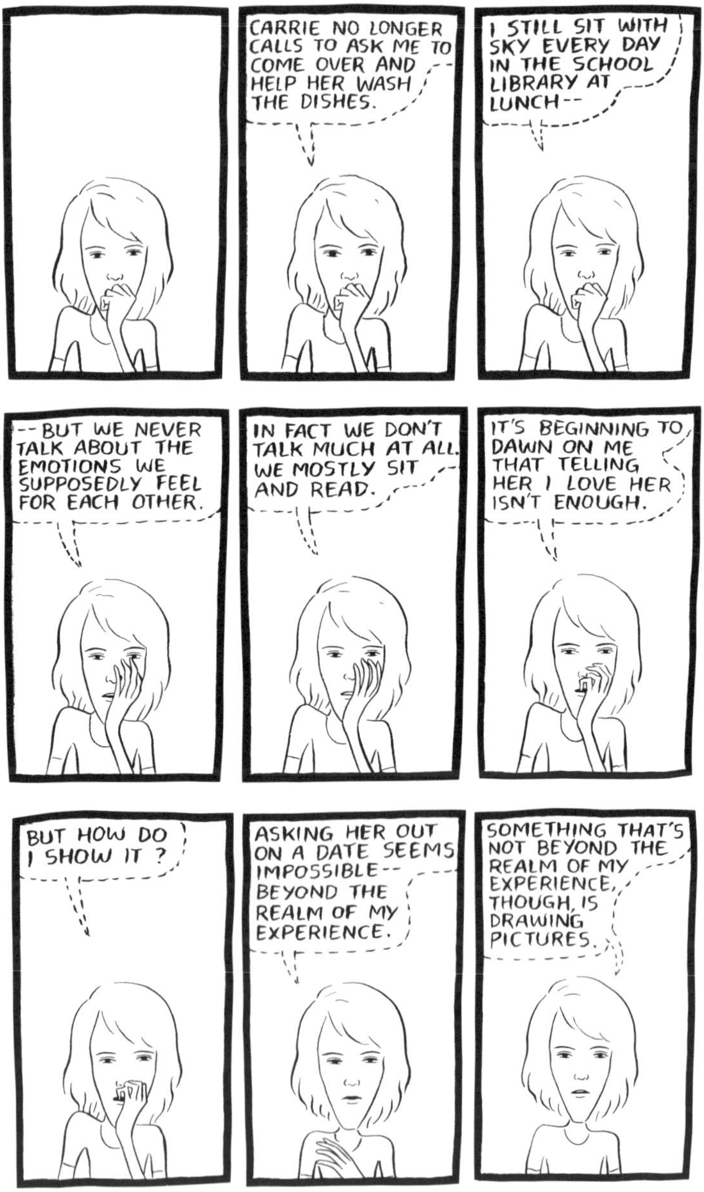

CARRIE NO LONGER CALLS TO ASK ME TO COME OVER AND HELP HER WASH THE DISHES.
I STILL SIT WITH SKY EVERY DAY IN THE SCHOOL LIBRARY AT LUNCH--
--BUT WE NEVER TALK ABOUT THE EMOTIONS WE SUPPOSEDLY FEEL FOR EACH OTHER.
IN FACT WE DON'T TALK MUCH AT ALL. WE MOSTLY SIT AND READ.
IT'S BEGINNING TO DAWN ON ME THAT TELLING HER I LOVE HER ISN'T ENOUGH.
BUT HOW DO I SHOW IT ?
ASKING HER OUT ON A DATE SEEMS IMPOSSIBLE-- BEYOND THE REALM OF MY EXPERIENCE.
SOMETHING THAT'S NOT BEYOND THE REALM OF MY EXPERIENCE, THOUGH, IS DRAWING PICTURES.

THE BIRD REPRESENTS SKY.

AND THE SKELETON REPRESENTS ME.

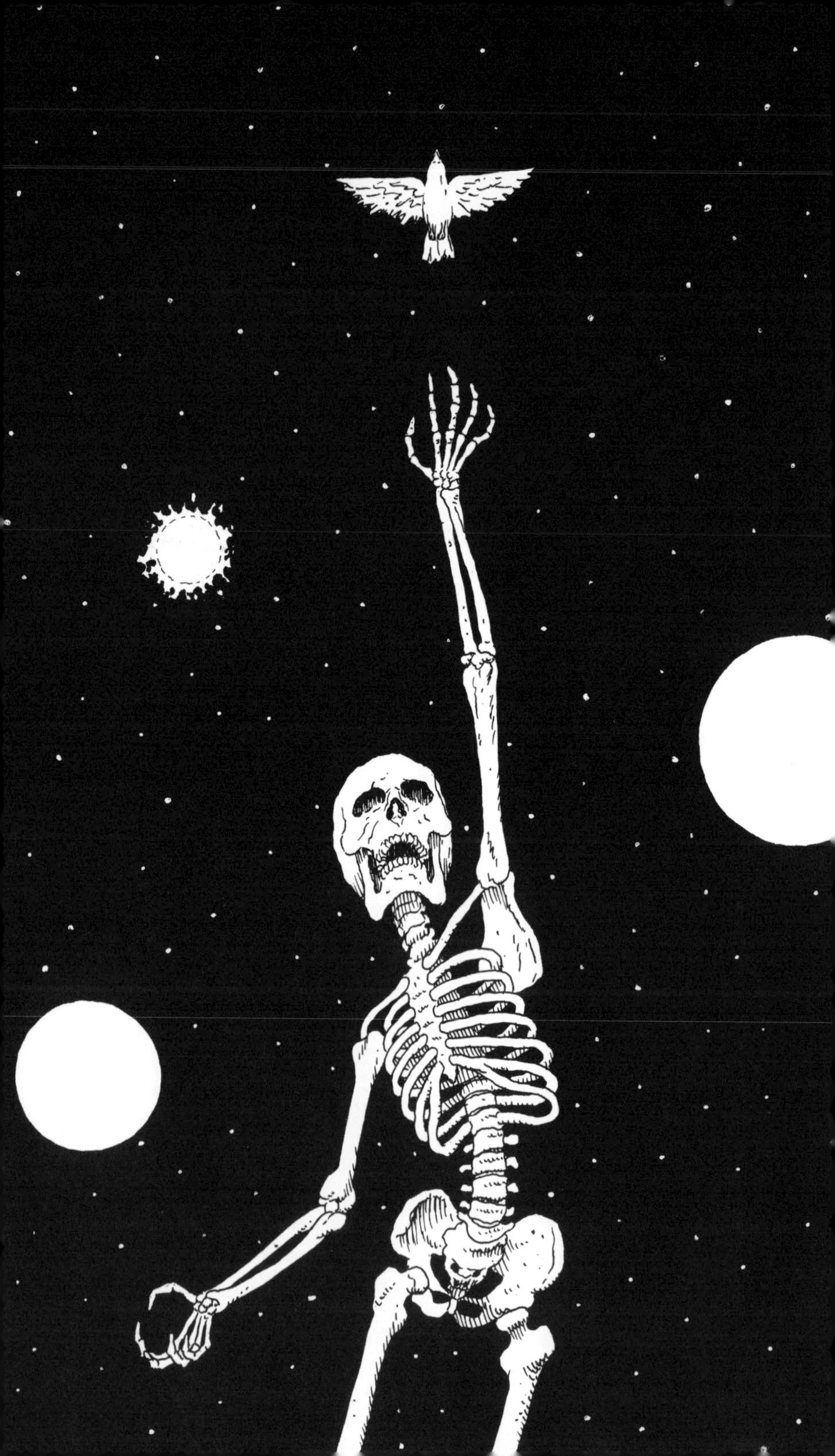

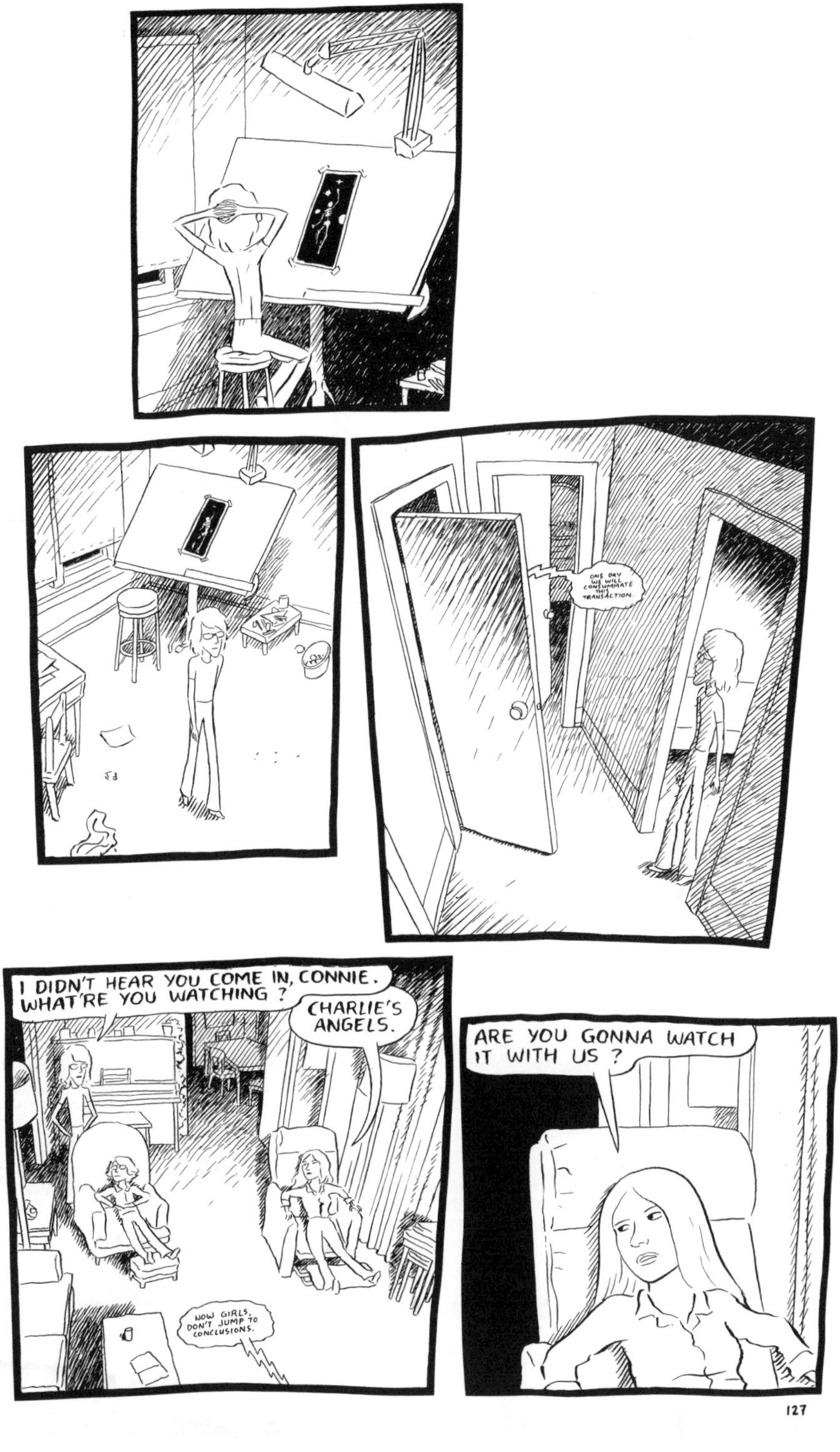
ONE DAY WE WILL CONSUMMATE THIS TRANSACTION.
I DIDN'T HEAR YOU COME IN, CONNIE. WHAT'RE YOU WATCHING ?
CHARLIE'S ANGELS.
NOW GIRLS, DON'T JUMP TO CONCLUSIONS.
ARE YOU GONNA WATCH IT WITH US ?

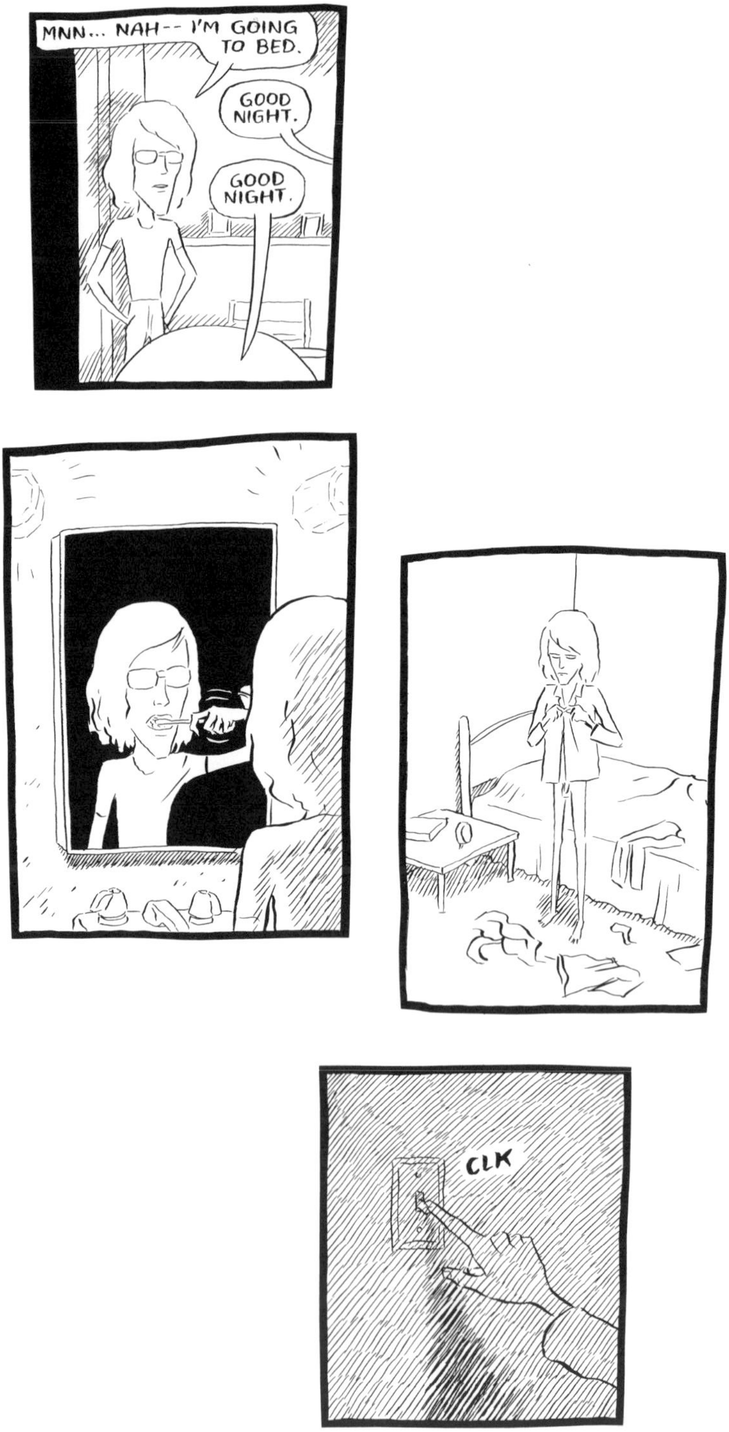
MNN... NAH-- I'M GOING TO BED.
GOOD NIGHT.
GOOD NIGHT.
CLK

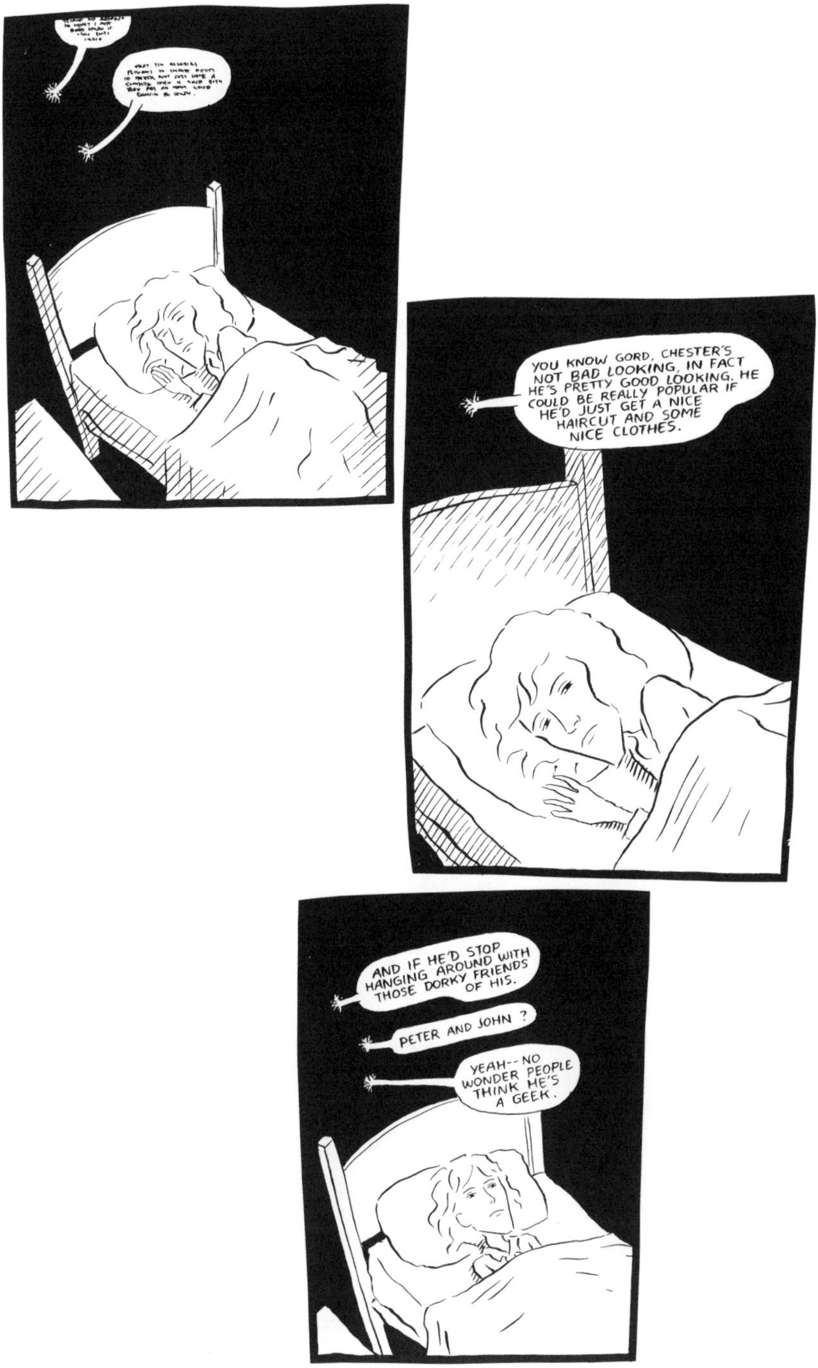
YOU KNOW GORD, CHESTER'S NOT BAD LOOKING, IN FACT HE'S PRETTY GOOD LOOKING. HE COULD BE REALLY POPULAR IF HE'D JUST GET A NICE HAIRCUT AND SOME NICE CLOTHES.
AND IF HE'D STOP HANGING AROUND WITH THOSE DORKY FRIENDS OF HIS.
PETER AND JOHN ?
YEAH-- NO WONDER PEOPLE THINK HE'S A GEEK.

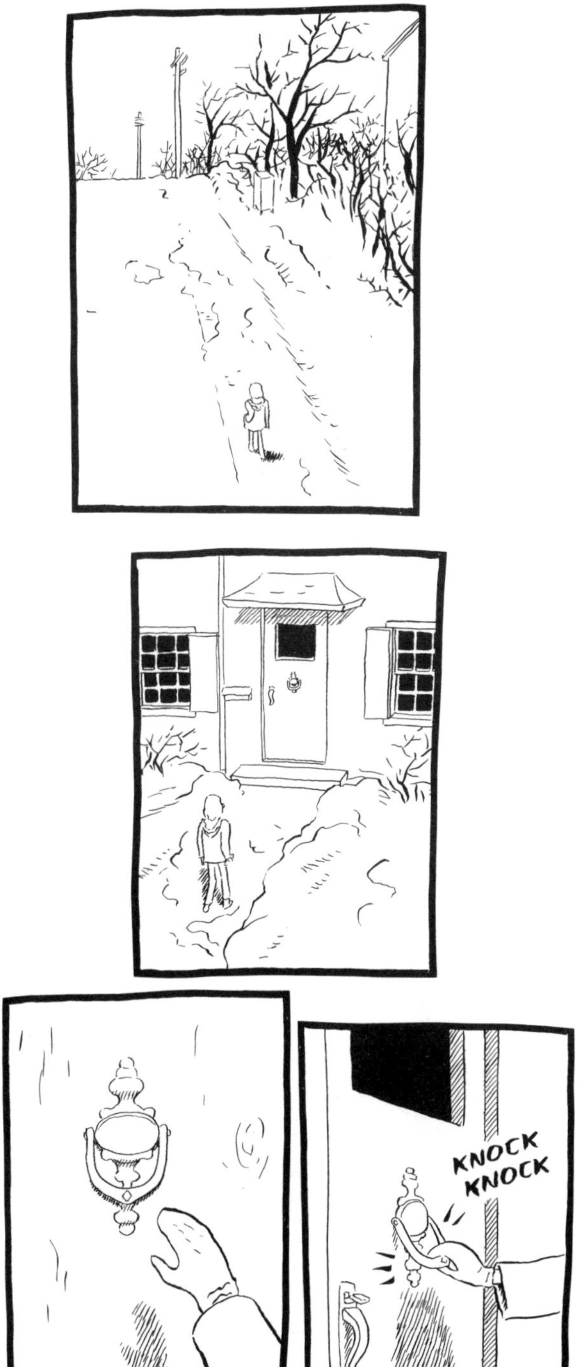
KNOCK
KNOCK

HELLO CHESTER-- MERRY CHRISTMAS.
HI MRS BAKER. IS SKY IN ?
OF COURSE -- JUST A SECOND.
SKY ! CHESTER'S HERE TO SEE YOU !
HI.
WANNA GO, UH, FOR A WALK ?
SURE.

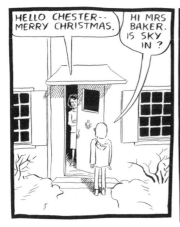

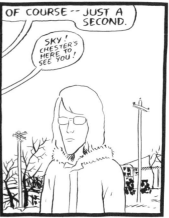

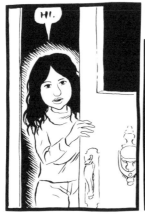

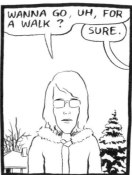

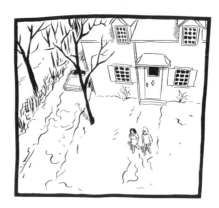

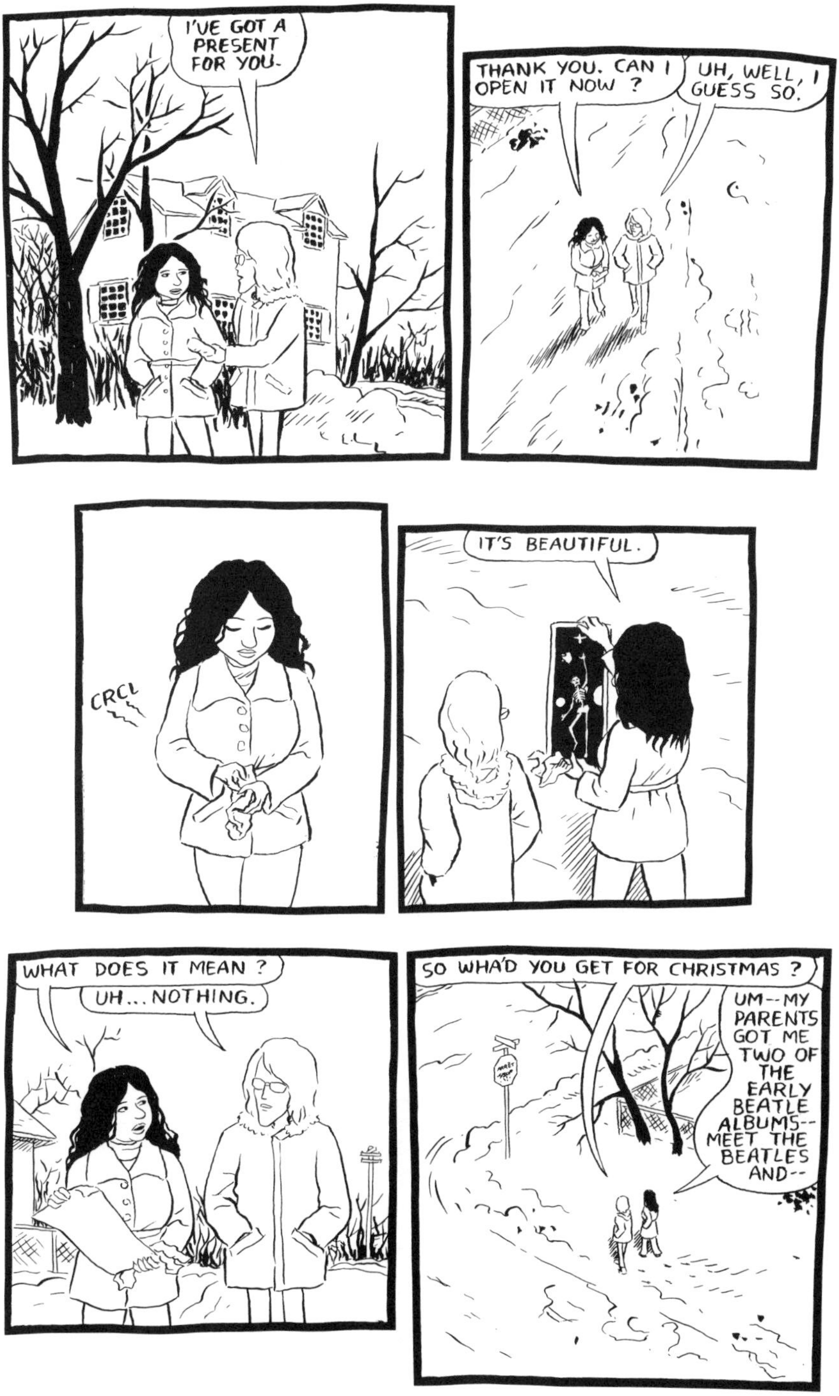
I'VE GOT A PRESENT FOR YOU.
THANK YOU. CAN I OPEN IT NOW ?
UH, WELL, I GUESS SO.
CRCL
IT'S BEAUTIFUL.
WHAT DOES IT MEAN ?
UH... NOTHING.
SO WHA'D YOU GET FOR CHRISTMAS ?
UM--MY PARENTS GOT ME TWO OF THE EARLY BEATLE ALBUMS--MEET THE BEATLES AND--

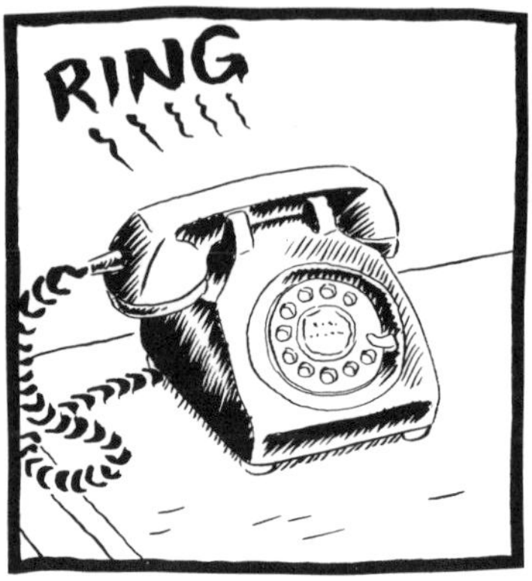
RING

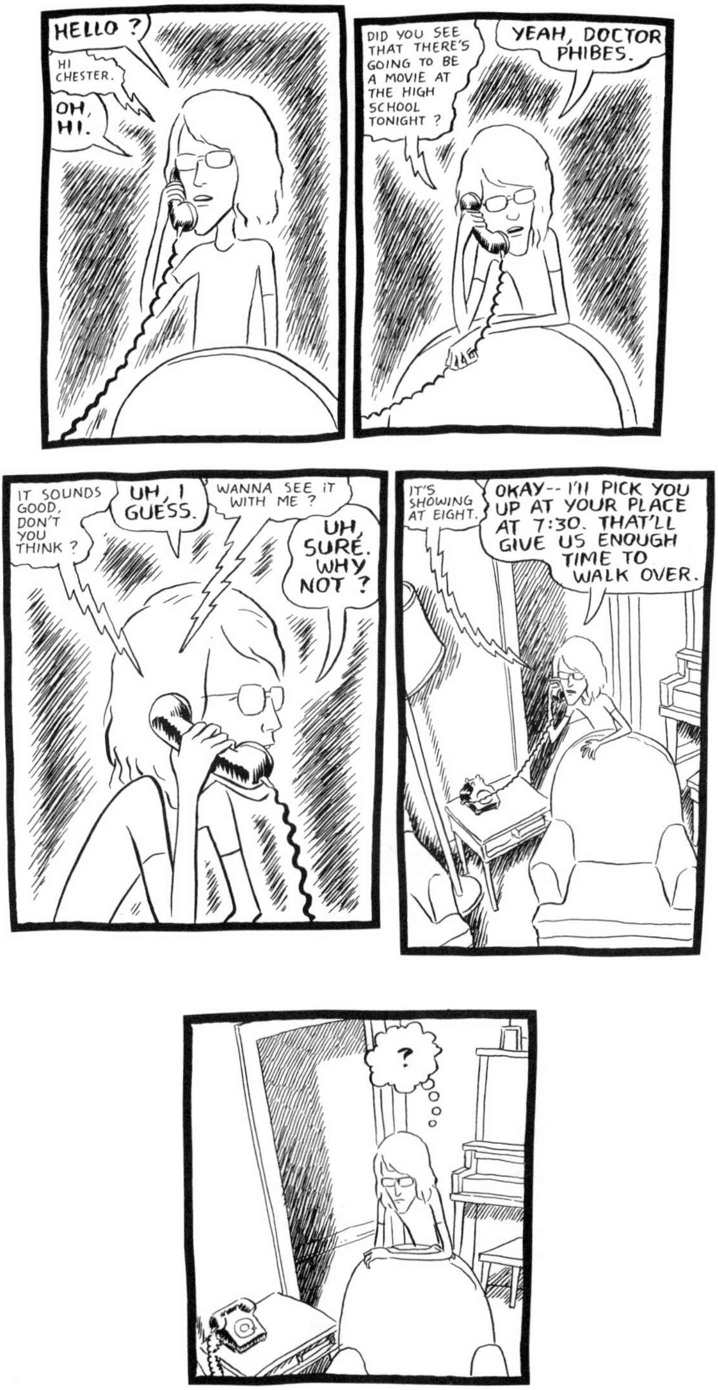
HELLO ?
HI CHESTER.
OH, HI.
DID YOU SEE THAT THERE'S GOING TO BE A MOVIE AT THE HIGH SCHOOL TONIGHT ?
YEAH, DOCTOR PHIBES.
IT SOUNDS GOOD, DON'T YOU THINK ?
UH, I GUESS.
WANNA SEE IT WITH ME ?
UH, SURE. WHY NOT ?
IT'S SHOWING AT EIGHT.
OKAY-- I'LL PICK YOU UP AT YOUR PLACE AT 7:30. THAT'LL GIVE US ENOUGH TIME TO WALK OVER.
?

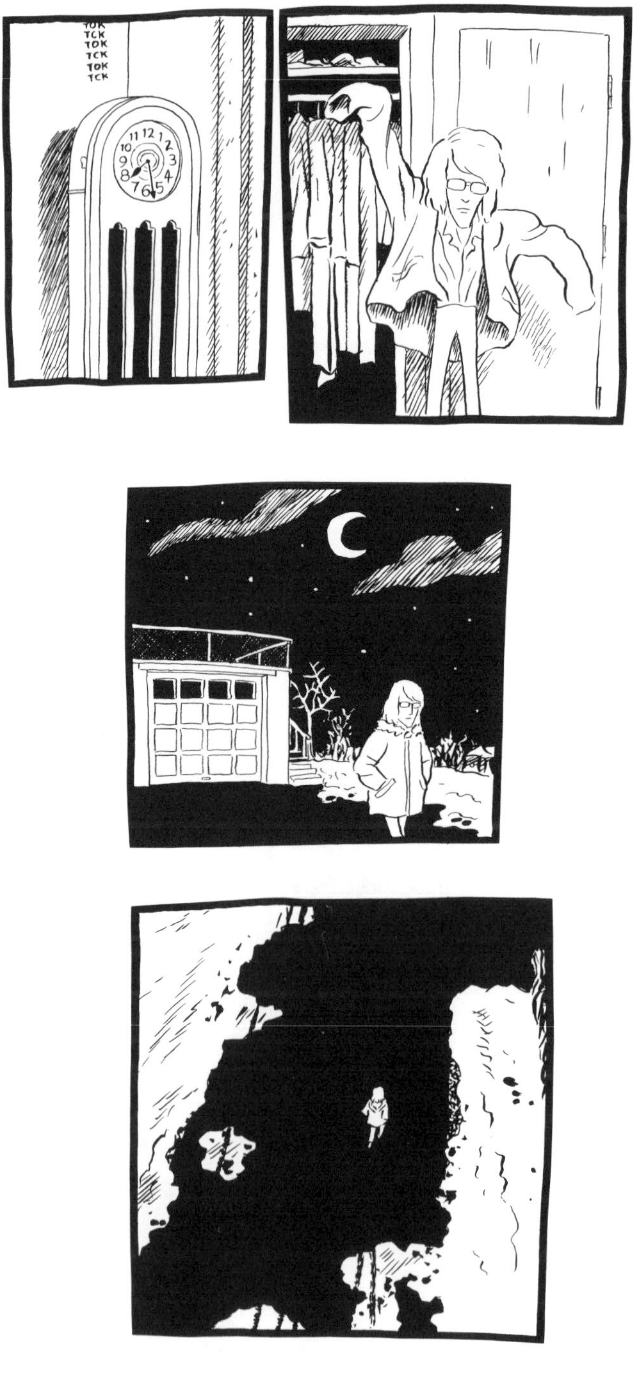
TOK
TCK
TOK
TCK
TOK
TCK

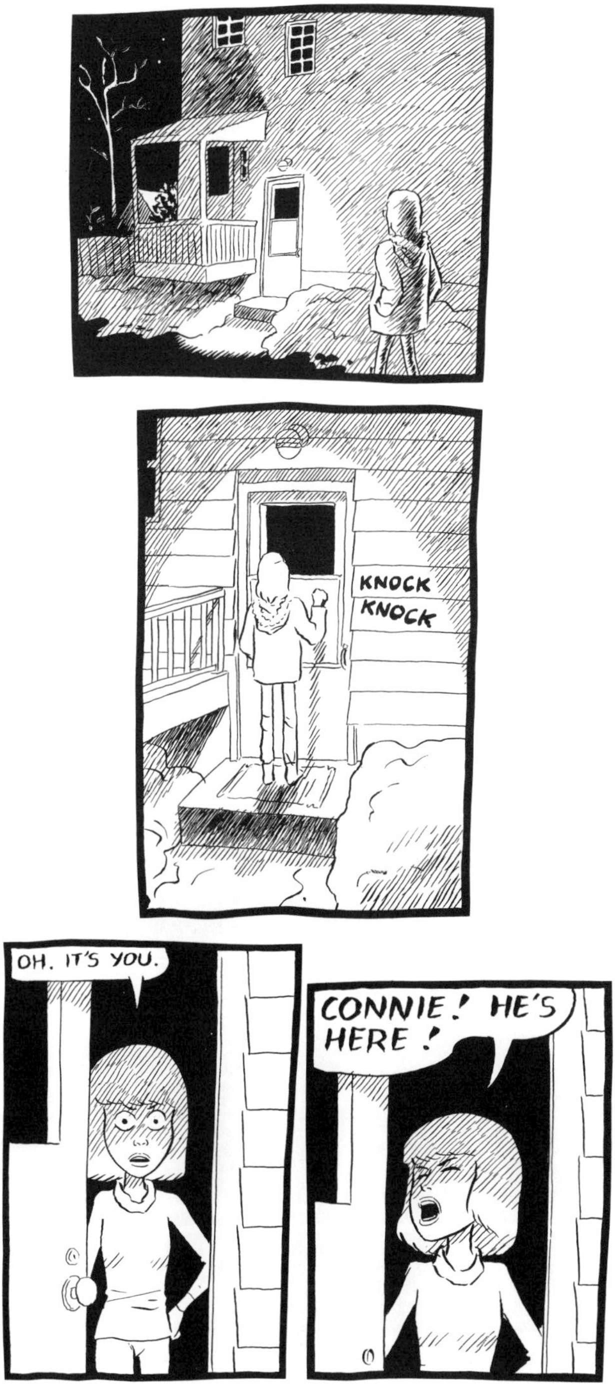
KNOCK
KNOCK
OH. IT'S YOU.
CONNIE! HE'S HERE!

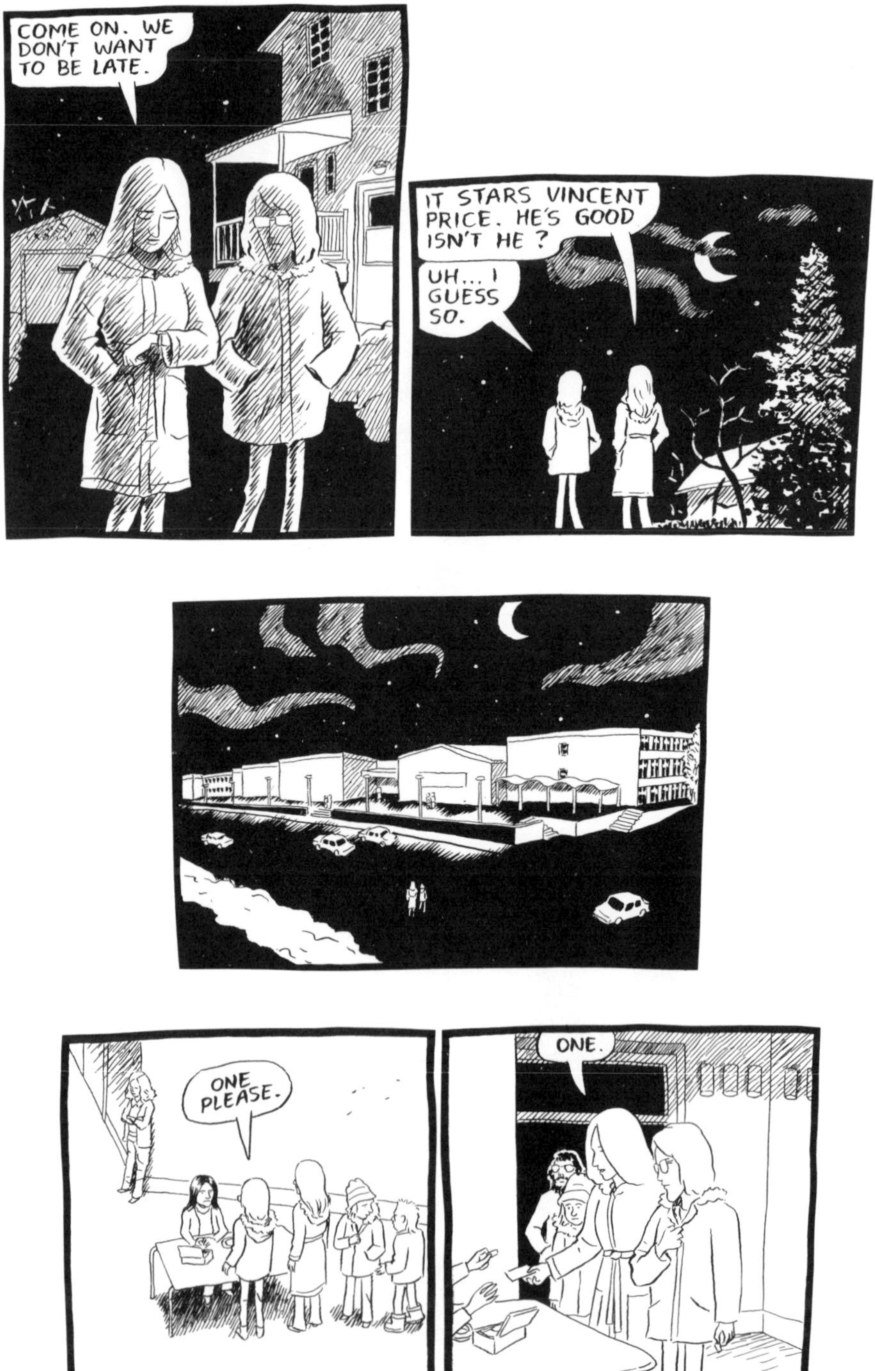
COME ON. WE DON'T WANT TO BE LATE.
IT STARS VINCENT PRICE. HE'S GOOD ISN'T HE ?
UH... I GUESS SO.
ONE PLEASE.
ONE.

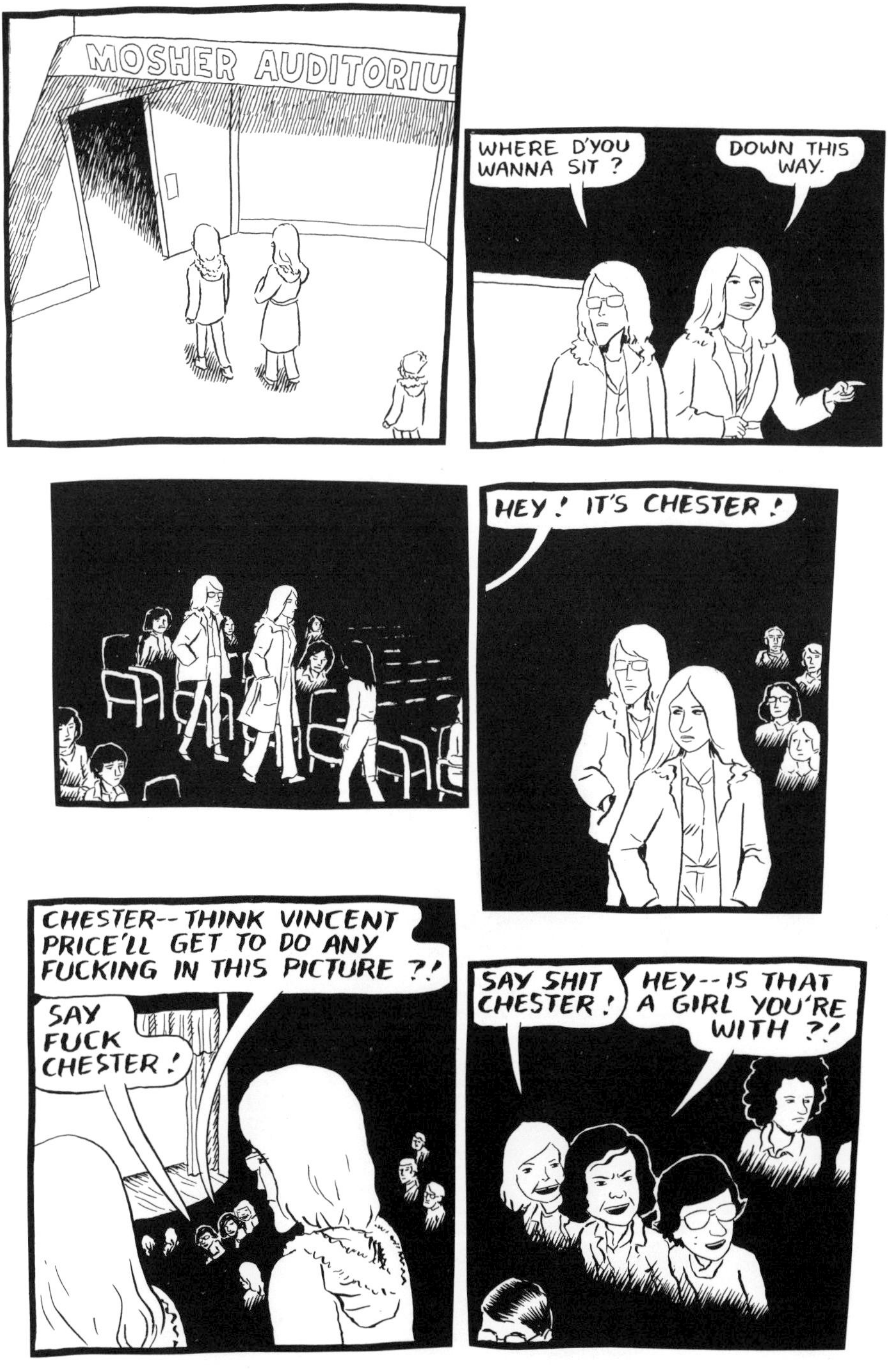
MOSHER AUDITORIU
WHERE D'YOU WANNA SIT ?
DOWN THIS WAY.
HEY ! IT'S CHESTER !
CHESTER--THINK VINCENT PRICE'LL GET TO DO ANY FUCKING IN THIS PICTURE ?!
SAY FUCK CHESTER !
SAY SHIT CHESTER !
HEY--IS THAT A GIRL YOU'RE WITH ?!

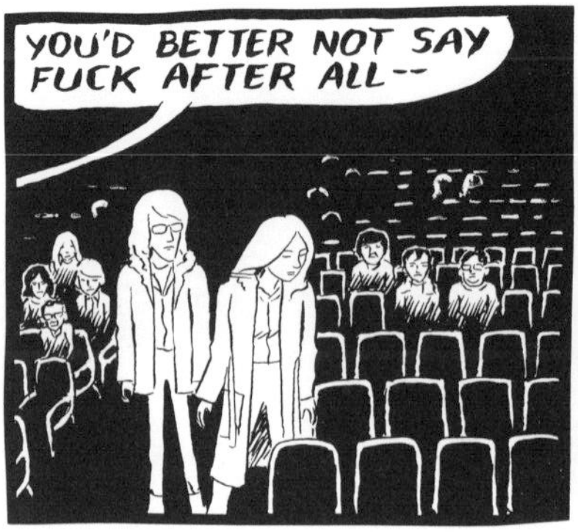
YOU'D BETTER NOT SAY FUCK AFTER ALL--

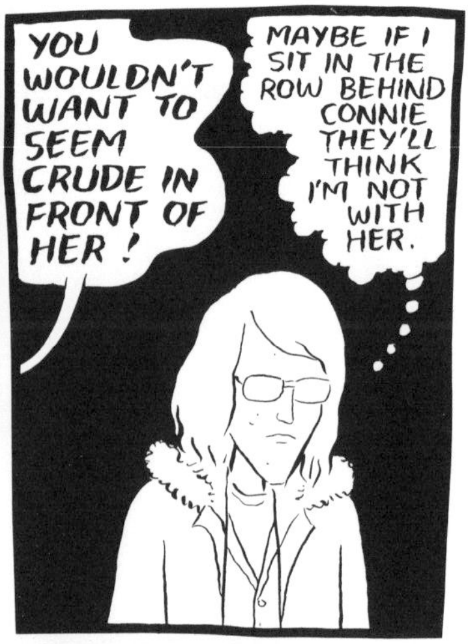
YOU WOULDN'T WANT TO SEEM CRUDE IN FRONT OF HER!
MAYBE IF I SIT IN THE ROW BEHIND CONNIE THEY'LL THINK I'M NOT WITH HER.

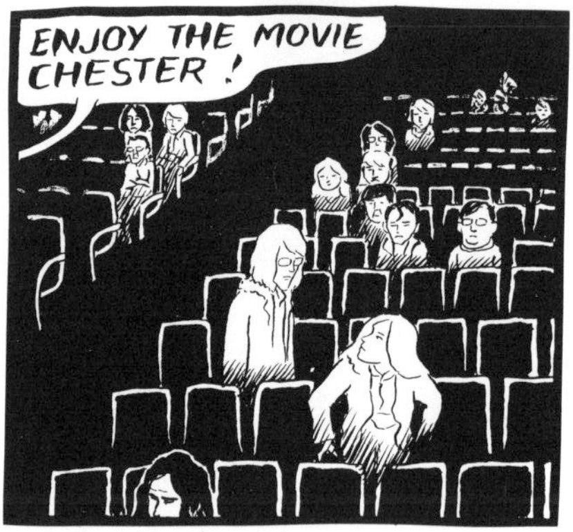
ENJOY THE MOVIE CHESTER!

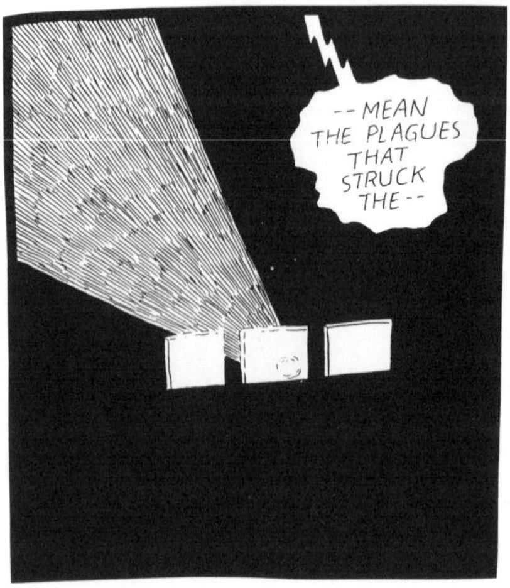
--MEAN THE PLAGUES THAT STRUCK THE--

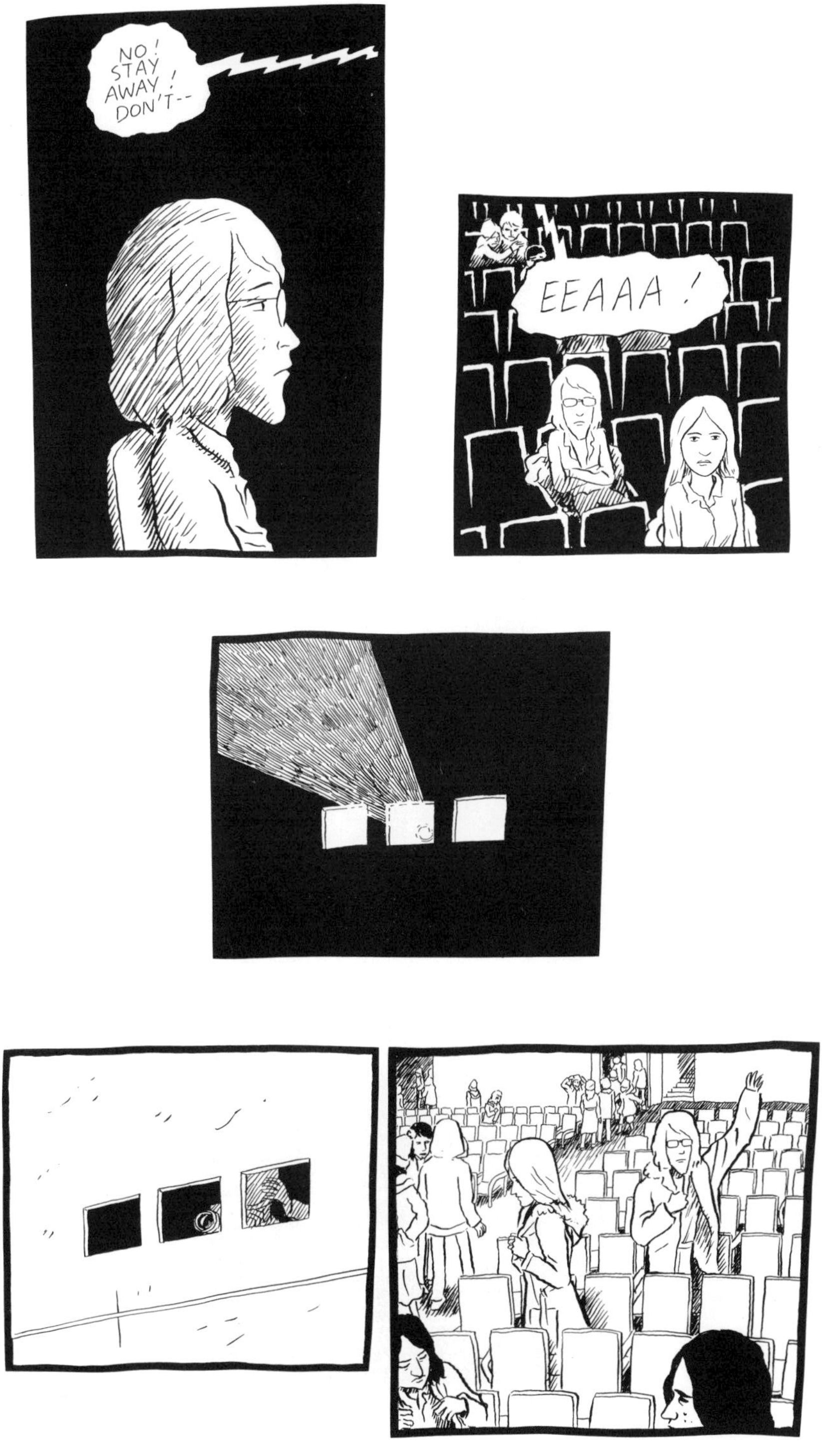
NO! STAY AWAY! DON'T--
EEAAA!

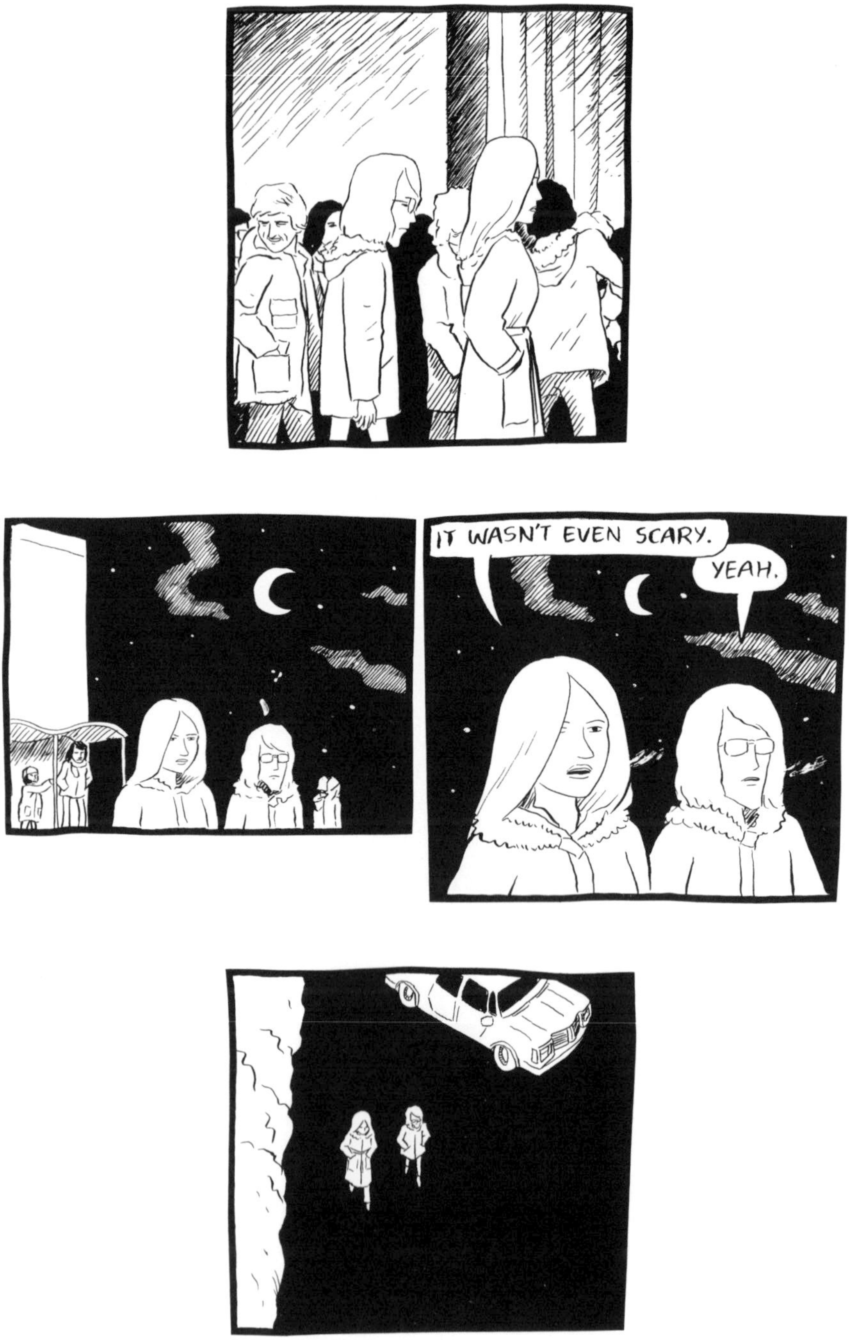
IT WASN'T EVEN SCARY.
YEAH.

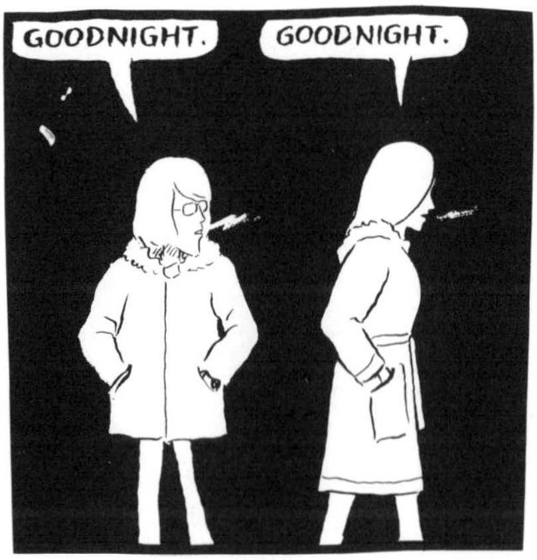
GOODNIGHT.
GOODNIGHT.

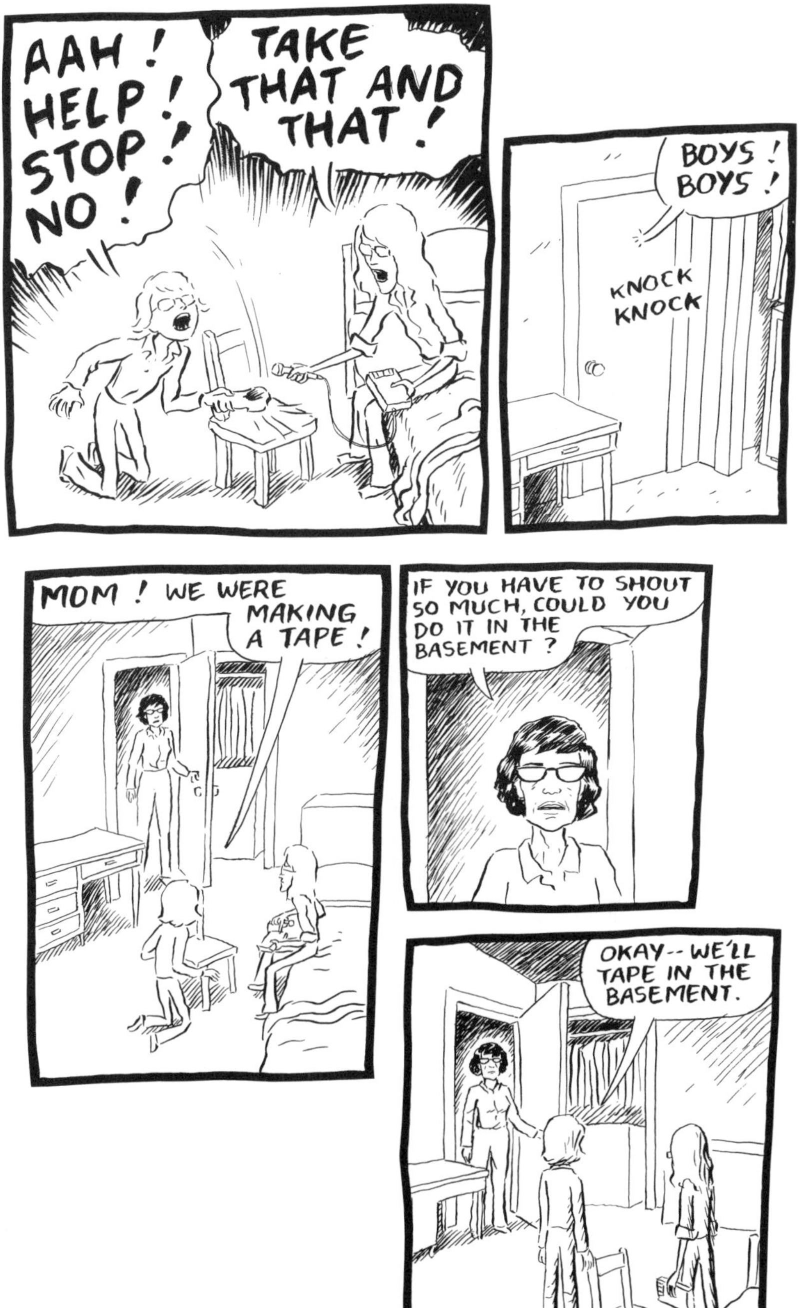
AAH! HELP! STOP! NO!
TAKE THAT AND THAT!
BOYS! BOYS!
KNOCK KNOCK
MOM! WE WERE MAKING A TAPE!
IF YOU HAVE TO SHOUT SO MUCH, COULD YOU DO IT IN THE BASEMENT?
OKAY-- WE'LL TAPE IN THE BASEMENT.

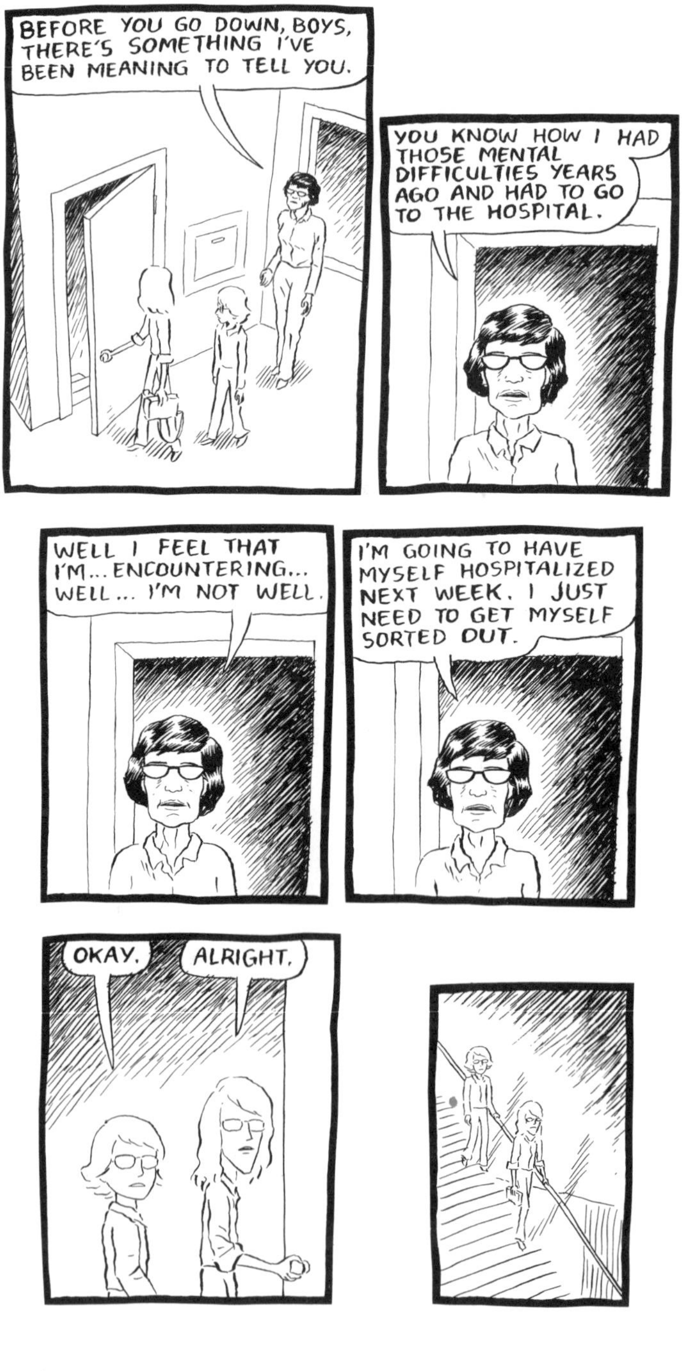
BEFORE YOU GO DOWN, BOYS, THERE'S SOMETHING I'VE BEEN MEANING TO TELL YOU.
YOU KNOW HOW I HAD THOSE MENTAL DIFFICULTIES YEARS AGO AND HAD TO GO TO THE HOSPITAL.
WELL I FEEL THAT I'M... ENCOUNTERING... WELL... I'M NOT WELL.
I'M GOING TO HAVE MYSELF HOSPITALIZED NEXT WEEK. I JUST NEED TO GET MYSELF SORTED OUT.
OKAY.
ALRIGHT.

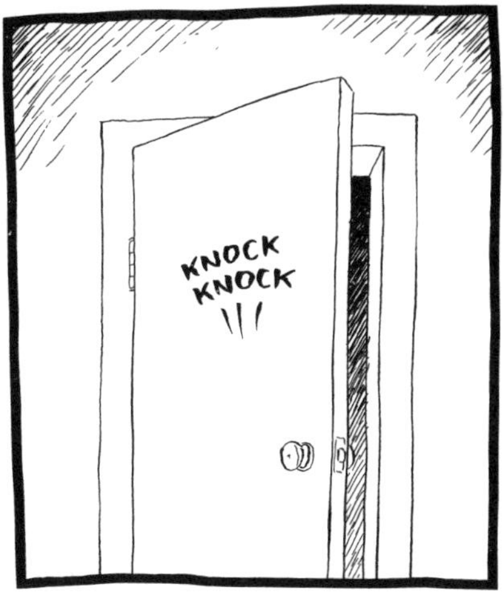
KNOCK
KNOCK

CHESTER--
--I DON'T KNOW IF I'LL BE BACK IN TIME FOR YOUR BIRTHDAY, SO... HERE'S YOUR PRESENT.
THANKS.

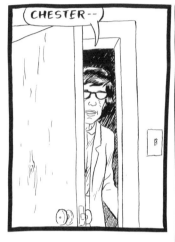

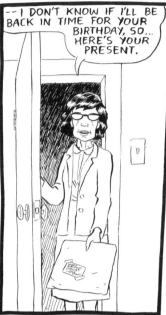

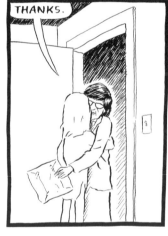

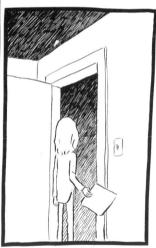

KRKL

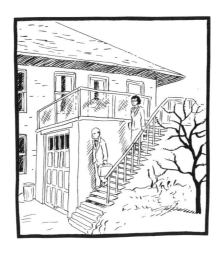

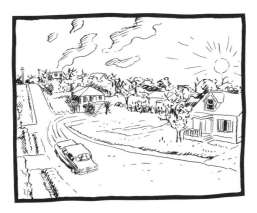

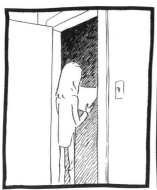

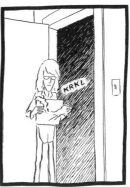

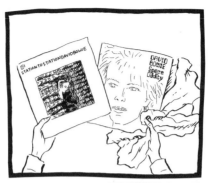

STATIONTOSTATIONDAVIDBOWIE
DAVID BOWIE Space Oddity
COULDN'T WAIT THE WEEK TILL YOUR BIRTHDAY ?
I KNEW WHAT THEY WERE GONNA BE. IT'S WHAT I ASKED FOR.

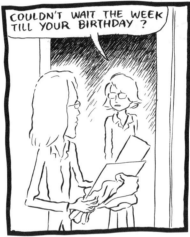

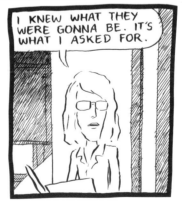

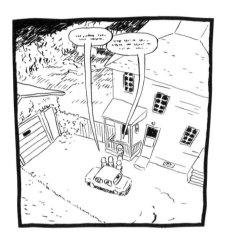

SKY SHOWED ME THAT PICTURE YOU DID FOR HER.

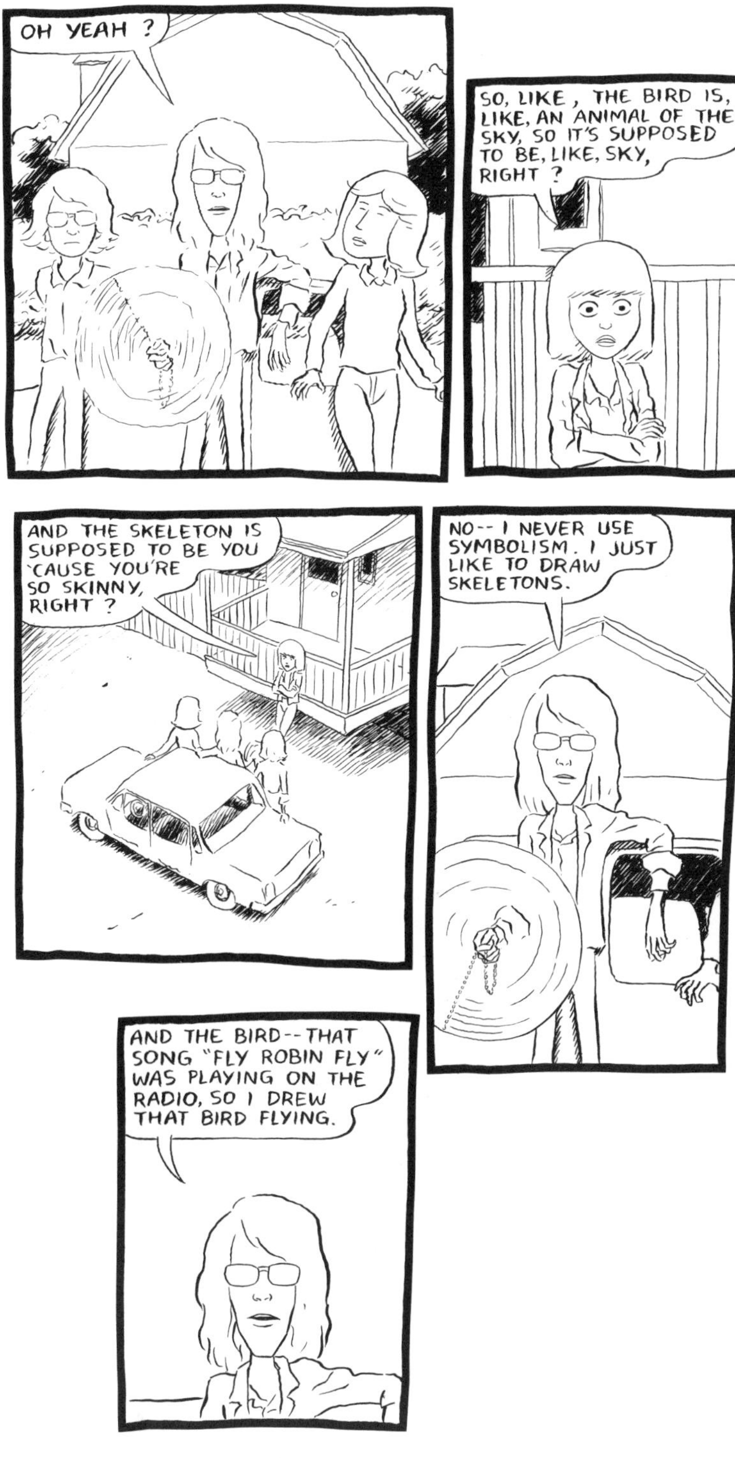
OH YEAH ?
SO, LIKE, THE BIRD IS, LIKE, AN ANIMAL OF THE SKY, SO IT'S SUPPOSED TO BE, LIKE, SKY, RIGHT ?
AND THE SKELETON IS SUPPOSED TO BE YOU 'CAUSE YOU'RE SO SKINNY, RIGHT ?
NO-- I NEVER USE SYMBOLISM. I JUST LIKE TO DRAW SKELETONS.
AND THE BIRD--THAT SONG "FLY ROBIN FLY" WAS PLAYING ON THE RADIO, SO I DREW THAT BIRD FLYING.

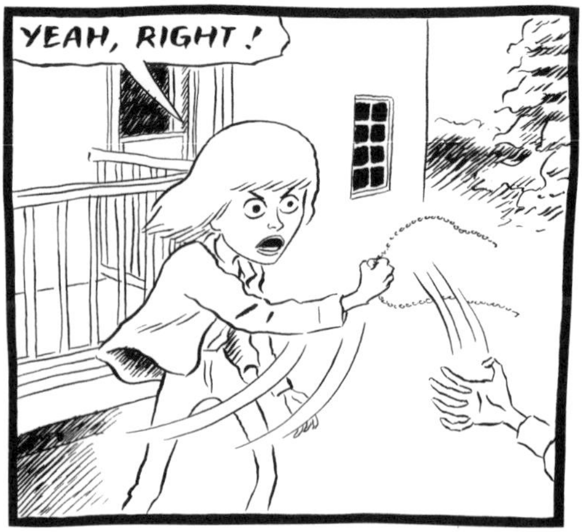
YEAH, RIGHT!

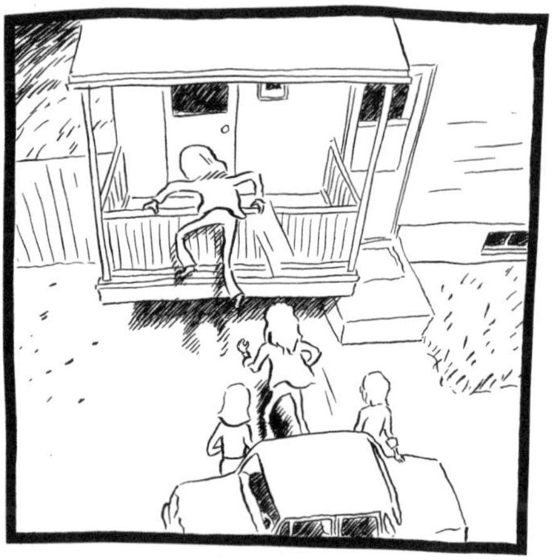

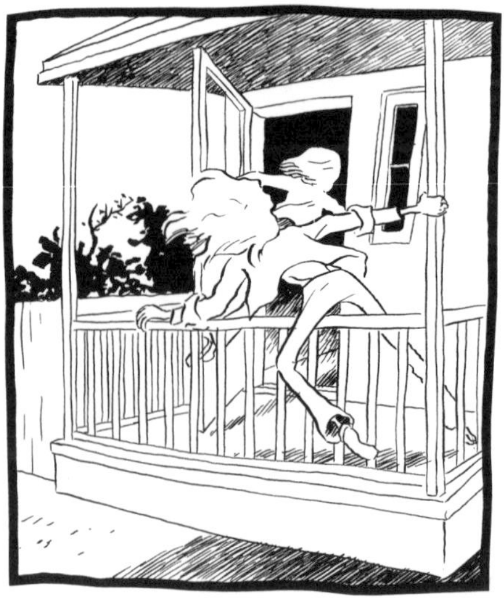

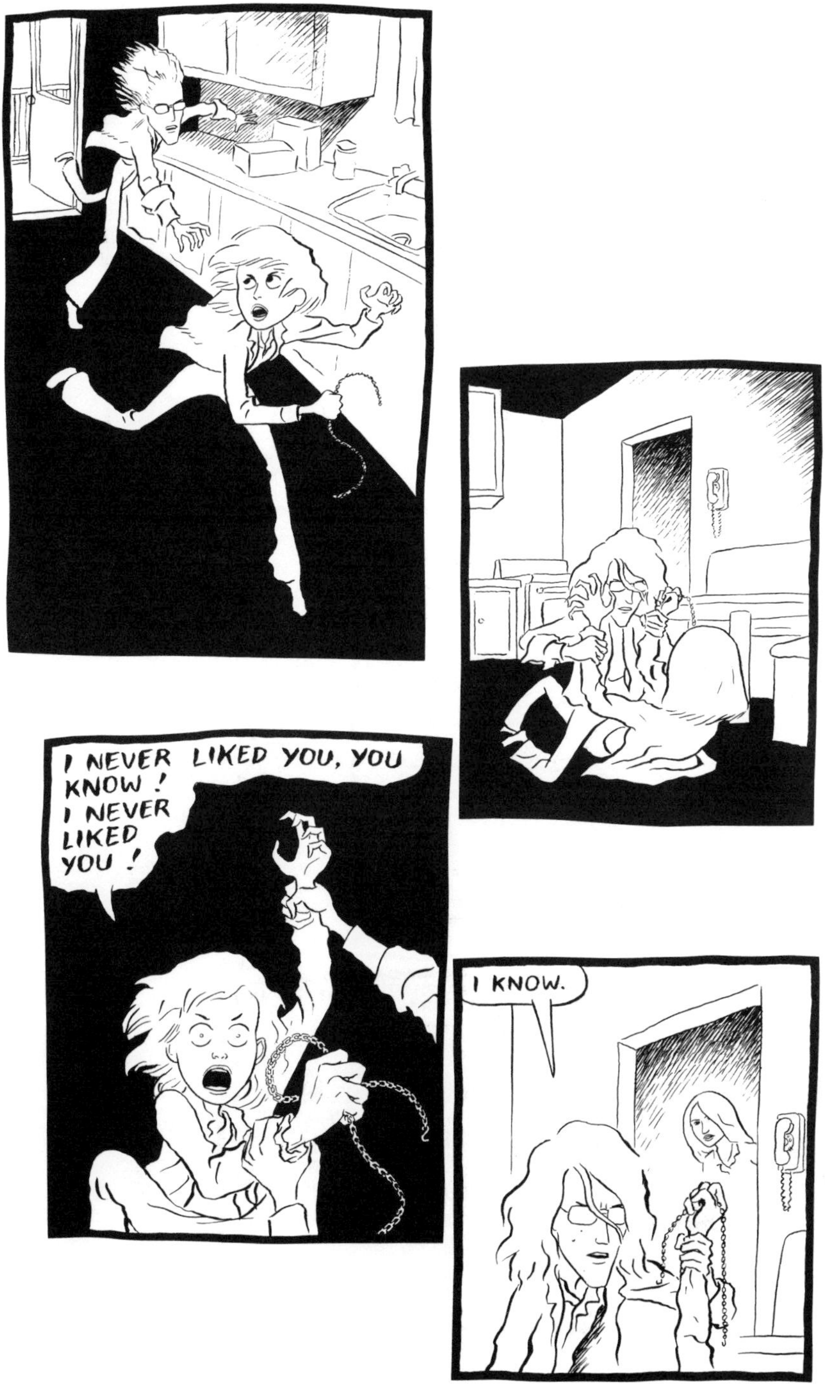
I NEVER LIKED YOU, YOU KNOW! I NEVER LIKED YOU!
I KNOW.

WHAT ARE YOU DOING ?!
I'M GETTING MY CHAIN FROM HER.
WHO INVITED YOU IN HERE ?
NOBODY.
GET OUT !

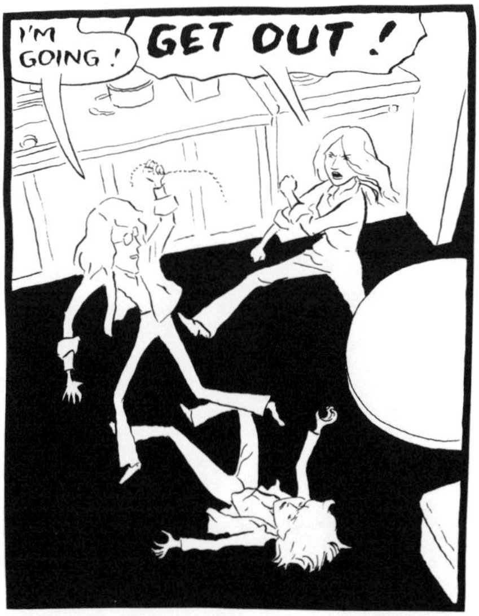
I'M GOING!
GET OUT!

AND, UH... SHE WAS APPARENTLY IN A CONFUSED... STATE.

SHE WANDERED AROUND THE HOSPITAL CORRIDORS AND FELL DOWN A FLIGHT OF STAIRS.

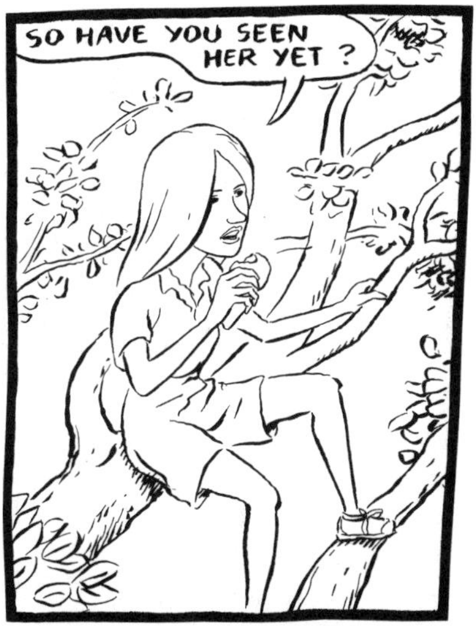
SO HAVE YOU SEEN HER YET ?

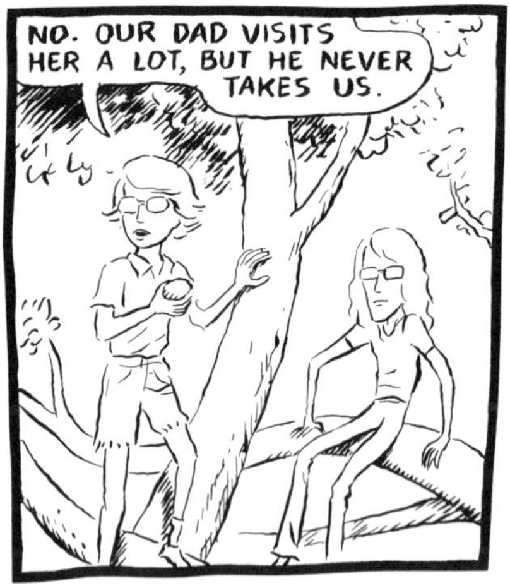
NO. OUR DAD VISITS HER A LOT, BUT HE NEVER TAKES US.

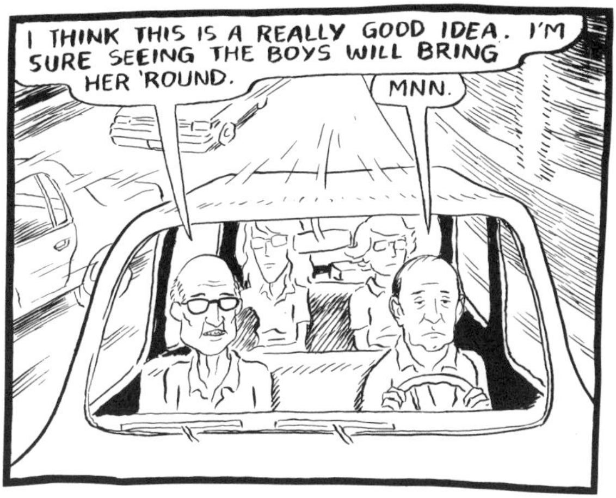
I THINK THIS IS A REALLY GOOD IDEA. I'M SURE SEEING THE BOYS WILL BRING HER 'ROUND.
MNN.

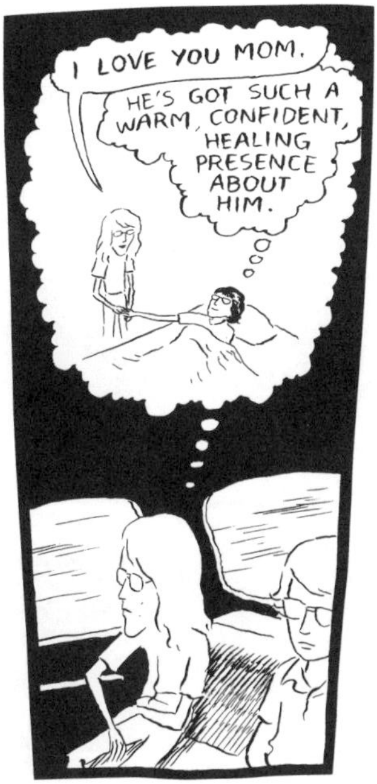
I LOVE YOU MOM.
HE'S GOT SUCH A WARM, CONFIDENT, HEALING PRESENCE ABOUT HIM.

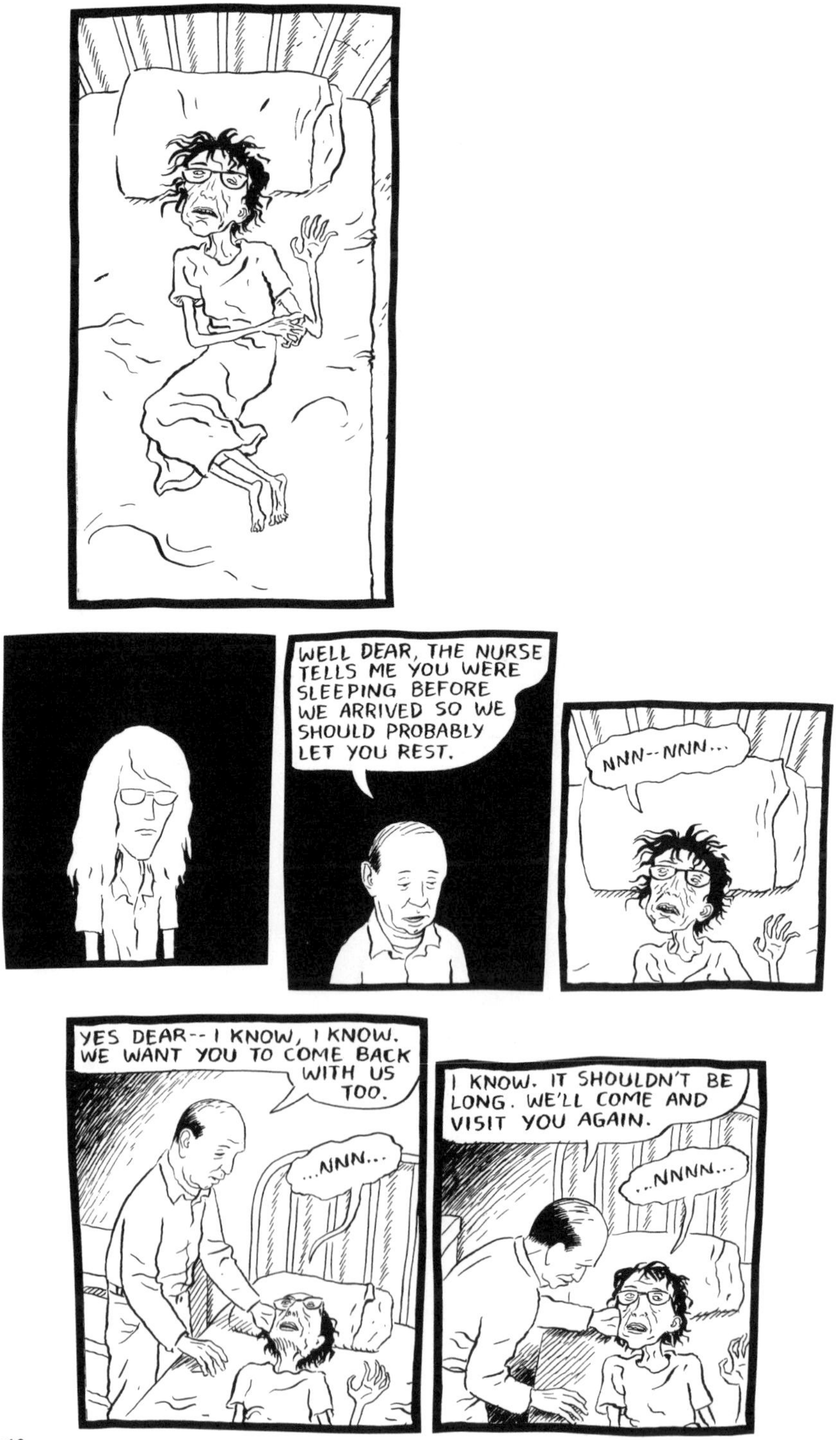
WELL DEAR, THE NURSE TELLS ME YOU WERE SLEEPING BEFORE WE ARRIVED SO WE SHOULD PROBABLY LET YOU REST.
NNN--NNN...
YES DEAR-- I KNOW, I KNOW. WE WANT YOU TO COME BACK WITH US TOO.
...NNN...
I KNOW. IT SHOULDN'T BE LONG. WE'LL COME AND VISIT YOU AGAIN.
...NNNN...

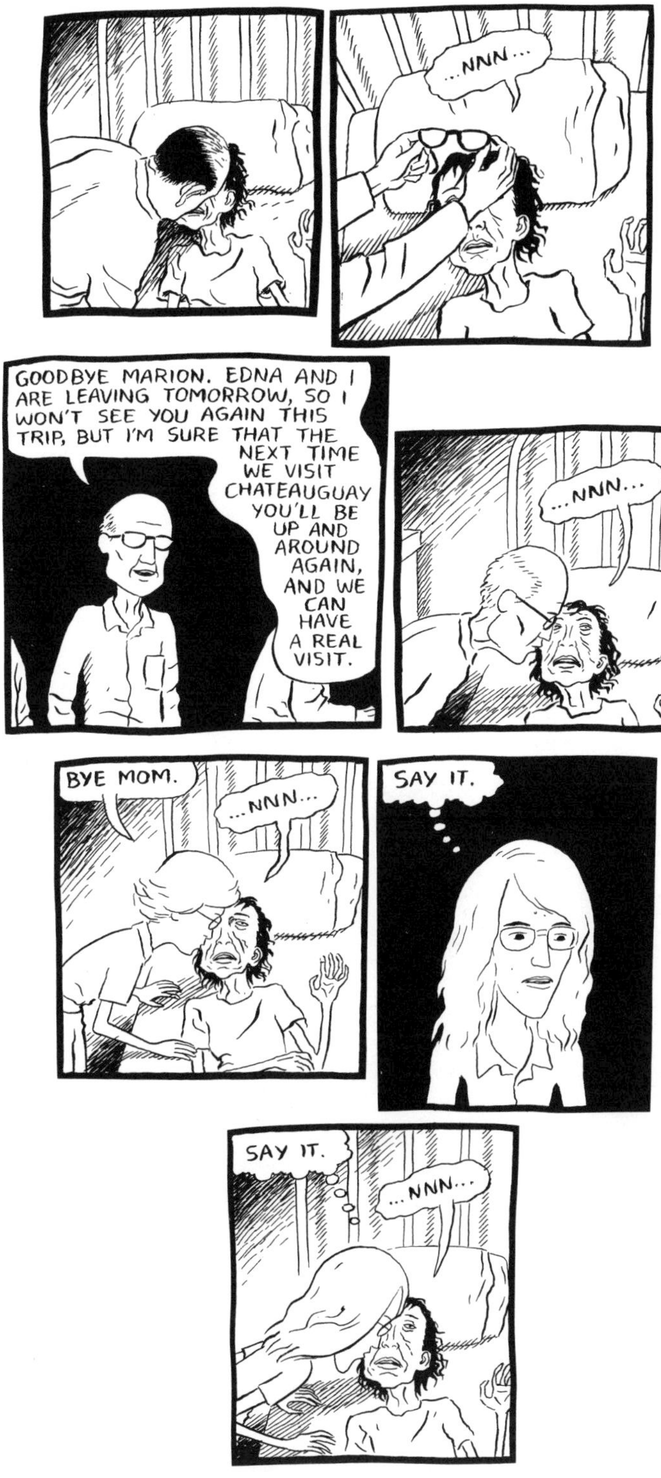
...NNN...
GOODBYE MARION. EDNA AND I ARE LEAVING TOMORROW, SO I WON'T SEE YOU AGAIN THIS TRIP, BUT I'M SURE THAT THE NEXT TIME WE VISIT CHATEAUGUAY YOU'LL BE UP AND AROUND AGAIN, AND WE CAN HAVE A REAL VISIT.
...NNN...
BYE MOM.
...NNN...
SAY IT.
SAY IT.
...NNN...

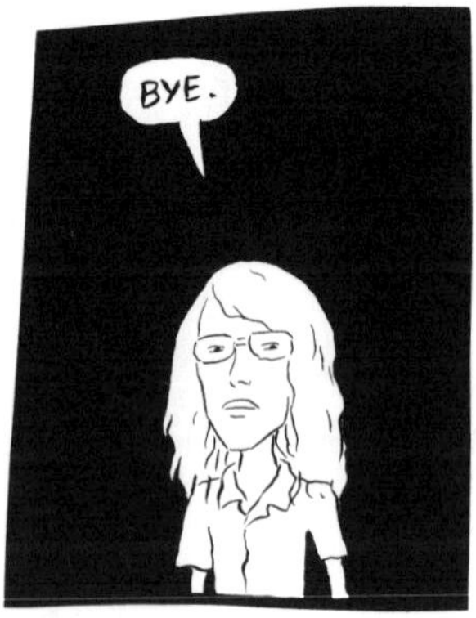
BYE.

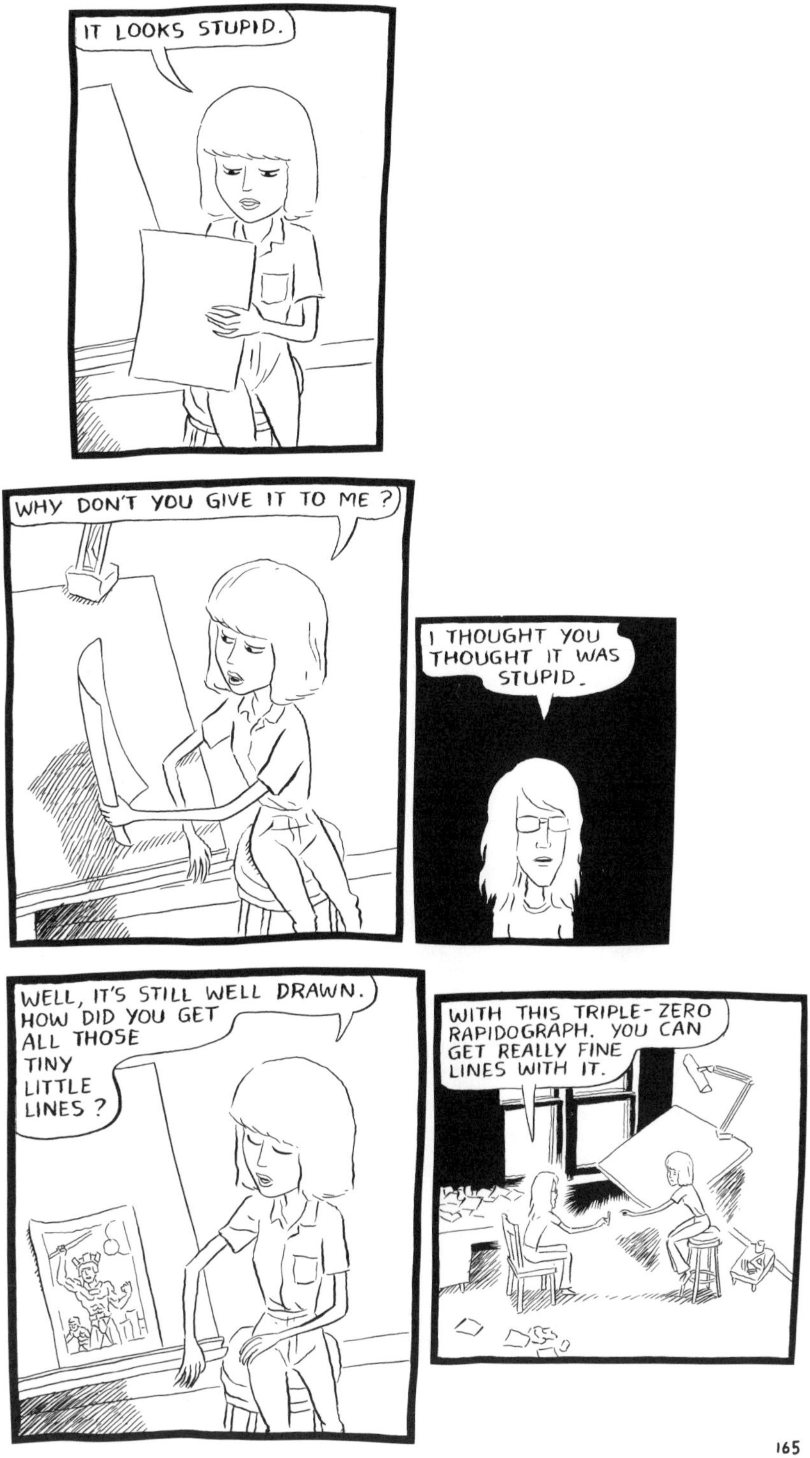
IT LOOKS STUPID.
WHY DON'T YOU GIVE IT TO ME?
I THOUGHT YOU THOUGHT IT WAS STUPID.
WELL, IT'S STILL WELL DRAWN. HOW DID YOU GET ALL THOSE TINY LITTLE LINES?
WITH THIS TRIPLE-ZERO RAPIDOGRAPH. YOU CAN GET REALLY FINE LINES WITH IT.

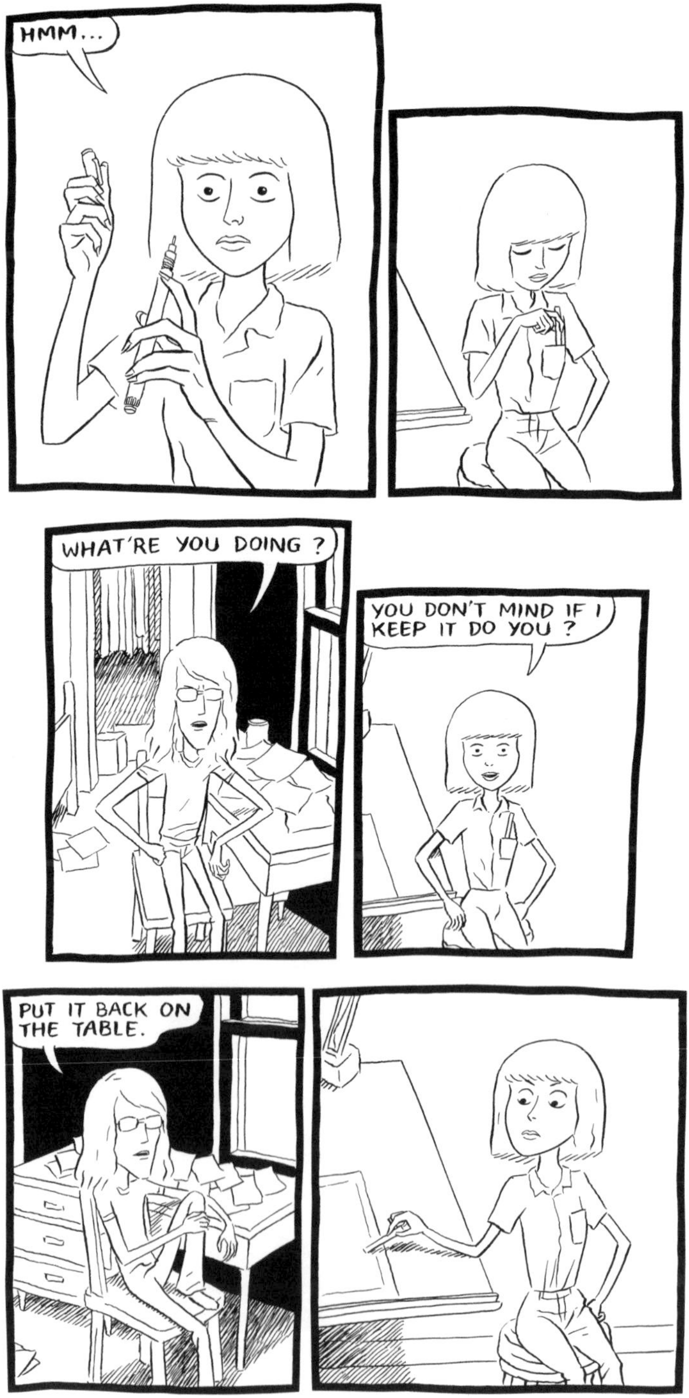
HMM...
WHAT'RE YOU DOING ?
YOU DON'T MIND IF I KEEP IT DO YOU ?
PUT IT BACK ON THE TABLE.

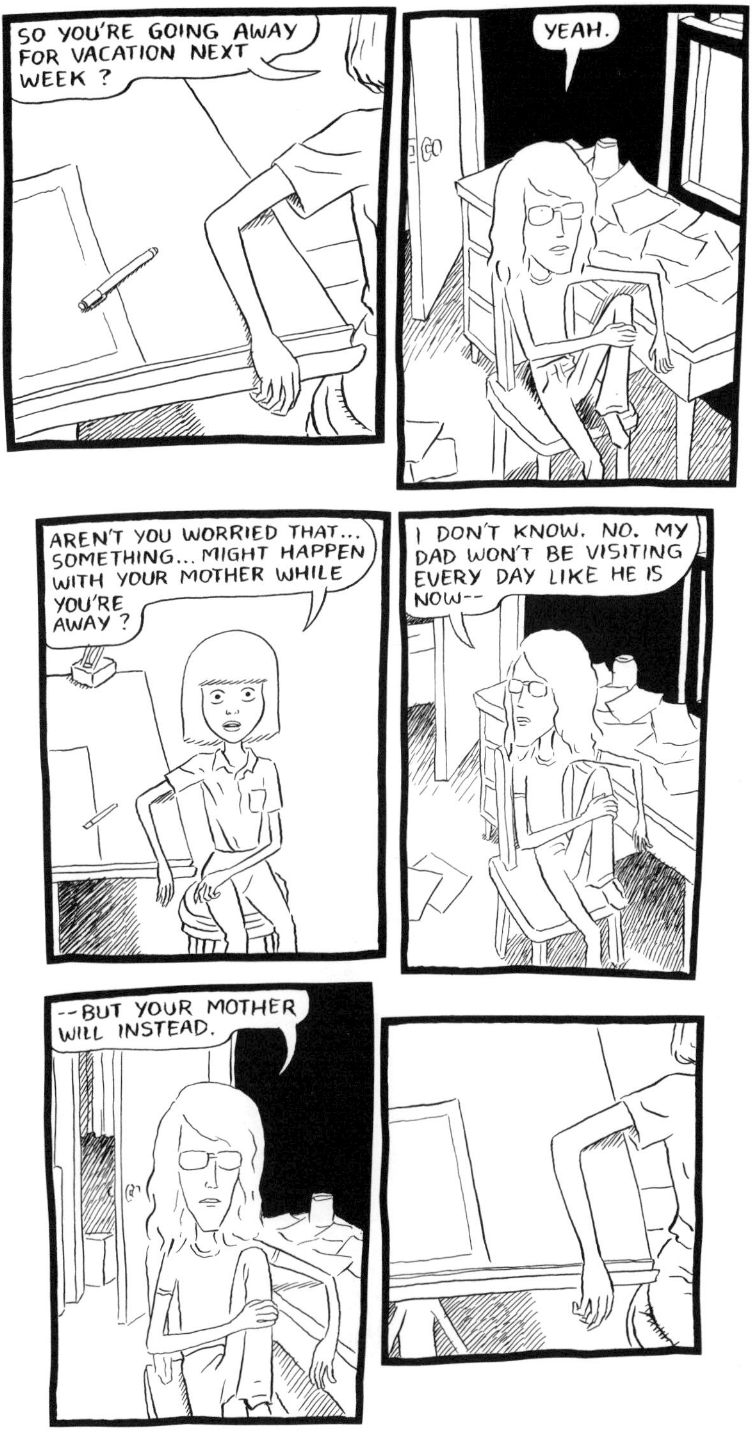
SO YOU'RE GOING AWAY FOR VACATION NEXT WEEK ?
YEAH.
AREN'T YOU WORRIED THAT... SOMETHING... MIGHT HAPPEN WITH YOUR MOTHER WHILE YOU'RE AWAY ?
I DON'T KNOW. NO. MY DAD WON'T BE VISITING EVERY DAY LIKE HE IS NOW--
--BUT YOUR MOTHER WILL INSTEAD.

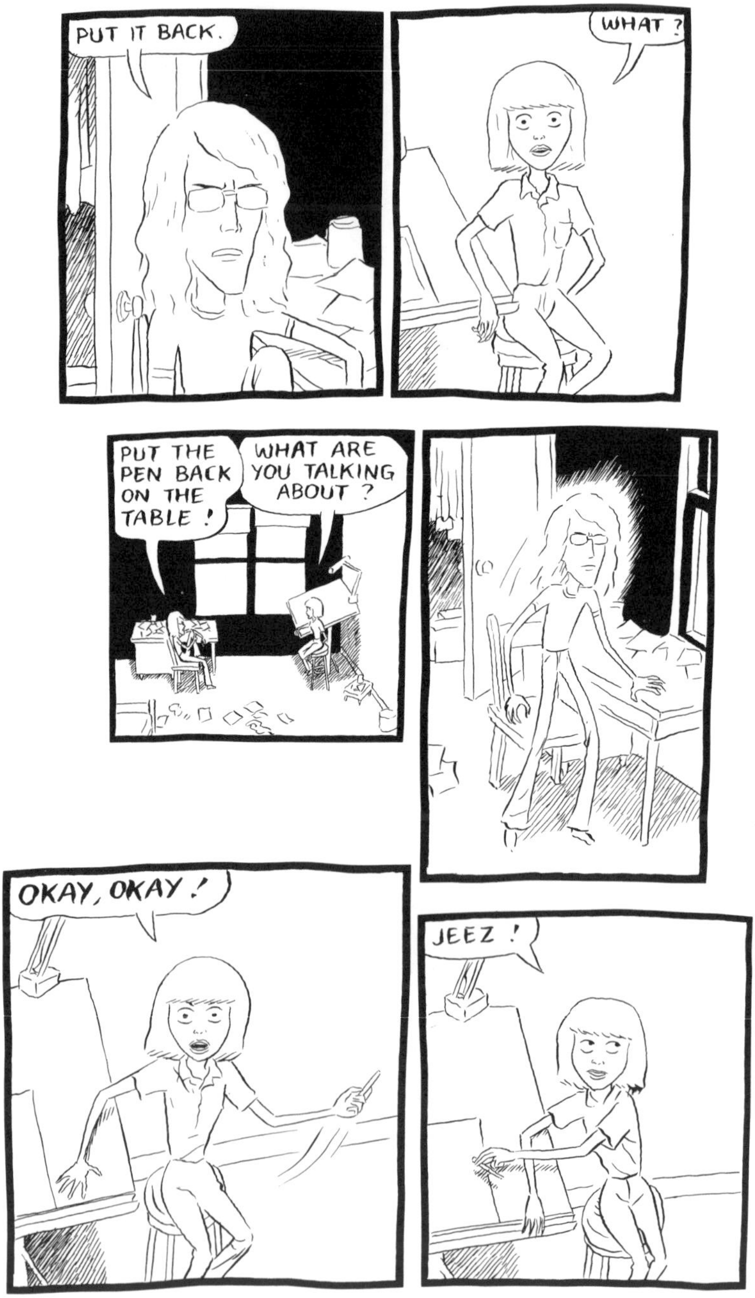
PUT IT BACK.
WHAT ?
PUT THE PEN BACK ON THE TABLE !
WHAT ARE YOU TALKING ABOUT ?
OKAY, OKAY !
JEEZ !

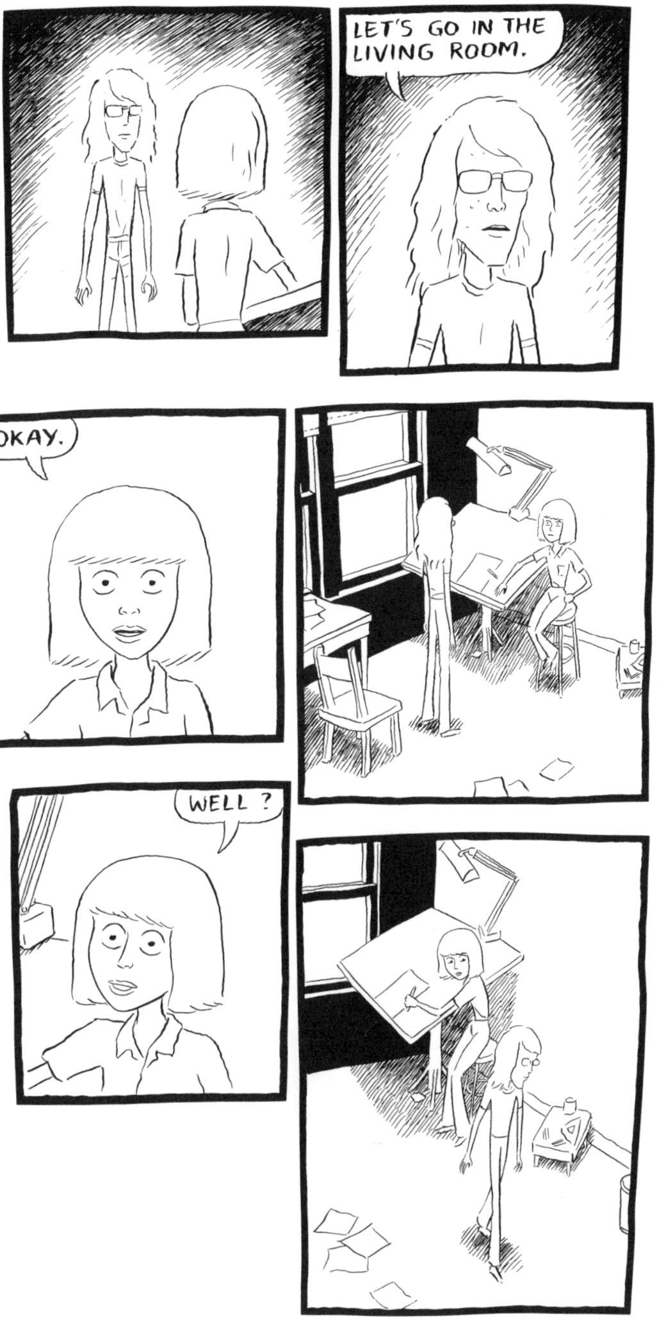
LET'S GO IN THE LIVING ROOM.
OKAY.
WELL ?

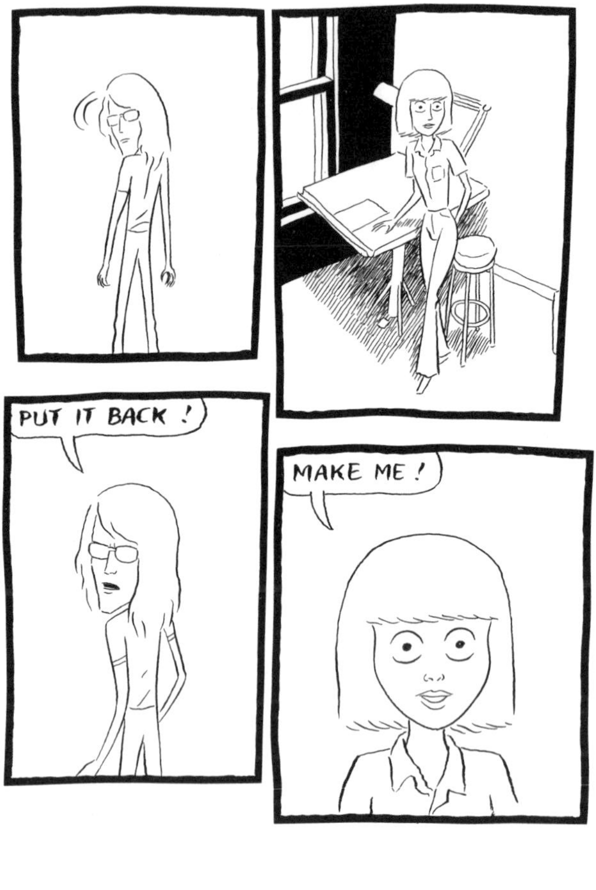
PUT IT BACK !
MAKE ME !

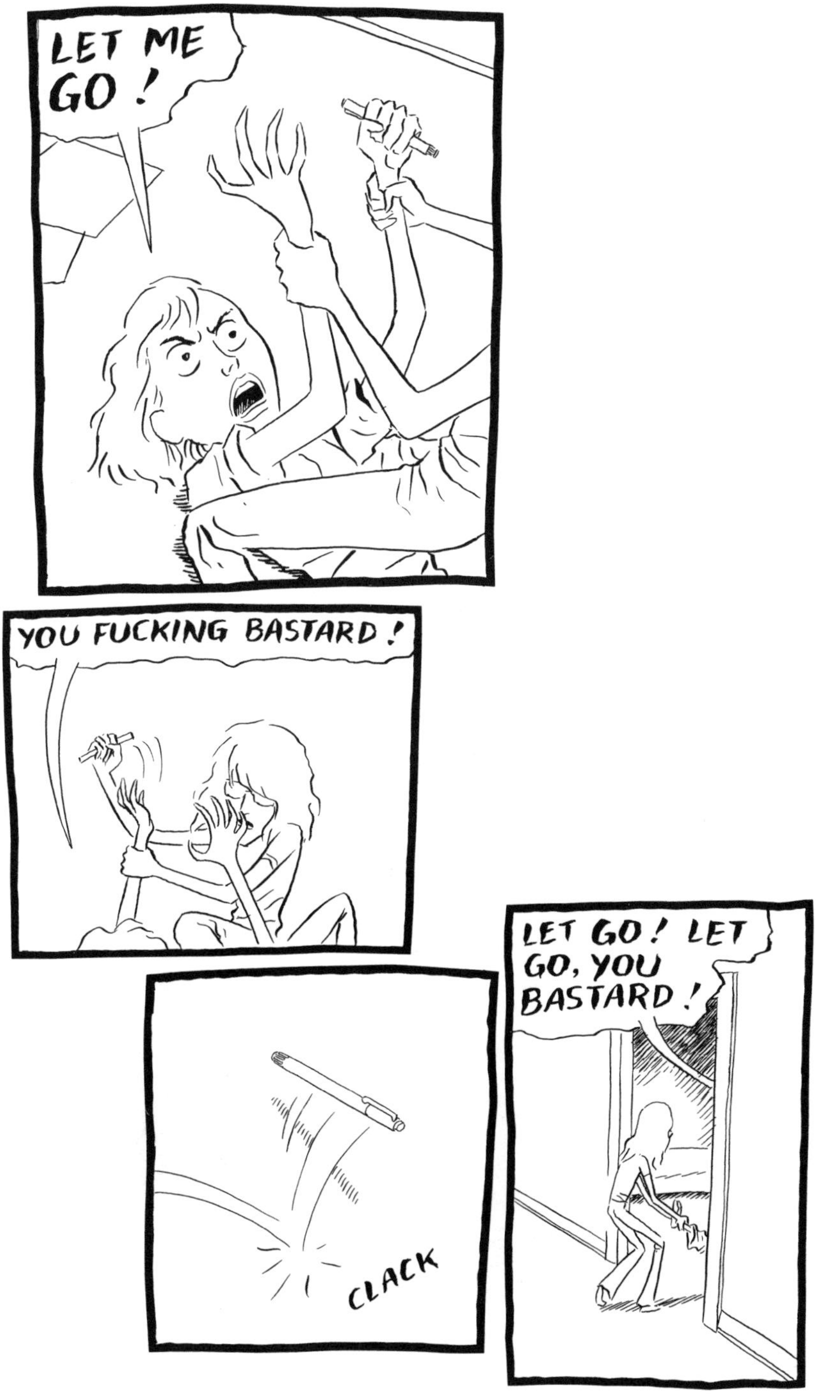
LET ME GO!
YOU FUCKING BASTARD!
CLACK
LET GO! LET GO, YOU BASTARD!

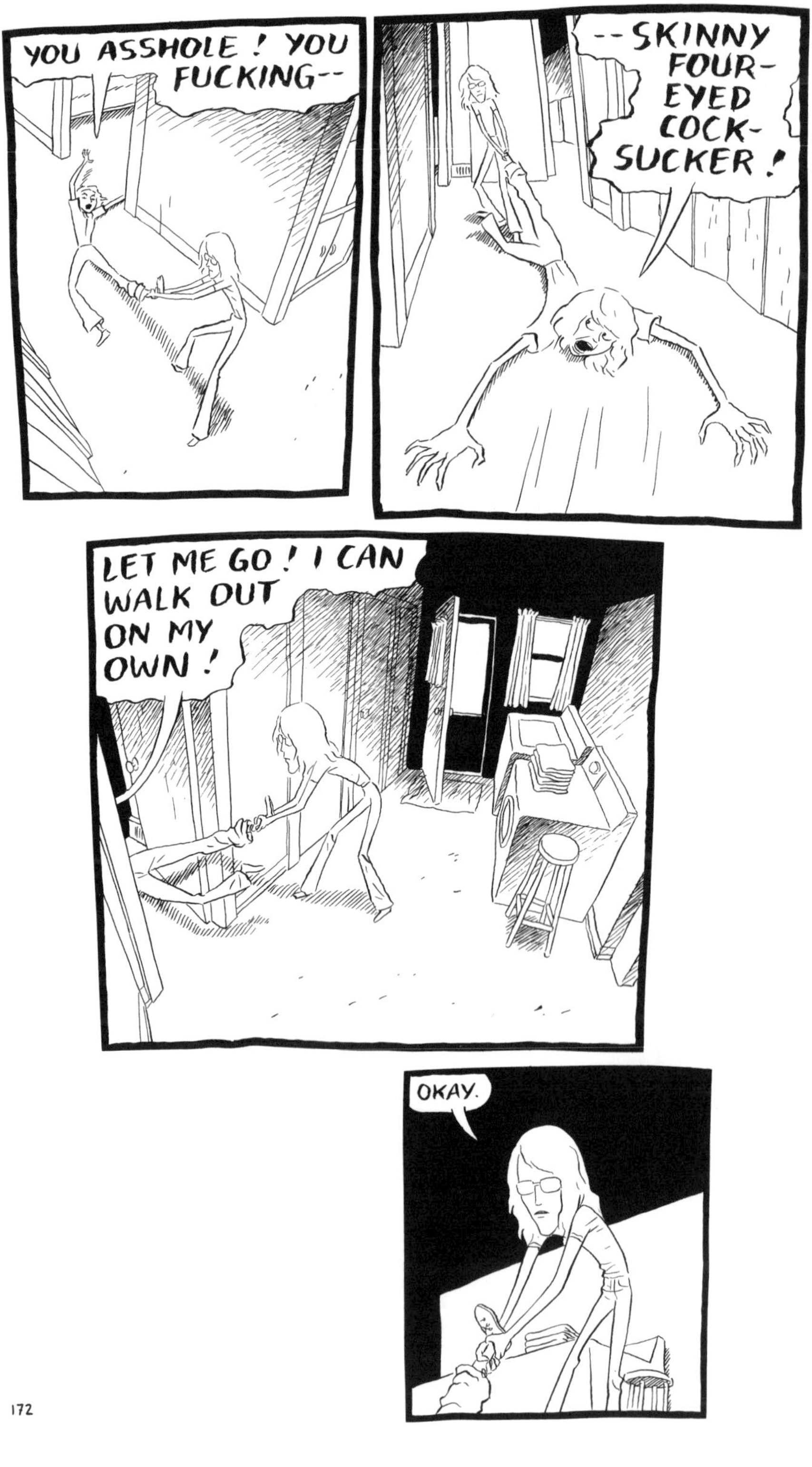
YOU ASSHOLE! YOU FUCKING--
--SKINNY FOUR-EYED COCK-SUCKER!
LET ME GO! I CAN WALK OUT ON MY OWN!
OKAY.

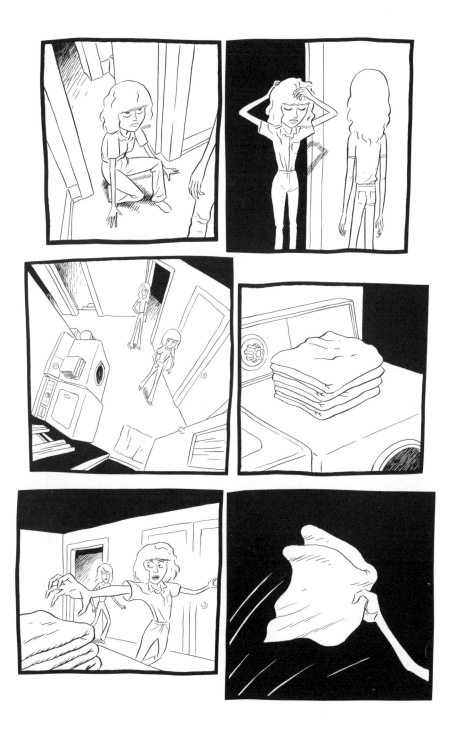

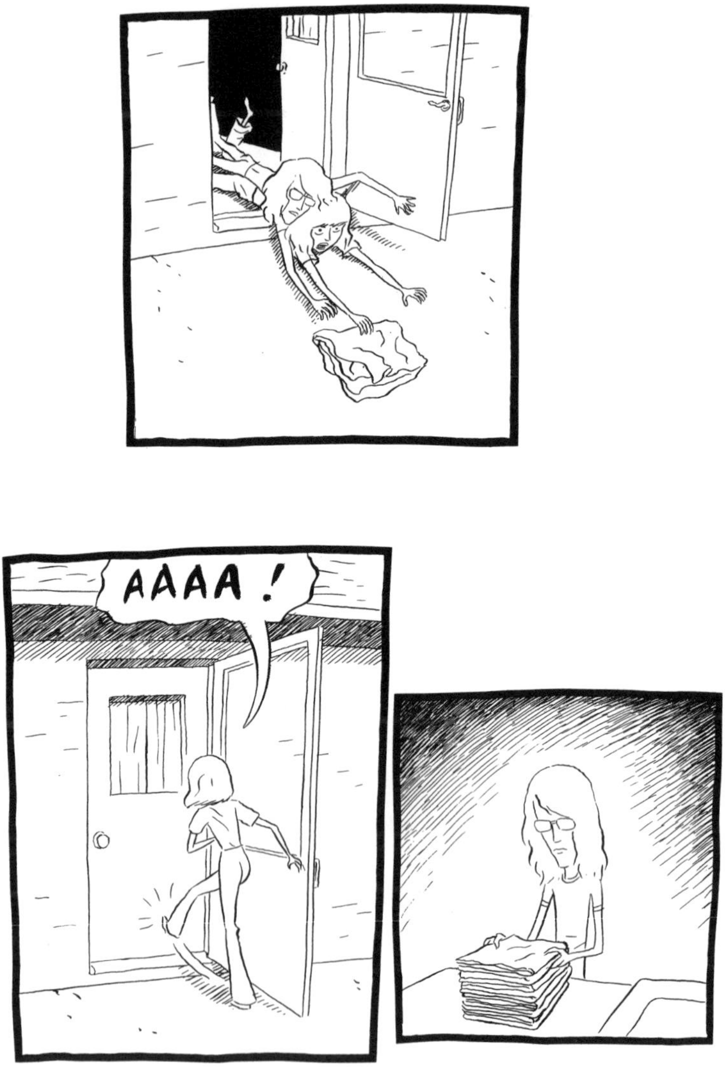
AAAA !

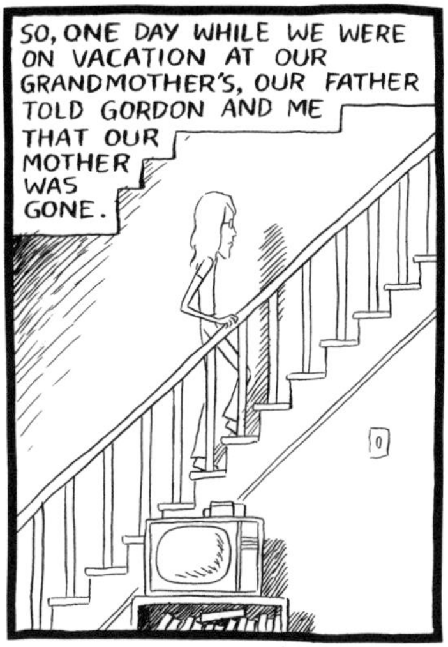
SO, ONE DAY WHILE WE WERE ON VACATION AT OUR GRANDMOTHER'S, OUR FATHER TOLD GORDON AND ME THAT OUR MOTHER WAS GONE.

"GONE?" I ASKED AS IF I HADN'T UNDERSTOOD.

I WENT UP TO THE ROOM MY BROTHER AND I WERE SHARING TO BE ALONE.

I TRIED TO CRY.

ONE TEAR CAME.

THAT WAS ALL.

MY FATHER CAUGHT A FLIGHT TO MONTREAL THAT DAY AND ARRANGED THE FUNERAL. NEITHER GORDON NOR I ATTENDED IT. WE WEREN'T ASKED IF WE WANTED TO.

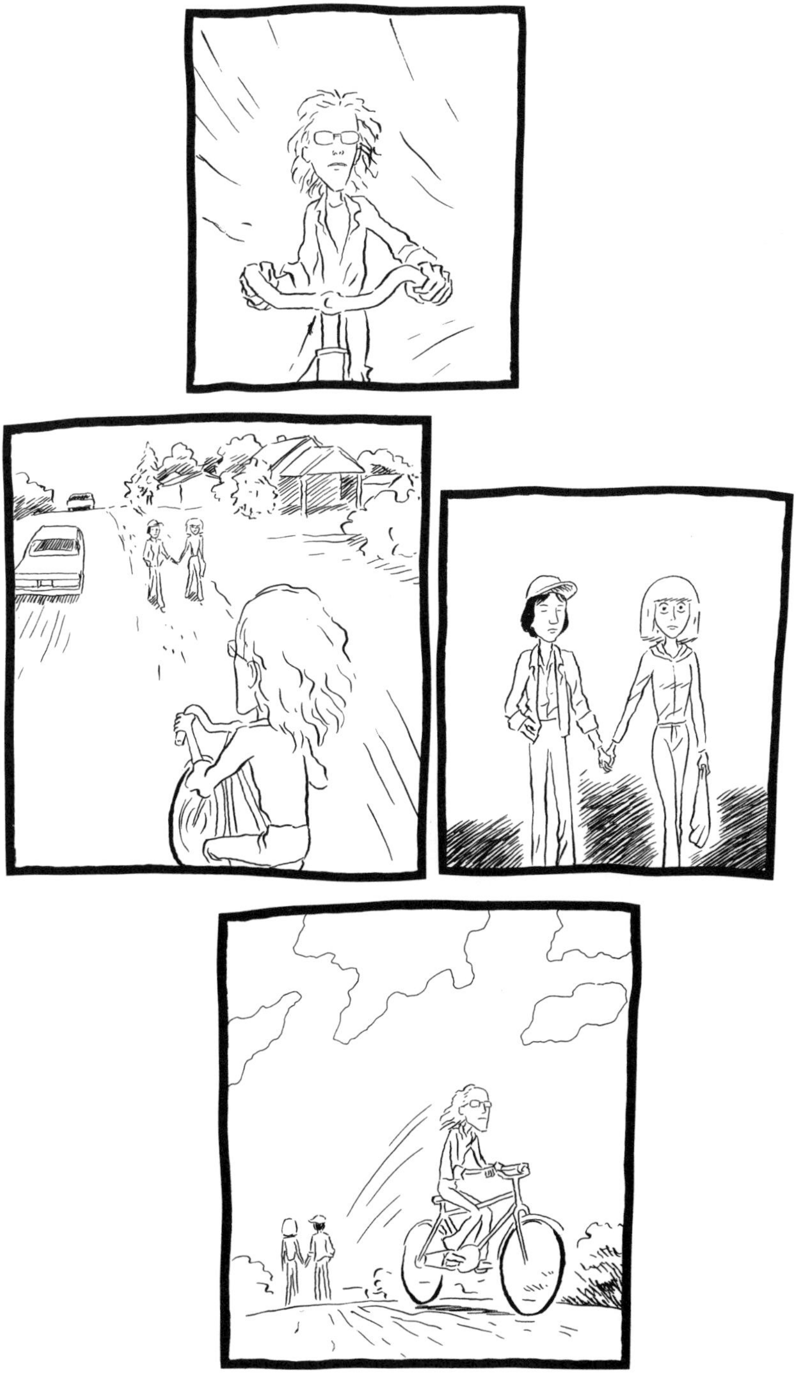

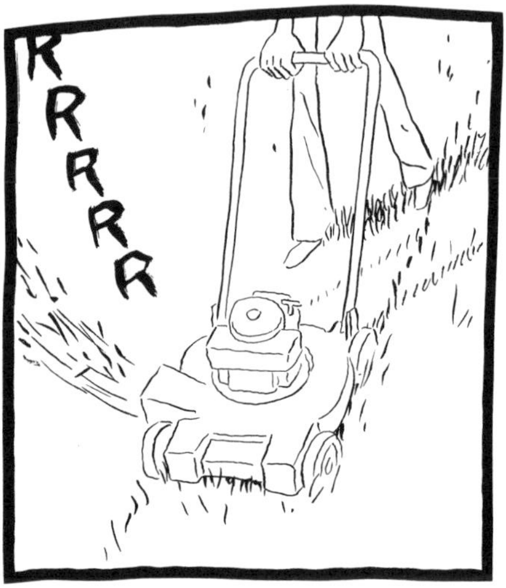
RRRRR

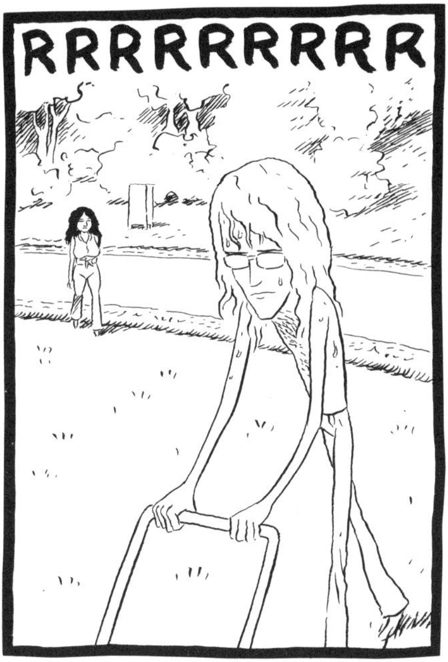
RRRRRRRRRR

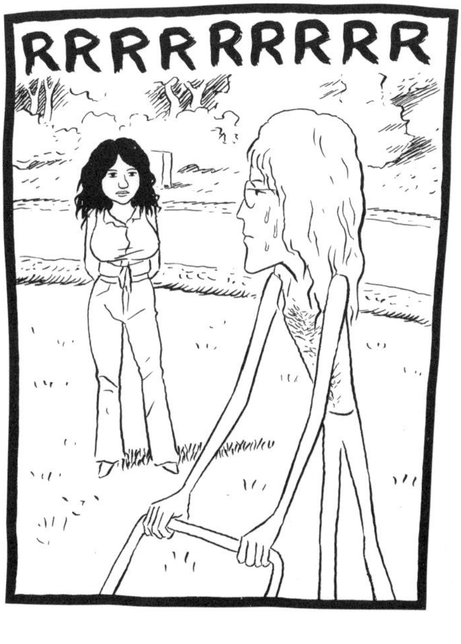
RRRRRRRRRR

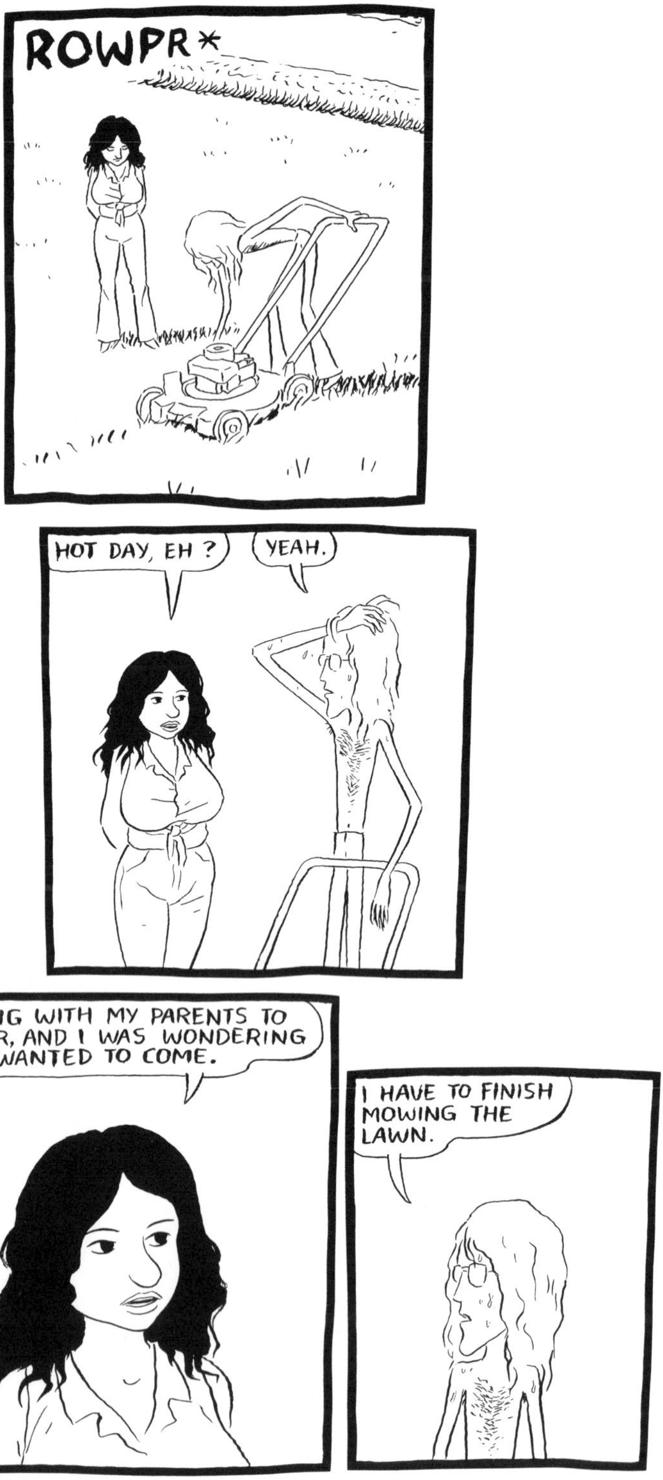
ROWPR*
HOT DAY, EH ?
YEAH.
I'M GOING WITH MY PARENTS TO THE FAIR, AND I WAS WONDERING IF YOU WANTED TO COME.
I HAVE TO FINISH MOWING THE LAWN.

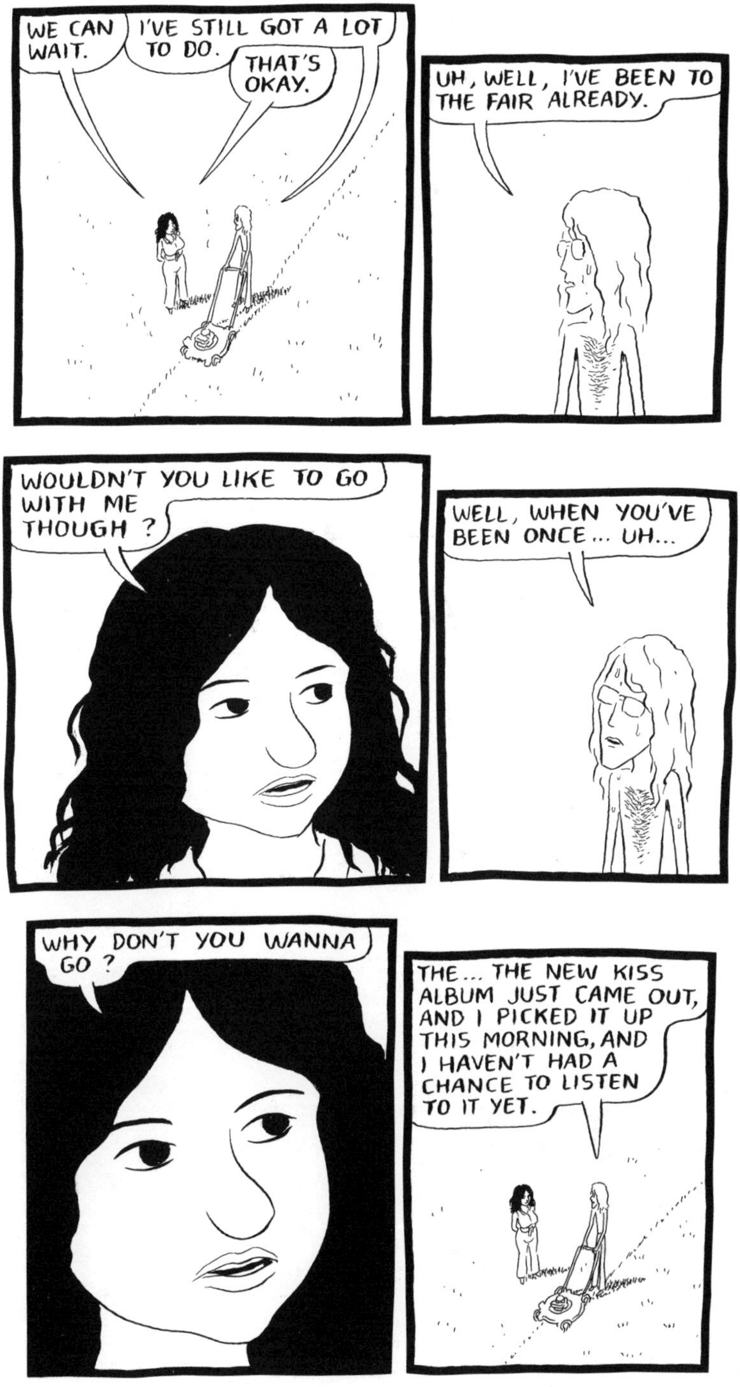
WE CAN WAIT.
I'VE STILL GOT A LOT TO DO.
THAT'S OKAY.
UH, WELL, I'VE BEEN TO THE FAIR ALREADY.
WOULDN'T YOU LIKE TO GO WITH ME THOUGH ?
WELL, WHEN YOU'VE BEEN ONCE... UH...
WHY DON'T YOU WANNA GO ?
THE... THE NEW KISS ALBUM JUST CAME OUT, AND I PICKED IT UP THIS MORNING, AND I HAVEN'T HAD A CHANCE TO LISTEN TO IT YET.

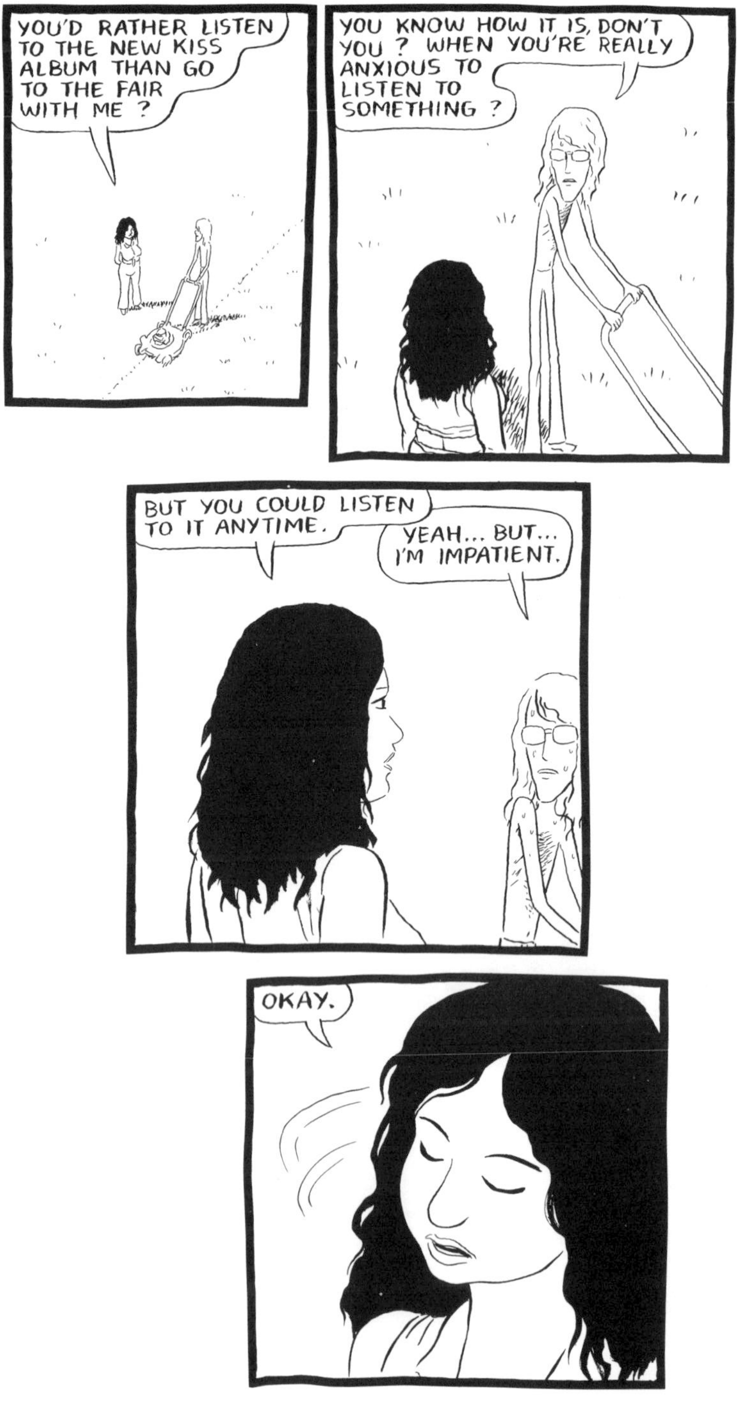
YOU'D RATHER LISTEN TO THE NEW KISS ALBUM THAN GO TO THE FAIR WITH ME ?
YOU KNOW HOW IT IS, DON'T YOU ? WHEN YOU'RE REALLY ANXIOUS TO LISTEN TO SOMETHING ?
BUT YOU COULD LISTEN TO IT ANYTIME.
YEAH... BUT... I'M IMPATIENT.
OKAY.

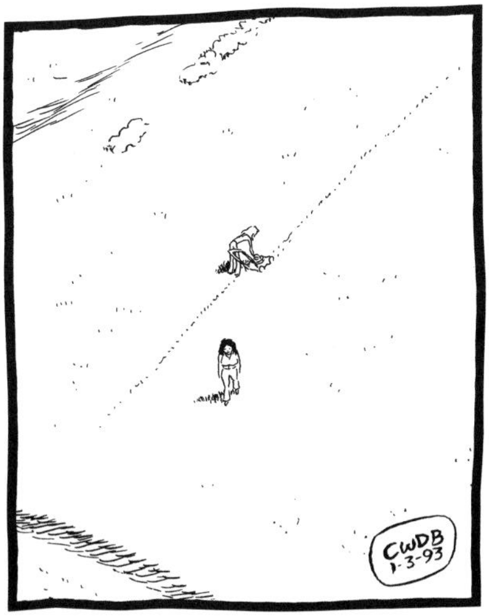
CWDB
1-3-93

I'm writing the following for those of you who are wondering when and where things happened.

I was born on May 16th 1960 at 10:17 AM in Montreal's Royal Victoria Hospital, and I grew up in Chateauguay, which is one of Montreal's suburbs. Most of this book is set in Chateauguay. The four scenes that aren't, are on pages 25 to 27, 111 to 115, 161 to 164, and 175 to 177.

PAGES 25-27 While I can remember that we were in the car when my mother delivered this little monologue, I'm not sure where the car was or where we were going, but I think we might have been on our way to or from Montreal, so I drew us on the Mercier Bridge which connects that island-city to the communities to its south.

What I have my mother saying isn't, of course, exactly what she said. Like almost all of the dialogue in I NEVER LIKED YOU, it's based on my memory of what was said. But I'm pretty sure that the lines I wrote for her are close to what she actually said.

PAGES 111-115 We were on a school field-trip to see a film in Montreal -- probably ONE FLEW OVER THE CUCKOO'S NEST.

PAGES 161-164 My mother was in the Montreal General Hospital.

PAGES 175-177 My grandmother, Grace Darling Brown, née Patterson, (1899-1992) lived in Fairfield, New Brunswick (near Saint John).

I'm not going to explain when every-thing in the book happened -- just the prologue (pages 1 to 5), the first scene proper (pages 9 to 12), and the last scene.

THE PROLOGUE On page two I wrote that I was in grade 4, but the truth is I'm not absolutely sure -- grade 4 is my best guess. That would have been 1969-1970, and I would have been nine for most of the school-year.

THE FIRST SCENE This happened when I was 12 and "Carrie" was 10. (The name is in quotes because that wasn't really her name.) I was in grade 7 at the time. The "educational" institution that I attended from grades 7 to 11, and where much of the book takes place, was Howard S. Billings High School. (In the Quebec school-system, high-school ended at grade 11.)

THE LAST SCENE The Kiss album in question was LOVE GUN, and according to page 29 of BLACK DIAMOND 2 : THE ILLUSTRATED COLLECTOR'S GUIDE TO KISS (by Dale Sherman, 1997) that record was released on either June 7th or June 17th 1977, so the exchange between "Sky" and me that's shown on pages 182 to 184 (or something very much like it) would have happened in June or early July of 1977, shortly after I'd graduated from high-school. I would have been 17, and "Sky" would have been 15.

I NEVER LIKED YOU was originally serialized in issues 26 to 30 of my comic-book YUMMY FUR (October 1991 to April 1993). My 1991 diary shows that I began writing it on May 20th and began drawing it on May 22nd. I was living in a rooming-house on Albany Avenue in Toronto, but at around that time the house was sold, and I had to leave. I moved to a rooming-house on Brunswick Avenue on July 15th and that's where I drew the rest of the piece. I drew the last panel on March 1st 1993.

The dedication to Sook-Yin Lee was written for the first book-edition of the strip in 1994. Our girlfriend-boyfriend-relationship lasted from late 1992 until mid-1996. We remain good friends -- she really is one of this planet's most delightful people. She took the photo on the next page in the summer of 1993 -- I'm the one on the left.

Chester
Brown

Toronto,
September, 2001